THE
PASTRY
BOOK

THE
PASTRY
BOOK

Rosemary Wadey

David & Charles
Newton Abbot   London   North Pomfret (Vt)

Colour photographs by John Lee
Line drawings by Jim Robins, Sharon Finmark,
Lee Robinson and Nick May

British Library Cataloguing in Publication Data

Wadey, Rosemary
    The pastry book.
    1. Pastry
    I. Title
    641.8' 65   TX773

    ISBN 0-7153-8344-2

Phototypeset by Typesetters (Birmingham) Limited,
and printed in Great Britain
by Butler & Tanner Limited, Frome and London
for David & Charles (Publishers) Limited
Brunel House Newton Abbot Devon

Published in the United States of America
by David & Charles Inc
North Pomfret Vermont 05053 USA

2234012

Contents

Introduction   9
1 Basic Pastries   14
2 Main Dishes   40
3 Puddings and Desserts   72
4 Teatime Fare   98
5 Suppers and Picnics   122
6 Starters and Cocktail Snacks   136
7 Traditional Recipes   150
What Could Go Wrong?   160
Index   163

For my father-in-law Sir Raymond Jennings whose
appreciation of good food has been an inspiration to me

Introduction

Weights and Measures

All spoon measures in the book are level unless otherwise stated.

1tsp = 5ml spoon
2tsp = 1dsp = 10ml (2 × 5ml spoons)
1tbsp = 15ml spoon
8tbsp = 150ml/¼pt

The size of eggs has been changed from large, medium and small to graded sizes from 1–7. The recipes in this book use sizes 2–3. If smaller ones are used remember to make allowances.

All the recipes in this book are metricated with the metric measurements appearing first. It is essential to follow one set of measurements or the other, but never to mix them.

Oven Temperature Guide

	Electricity		Gas Mark
	°C	°F	
Very Cool	110	225	¼
	120	250	½
Cool	140	275	1
	150	300	2
Moderate	160	325	3
	180	350	4
Moderately hot	190	375	5
Fairly hot	200	400	6
Hot	220	425	7
Very hot	230	450	8
	240	475	9

The oven should always be preheated to the suggested temperature given in the recipe before putting in the food. If insufficiently heated this will seriously affect the finished dish.

Introduction

It is sometimes said that British food is plain and unimaginative, but I cannot agree. Who can resist a succulent steak and kidney pudding or pie, crisp little mince pies that melt in the mouth or one of those extravagantly filled cream slices or chocolate eclairs? And the cook enjoys preparing this sort of food just as much as working on some exotic foreign dish, for it requires skill as well as imagination and her efforts will be well received.

All the recipes in this book are based on pastry of one type or another. There is a real art to making good pastry. Any cook should be keen to learn pastry making, beginning with the simple and straightforward shortcrusts; when you have acquired the correct 'feel' of these you will be ready to embark on the more difficult and time-consuming flaked pastries and special types such as choux and pâte sucrée. It is very pleasing to be known as a good pastry cook, for so many recipes call for pastry. It is worthwhile taking the time to learn properly and you can then achieve the all-important 'light touch'; it will soon come, given a little patience and a good teacher.

The 'feel' of a pastry is mainly governed by the amount of water added. Too much produces a sticky mass, which cannot be cured by adding more flour—this only upsets the balance of the ingredients. Too little water will produce a dry or very short dough, and if you add extra water at a late stage you only create a rather slimy mess hardly reminiscent of any sort of pastry. Both these mistakes make the pastry almost impossible to roll out and the finished baked dish unpalatable. But once you have learned how pastry should feel, you will never forget—and whether male or female you will surely be on the way to reaching somebody's heart through their stomach!

Traditional British food has been evolved to fulfil a need—to make substantial meals that will satisfy healthy outdoor appetites. Right up until not so long ago most men worked out in the fresh air, and in a damp and often chilly climate this called for something good and filling to eat. All the home-baked breads, scones and teacakes became firm favourites, with the various regions producing their own versions, many quite similar but with different names. Pastry became popular not only because it was good, sound enjoyable food but because it could be used in so many ways; the traditional pasties, pies and tarts which first appeared many years ago are still found all over the country. Almost anything—meat, fish, game, eggs, vegetables or fruit—could be enclosed or baked in pastry, and could then easily be carried to places of work or used for a hearty evening meal.

Climatic conditions and type of landscape often explain why certain foods have been popular in particular areas. Many centuries ago the Highlanders of Scotland lived in barren conditions. There was plenty of game and fish available if they wanted it, but because it was difficult to produce high-quality crops or feed their animals properly, they became poor in physique and not sufficiently interested in making use of the better foods available to them. Instead they concentrated on the abundance of oatmeal available; this kept them well—often washed down by large quantities of whisky—though they could have lived much better with a little thought. They baked with oatmeal, making a type of pastry, and produced the forerunners of the oatcakes which are still famous in Scotland and all over the world. The Lowlanders made the most of their better land and became better off through proper use and cultivation of what they had. Consequently they could afford to buy ingredients for baking breads, scones and pastries, and through the years have become known as the people with that 'special touch' necessary for baking light-textured breads, buns and pastries; many Scotswomen are excellent pastrycooks.

The Welsh were better equipped to feed themselves than the Highlanders, and although they were isolated up to the time of the Industrial Revolution they were spared the clan problems of the Scots. There was plenty of fresh natural food, the animals fed well on the hillsides and most homesteads had small plots of land. The South Wales coal mines in due course brought more employment and more people with money eager to buy local produce. The Welsh too were famous for their breads and scones, usually cooked on the bakestone over the open fire, again often containing oatmeal. They used leeks widely, in their native dishes, probably because they were plentiful, as well as the excellent lamb and the fish from their abundant rivers.

England had its regions too, but was less markedly divided; although the terrain changes from north to south, communications have always been easier and nothing was thought of walking 300 or so miles to market with a flock of turkeys and hens, pigs and sheep. They must have required long slow cooking after all that exercise, or perhaps people just had stronger stomachs. The West Country often used apples in its recipes, probably because of the quantities of cider apples grown locally and the fact that the apple pulp available after the cider pressing was often to be had for nothing; this was a good enough reason for adding it to savoury pies, particularly those containing pork or lamb, in which it was thought to draw off some of the fattiness. Pilchards and herrings caught off Cornwall were baked in pies with heads 'star-gazing' out of the pastry, said to be the best way of cooking these fish, for all the oils, usually lost when the heads are removed, seep back into the flesh, and all the juices are caught in the pastry. Cornish pasties were said once to contain a savoury filling at one end and a sweet one at the other, to provide a complete meal; perhaps wrapped in the old red-and-white-spotted handkerchief, they were taken to the tin mines or the fields. Perhaps we ought to try something similar for the school lunch boxes and other packed meals so often called for today.

The pieman was a familiar sight in old London, walking the streets with pies held high in a basket covered with a cloth, starting out when they were still hot from the oven. The old nursery rhyme 'Simple Simon met a pieman' reminds us of this and the fact that they used to cost a penny. With the muffin man and the crumpet seller he must have been a colourful and welcome sight.

The old Chelsea Bunhouse was a favourite spot where people from Royalty downwards would sit and eat their buns whilst watching the world go by. Cockney London boasted eel and pie shops early this century, and there is still the odd one to

be found hidden away in the City, although eels are not so popular now as in Victorian times. The shops used to sell jellied eels, stewed eels, eel pie and a selection of meat pies, which could be eaten on the premises or taken away. The live eels were kept in tanks at the back of the shop, ready and waiting! There are still eel stalls around, now mostly to be found at the seaside, large race meetings and fairgrounds. They remind us that in Victorian times it was common to see plates of jellied eels being eaten at the stall with the bones being spat out onto the pavement. An island in the River Thames near Richmond was named after the eels captured nearby.

When the Normans invaded England they introduced savoury pastry pies to the country. The fillings they used sound peculiar, often including mixtures such as eggs, ginger, bone marrow, raisins and saffron. But these improved through the centuries and pies became either sweet or savoury. The sweet ones were good and are still great favourites; at first the savoury ones contained more or less anything in the meat or game line, highly seasoned with herbs and spices—no doubt to overcome the powerful taste and smell of the rotting meats commonly consumed in those times. How often did salmonella raise its ugly head? It was probably known then as some type of plague, for it must have been a common killer.

One of the first-known pastries was 'huff paste', more or less a flour-and-water dough, obviously without much flavour but used to wrap round foods which were to be baked for many hours in the fire; it would be inedible itself, more often than not, but protected the food inside. We use a flour-and-water paste today if a casserole dish has a badly fitting lid or needs to be completely sealed. An old recipe from 1750–1800 used a type of pastry for 'coffins' or 'coffers', casings some 2–3 inches thick, into which raw meats were put; they were then sealed and cooked long and slow. When opened out the meats were well cooked and tender—this must have been one of the earliest types of casserole.

Today, pastry still plays an important part in our kitchens. You do not now always have to make your own; you can buy it in mix form, simply adding water, or buy it ready-made, fresh or frozen. More and more of the delicatessens and larger supermarkets sell ready-cooked pastry flan cases, some sweet, some savoury, one type made with brown-flour pastry, another using cheese pastry; then come the individual tartlet cases, some of plain pastry, others using a rich flan crust; pastry hors d'oeuvre shells, cocktail bases and who knows what else. I think they take the fun out of cooking, but again they are ideal for the busy cook who now probably has a full-time job and who finds time for cooking very limited. The food processor has arrived too, and this marvellous machine can rub in your pastry in a few seconds; add the water and it is ready to use, almost more quickly than getting out the scales and utensils, and provided you don't overprocess, it makes perfect pastry every time.

And what of the future? We are still going to eat pastry, well into the next century and, if the past is anything to go by, for centuries to come. The most recent pastry 'find' must be the quiche: versatile, easy to make, cook and eat, and fit for any occasion. Even if it is a French idea, we have adopted it and certainly produced plenty of British versions. What will emerge as the next pastry favourite—any ideas? I have a few, but perhaps I'll keep those for another book.

1
Basic Pastries

1

Pastry making is an art said to be passed down from one generation to the next for as long as anyone can remember. It has its simple rules, which if followed will guarantee success. However, it is true that some people have an 'extra special' touch when it comes to making pastry—something that cannot be taught but is much envied. The do's and don'ts below may help beginners and also include the points that may have given you trouble in the past.

Probably the most important thing to remember with pastry making is to keep everything cool—that is except with choux and hot-water crust pastries (which require the fat to be melted and then brought up to the boil with the measured water). The fat should be cool and firm but not too hard, so that it will easily cut into pieces to rub into the flour until the mixture resembles fine breadcrumbs, or will stay in flakes or cubes if being used for one of the flaked pastries. If the fat is too soft a rubbed-in mixture will become greasy and not absorb the correct amount of liquid, giving a disappointing result.

Always use cold water and the coldest possible surface for rolling out—marble is the best but as not many kitchens contain a marble slab, formica or any cool even working surface will do. The idea is to start with all the ingredients at the same temperature so they blend evenly, and then to carry out the rolling process on something cool so the temperature is still kept at much the same level. If the pastry should become too soft to roll, then simply wrap it in foil or a polythene bag and rest it in the refrigerator for a short while; flaked pastries need to be rested and chilled between rollings in case the fat becomes too soft and prevents the layers forming correctly.

The type of flour used is important too. Plain flour is most often used, the exceptions being for suet crust and any other special pastries such as special shortcrust which use self-raising flour, as they require a certain amount of 'rise' to give their characteristic finish. White flour is mostly preferred but some of the shortcrusts can be made using all or a proportion of brown flour. The type of brown flour you choose is a matter of personal preference—it gives an excellent flavour. With the flaked pastries—puff, rough puff and flaky—a strong plain flour as used in yeast cookery can also be satisfactory, for the rolling and folding processes involved develop the gluten sufficiently for excellent results. The flour and salt (added for flavour even in sweet dishes) should be sifted into the mixing bowl to incorporate as much air as possible. Pastry requires the least amount of handling possible to keep it light and crisp; and as much extra air should be incorporated as possible, so always rub in with the fingertips only, lifting the mixture a few inches above the bowl allowing the ingredients to be thoroughly aerated as they fall back into the bowl.

The type of fat used governs the flavour of the pastry. Generally, for short and flaked pastries an equal amount of butter or margarine and lard give the best results. Using all lard gives a good short texture but it lacks the flavour obtained by using a proportion of butter or margarine. Again using all butter or all margarine gives the best flavour but with some of the short pastries a very short-textured pastry results making it difficult to roll out; flan pastries, pâte sucrée and choux pastry should contain all butter.

Take care when adding liquid; too much gives a sticky unmanageable dough which bakes into a hard and brittle pastry and adding extra flour will only upset the balance of the ingredients and result in a spoilt texture. Keep the proportions correct: always weigh accurately and then add almost the amount of liquid suggested, and a little more if and as necessary. Take care also with the amount of flour dredged onto the rolling surface. It is easy to incorporate too much into the pastry, again upsetting the balance of ingredients.

One last hint: always roll the pastry in one direction—straight in front of you. Turn it round gradually whilst continuing to roll to keep a good shape. Do not turn it over or over-stretch it during rolling, or it will simply shrink back whilst baking. The rolling should be light but firm, and do not roll out any more than necessary—remember the less handling it receives, the better the pastry.

Shortcrust Pastry

This is probably the most used basic pastry for both sweet and savoury dishes. It is made by the rubbing-in method and the quantities are half the amount of fat to flour. Always use plain flour for a true shortcrust pastry. The fat content is usually made up of half butter or margarine and half lard or other type of white fat; however, other proportions can be used to suit your taste. For instance, all whipped white fat can make a good pastry, whilst some people prefer to use all butter or margarine—this gives a very short pastry which is difficult to handle but has an excellent flavour. It is important to add the correct amount of water, for too little gives a hard pastry whilst too much results in a brittle and uninteresting texture. Take care not to overknead or incorporate too much extra flour during rolling for both of these will spoil the texture.

The rubbed-in mixture can be kept in an airtight container in the refrigerator for up to 2 weeks, ideal if large quantities are to be made and stored ready for use. The ready-made pastry will keep for 2–3 days if wrapped in foil or polythene and chilled; or will freeze raw for 3–6 months.

200g/8oz plain flour
good pinch salt
50g/2oz butter or margarine
50g/2oz lard or white fat
4tbsp (approx) cold water to mix

1 Sift the flour and salt into a bowl.
2 Add the fats cut into small pieces and rub in with the fingertips until the mixture resembles fine breadcrumbs. This stage can be

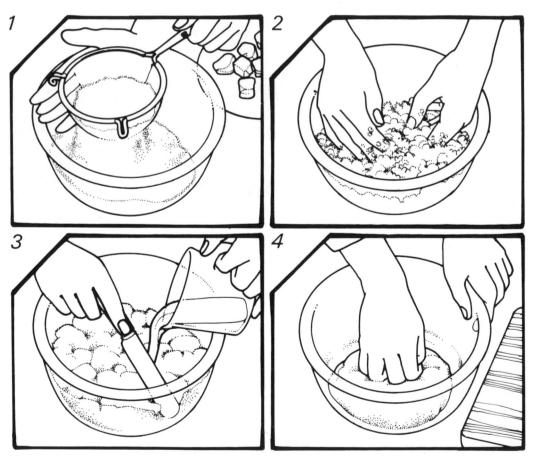

Shortcrust Pastry

done in a food processor or large electric mixer fitted with a dough hook. If using a food processor, turn it on and off to give short bursts until the mixture is blended.

3 Add sufficient water to mix to a firm but pliable dough, using a round-bladed knife or a fork.

4 Knead very lightly then turn onto a lightly floured surface ready for rolling. If time allows, wrap and chill for 30 minutes before rolling out.

5 Bake in a fairly hot to hot oven (200–220°C/400–425°F, Gas Mark 6–7).

Note Pastries are usually measured by their weight of flour: 200g/8oz shortcrust pastry is made from 200g/8oz plain flour etc.

VARIATIONS

Curry Add 1–2 level tsp curry powder to the flour before rubbing in the fat.

Herb Add 1½–2 level tsp any dried herbs to the rubbed-in mixture.

Spicy (for sweet pies and flans) Add 1 level tsp ground cinnamon or mixed spice to the flour before rubbing in the fat.

Wholemeal Pastry

The use of a brown flour in pastry making is becoming increasingly popular and gives an excellent flavour to pies and flans. The appearance may not be quite so attractive but the flavour makes up for this. Try any type of brown flour—wholemeal, wholewheat, stoneground, etc—or a combination of brown and white flours. Brown-flour pastry needs more salt and usually absorbs a little more water.

200g/8oz plain brown flour (any type), or
   100g/4oz each brown flour and plain white
   flour
½ level tsp salt
50g/2oz butter or margarine
50g/2oz lard or white fat
5 tbsp (approx) cold water to mix

1 Put the flour and salt into a bowl (do not sift the flour) and mix well.

2 Cut the fats into small pieces and rub in until the mixture resembles fine breadcrumbs; alternatively use a food processor.

3 Add sufficient water to mix to a firm but pliable dough, using a round-bladed knife or fork.

4 Knead lightly, then wrap and chill the pastry for 15–30 minutes before rolling out.

5 Bake in a fairly hot to hot oven (200–220°C/400–425°F, Gas Mark 6–7).

Note This pastry will freeze when raw for 3–6 months.

Cheese Pastry

A very tasty addition to most savoury pies and flans. It is made in the same way as shortcrust, with the cheese added just before the liquid. It is best to use a strong-flavoured Cheddar, finely grated, but a combination of Cheddar and Parmesan gives a good strong flavour. One of the red cheeses such as Cheshire, Leicester, etc, gives an interesting colour and taste to the pastry. Both salt and pepper are added to bring out the flavour, with often a pinch of cayenne pepper or a little dry mustard. Once made up this pastry is best cooked within 24 hours, but it will keep in the freezer for 2–3 months.

200g/8oz plain flour
½ level tsp salt
good shake pepper
pinch cayenne pepper and/or ½ level tsp dry
   mustard
50g/2oz butter or margarine
50g/2oz lard or white fat
40g/1½oz mature Cheddar cheese, finely grated
2–3 level tsp ready-grated Parmesan cheese
4 tbsp (approx) cold water to mix

1 Sift the flour, salt, pepper, cayenne and mustard into a bowl.

2 Rub in the fats until the mixture resembles fine breadcrumbs; alternatively use a food processor or large electric mixer fitted with a dough hook. Stir in the Cheddar and Parmesan cheese.

3 Bind to a firm but pliable dough with water and knead until smooth (a little more than with normal shortcrust pastry, in order to distribute the cheese evenly).

4 Wrap and chill the pastry for 15–30 minutes before rolling out, if time permits.

5 Bake in a fairly hot oven (200°C/400°F, Gas Mark 6).

Note Parmesan cheese may be omitted, in which case increase the amount of Cheddar to 50g/2oz.

Rich Cheese Pastry

This is ideal for cheese straws, garnishes for soups or cocktail snack bases. It is made by a different method and is more difficult to roll out to a large shape without cracking, so use it for small items.

75g/3oz butter, block margarine or lard
75g/3oz mature Cheddar cheese, finely grated
100g/4oz plain flour
pinch salt
good pinch dry mustard

1 Cream the fat until soft, add the cheese and cream again until very soft.

2 Sift the flour, salt and mustard into the mixture and gradually work in using a palette knife or fork, until the mixture begins to stick together.

3 Knead together into a ball, then knead lightly until the mixture is smooth.

4 Cover the bowl with cling film or wrap the pastry in polythene or greaseproof paper, then chill for about 30 minutes before rolling out.

5 Bake in a fairly hot oven (200°C/400°F, Gas Mark 6).

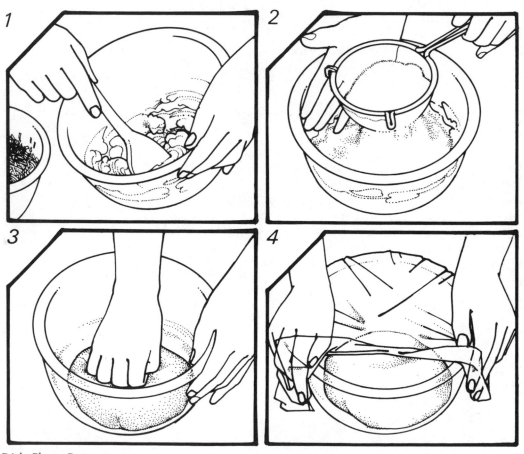

Rich Cheese Pastry

Flan Pastry

A richer pastry than shortcrust but made by the same method. It is slightly sweetened for use in sweet dishes but the sugar can be omitted for use with savoury flans.

100g/4oz plain flour
pinch salt
50g/2oz butter or block margarine
25g/1oz lard or white fat
1 level tsp caster sugar
1 egg, beaten

1 Sift the flour and salt into a bowl.
2 Add the fats, cut into small pieces, and rub in carefully with the fingertips until the mixture resembles fine breadcrumbs (if using a food processor take care, for being a rich pastry it is easy to over-process).
3 Mix in the sugar, then add sufficient beaten egg and mix with a fork or round-bladed knife until the ingredients come together.
4 Knead lightly, then wrap and chill for about 30 minutes.
5 Roll out and use as shortcrust pastry.
6 Bake in a fairly hot oven (200°C/400°F, Gas Mark 6).

Note This pastry will freeze when raw for up to 2 months.

FLAN SIZES
100g/4oz flour etc fits a 15cm/6in flan ring
125g/5oz flour etc fits a 18cm/7in flan ring
150g/6oz flour etc fits a 20cm/8in flan ring
175g/7oz flour etc fits a 23cm/9in flan ring
200g/8oz flour etc fits a 25cm/10in flan ring

Pâte Sucrée

This is the famous French flan pastry, equivalent to our own enriched flan pastry. It is thin and crisp when baked and a favourite choice for all continental-style pastries and flans. It is made in a very special way. This recipe gives sufficient pastry to line an 18cm/7in flan tin or 10–12 tartlet tins.

100g/4oz plain flour
pinch salt
50g/2oz caster sugar
50g/2oz butter
1½–2 egg yolks

1 Sift the flour and salt into a pile on a working surface and make a well in the centre.
2 Put the sugar into the well.
3 Cut the butter into small pieces and add with the egg yolks to the sugar.
4 Use a palette knife to tip the flour over the egg yolks and cover up the 'well'.
5 Gradually pinch the mixture together, using one hand only, until all the flour is incorporated; then work the dough quickly and lightly until smooth, using the palm of the hand, and form into a ball.
6 Wrap the pastry in clingfilm, polythene or foil and chill for 1 hour.
7 Roll out thinly and bake in a moderately hot oven (190°C/375°F, Gas Mark 5).

Special Shortcrust Pastry

Excellent for individual sweet pies and smallish flans; without the sugar, it can also be used for savoury dishes. It is a rich pastry with a very short texture, made with self-raising flour and a higher proportion of fats than usual. It is a little more difficult to roll out than most pastries. If you have trouble, try rolling it between two layers of polythene or greaseproof paper. For best results use the fats straight from the refrigerator. This pastry breaks the pastry rule by using self-raising flour, which gives a certain amount of rise.

200g/8oz self-raising flour
pinch salt
1 level tsp caster sugar (optional)
50g/2oz butter
50g/2oz block margarine
25g/1oz lard or white fat
1 egg yolk
milk to mix

1 Sift the flour, salt and sugar into a bowl.
2 Cut the fats into small pieces and rub into

the flour until the mixture resembles fine breadcrumbs.

3 Bind to a firm but pliable dough with the egg yolk and sufficient milk to mix. Knead lightly until smooth.

4 Wrap the pastry and chill for about 30 minutes before rolling out.

5 Bake in a fairly hot oven (200°C/400°F, Gas Mark 6).

Note this pastry will freeze when raw for up to 2 months.

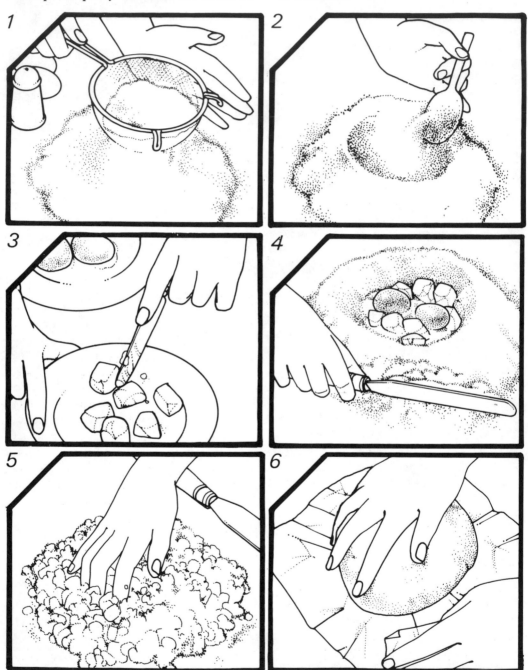

Pâte Sucrée

One-Stage Shortcrust Pastry

So speedy it is ready before you realize and you hardly even use your hands.

100g/4oz soft (tub) margarine
1 tbsp water
150g/6oz plain flour
pinch salt

1 Cut the margarine into small pieces and put into a bowl with the water and 2 tbsp flour. Beat together until smooth and creamy (about 30 seconds).
2 Sift in the remaining flour and salt and mix to form a fairly soft dough.
3 Turn onto a lightly floured surface and knead lightly until smooth.
4 Wrap the pastry in foil or polythene and chill. The pastry is ready for use but should be rolled out fairly thinly.
5 Cook in a moderately hot oven (190°C/ 375°F, Gas Mark 5).

Puff Pastry

Home-made puff pastry takes time and effort to produce but the result is well worthwhile. This is the richest of all the pastries, using equal quantities of fat and flour, and should have the most even rise of all because of the amount of air rolled and folded into it. For the best flavour use all butter, but a combination of butter and block margarine, or butter/margarine and lard may be used. Once made the pastry will keep, wrapped in foil, in the refrigerator for 3–4 days or in the deep freeze for 3–6 months. It is a good idea to make large batches at one time and freeze for later use. The first rolling gives the most even rise and should be used for vol-au-vents, cream slices etc, whilst the trimmings can be re-rolled and used for small pastries such as Eccles cakes, sacristans, cream horns etc. Roll out to a thickness of 0.3cm/⅛in as the rise should be very good. Bought frozen puff pastry is a good alternative if you cannot manage the time needed to produce your own.

450g/1lb plain flour
1 level tsp salt
450g/1lb butter, firm but not too hard
300ml/½pt (approx) iced water
squeeze lemon juice

1 Sift the flour and salt into a bowl.
2 Take about 75g/3oz butter and rub into the flour.
3 Bind to a fairly soft dough with iced water and lemon juice and knead lightly in the bowl.
4 Roll out the pastry to a square measuring approx 30cm/12in.
5 Soften the remaining butter a little and form into an oblong block; place on one half of the pastry. Fold the pastry over to enclose it and seal the edges with the rolling pin. 'Rib' the pastry by pressing the rolling pin across the pastry at regular intervals—this helps to distribute the air evenly.
6 Turn the pastry so the fold is to the right and roll into a long strip, three times as long as it is wide.
7 Fold the bottom third upwards and the top third downwards evenly. Seal the edges, rib the pastry and put it into a polythene bag. Chill for 30 minutes.
8 Repeat the rolling and chilling process 5 times more, giving the pastry a quarter turn each time so the fold is always on the right.
9 Chill for at least 1 hr after the final rolling and preferably overnight. The pastry is even better if given 3 rollings one day and 3 more the following day, followed by a chilling period of 1–2 hrs. The pastry is now ready for use.
10 Bake in a hot to very hot oven (220– 230°C/425–450°F, Gas Mark 7–8).

Flaky Pastry

This is the most common of the 'flaked' pastries, having an excellent flavour and lightness. It is a rich pastry but not so rich as puff pastry, and it can be used for all types of sweet and savoury dishes, for it has a medium rise. For first-time makers of a 'flaked' pastry the instructions may sound a little daunting

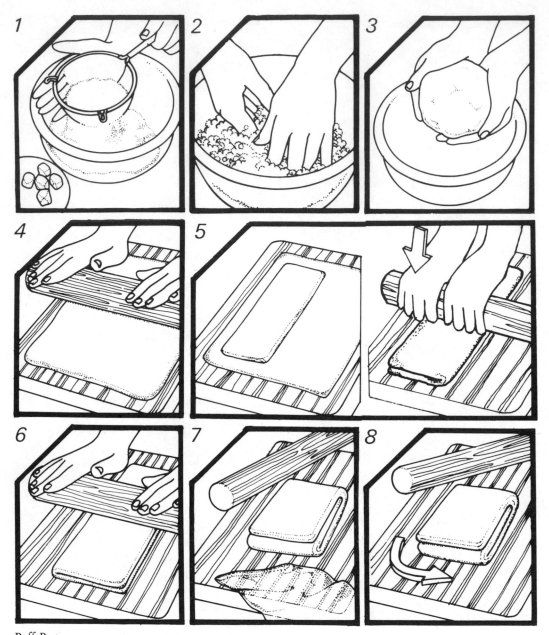

Puff Pastry

but if followed carefully good results are guaranteed and the process becomes easier each time attempted. It requires proportions of three-quarters fat to flour and as the name implies flakes of the fat are put over the pastry dough during the rolling and folding process. Use all butter for the best flavour but a mixture of butter or margarine and lard is quite satisfactory. Remember that flaked pastries must be made using cold ingredients on a cold surface, and that the chilling and resting periods are most important for good results. Extra chilling will do no harm but a shorter time will cause the fat to over soften and not form the proper flakes. Once made, the pastry will store wrapped in the refrigerator for 3–4 days or keep in the freezer for up to 6 months.

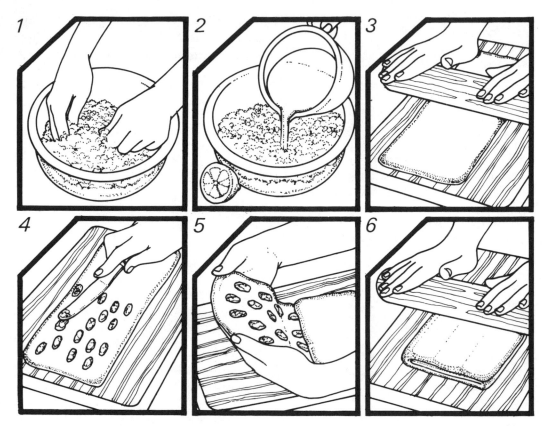

Flaky Pastry

450g/1lb plain flour
1 level tsp salt
350g/12oz butter (or butter/margarine and lard mixed)
1 tsp lemon juice
300ml/½pt (approx) iced water

1 Sift the flour and salt into a bowl and rub in 75g/3oz fat until the mixture resembles fine breadcrumbs.

2 Add the lemon juice and sufficient water to the dry ingredients to mix to a fairly soft elastic dough.

3 Knead lightly on a floured surface then roll out to a strip three times as long as it is wide.

4 Divide the remaining fat into three equal portions and use one part to cut into small flakes which should be laid evenly over the top two-thirds of the pastry.

5 Fold the bottom third of the pastry upwards and the top third downwards, seal the edges and 'rib' with the rolling pin (*see* puff pastry, page 21). Put into a polythene bag and chill for 15 minutes.

6 Remove the pastry from the refrigerator and, with the folded side of the pastry to the right, roll out again to a strip three times as long as it is wide. Repeat the 'flaking' process with the second portion of fat, fold up as before and chill again for 15 minutes.

7 Repeat stage 6 using the final portion of fat, folding and chilling for 15 minutes.

8 A further rolling and folding process may be done without adding any fat.

9 Chill the pastry for about 1 hour after which it is ready for use.

10 Bake in a hot oven (220°C/425°F, Gas Mark 7).

Rough Puff Pastry

A pastry with a similar texture to flaky pastry, this is quicker and easier to make—hence the name. It uses the same proportions of ingredients as flaky pastry—three-quarters fat to flour—and can be used in place of flaky pastry for both sweet and savoury dishes. The fat used can be all butter or margarine or a combination of butter or margarine and lard; butter of course gives the best flavour. In this pastry none of the fat is rubbed in, it is simply cut into pieces and mixed into the flour. Once made it will keep wrapped in the refrigerator for 3–4 days, or in the freezer for up to 6 months.

450g/1lb plain flour
1 level tsp salt
350g/12oz firm butter (or butter/margarine and lard)
1tsp lemon juice
300ml/½pt (approx) iced water

1 Sift the flour and salt into a bowl. Cut the fats into neat pieces—about 1cm/½in square and toss into the flour without breaking up the pieces.
2 Add the lemon juice and sufficient water to mix to a fairly stiff dough—do not knead.
3 Turn onto a floured surface and roll out carefully to a strip three times as long as it is wide.
4 Fold neatly into three as for the other flaked pastries, seal the edges and rib with the rolling pin (see puff pastry, page 21).
5 Give the pastry a quarter turn so the fold is at the right and repeat the rolling and folding process twice.
6 Wrap in polythene or foil and chill for 30 minutes then repeat the rolling and folding process twice more.
7 Chill for 30–60 minutes when the pastry will be ready for use.
8 Bake in a hot oven (220°C/425°F, Gas Mark 7).

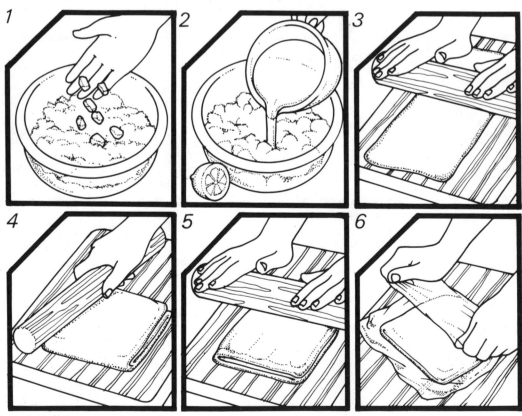

Rough Puff Pastry

Quick Puffy Pastry

A big cheat but a very quick and delicious pastry to top a pie. The butter or block margarine (soft tub margarine will not work) must be thoroughly chilled or preferably be part frozen before grating. Once made the pastry must be used at once—so have the filling ready and cooled first and then bake immediately.

300g/10oz plain flour
1 level tsp salt
200g/8oz block margarine or butter, thoroughly chilled
iced water to mix

1 Sift the flour and salt into a bowl.
2 Coarsely grate the fat into the flour and mix lightly with a palette knife until evenly distributed.
3 Add sufficient iced water—approx 4–6 tbsp—to mix to a stiff dough. Do not knead.
4 Turn onto a floured surface and either pat out to the size required or gently roll using a well-floured rolling pin. Use to cover the pie, decorate with trimmings and then glaze.
5 Bake in a hot oven (220°C/425°F, Gas Mark 7).

Quick-Mix Pastry (using oil)

Very speedy but a little more greasy than normal pastry so best for savoury dishes.

2½ tbsp oil (vegetable, corn etc)
1 tbsp cold water
squeeze lemon juice
100g/4oz plain flour
pinch salt

1 Put the oil, water and lemon juice into a bowl and beat or whisk until thoroughly emulsified.
2 Sift the flour and salt together then gradually whisk or beat into the oil mixture to form a dough.
3 Knead lightly and roll out on a floured surface or between sheets of polythene, greaseproof paper or non-stick silicone paper.
4 Bake in a fairly hot oven (200°C/400°F, Gas Mark 6).

Suet-Crust Pastry

This is the traditional 'roly poly' pastry for both sweet and savoury dishes and breaks the pastry rule by using self-raising flour. It is best boiled or steamed but can also be baked with care although it may be a little on the tough side, particularly on the outer crust. To minimize the cooking time it is best to use pre-cooked fillings only when baking this pastry.

I like to use half suet to flour but some people prefer a lesser proportion of suet. Use a commercially packaged shredded suet or buy lumps of suet from the butcher and grate it yourself.

Quick-Mix Pastry

The quantities given here provide sufficient pastry to line a 900ml/1½pt pudding basin.

200g/8oz self-raising flour
½ level tsp salt
75–100g/3–4oz shredded suet
150ml/¼pt (approx) cold water to mix

1 Sift the flour and salt into a bowl and mix in the suet.
2 Add sufficient water to mix to a soft elastic dough and knead lightly until smooth.
3 Roll out to 0.5cm/¼in thick.
4 The pastry is now ready for use.

VARIATIONS
Herb Add 1–2 level tsp any dried mixed herbs to the dry ingredients.
Onion Add 1 small onion, either finely chopped or minced, to the dry ingredients.

Yeast Pastry

As a change from flaky pastry a yeast dough pastry can be used. It is especially good for such things as sausage rolls, savoury puffs etc and can be made plain or in fancy plaits. It can also be used for some sweet pastries such as Banbury or Eccles cakes. It requires risen white bread dough so is a good thing to make when there is a surplus of bread dough.

450g/1lb risen white bread dough
150g/6oz block margarine or butter and lard
  mixed

1 Knock back the dough as usual and roll out thinly to a strip three times as long as it is wide.
2 Divide the fat into three and use one portion to dot over the top two-thirds of the pastry.
3 Fold into three as for puff pastry (page 21) by bringing the bottom third upwards and the top portion downwards. Seal the edges with the rolling pin and place in a lightly oiled polythene bag. Chill for 15 minutes.
4 Roll out to a strip as before making sure the folded edge is on the right-hand side. Use another fat portion to dot as before.

5 Fold as before, seal and rest for 15 minutes.
6 Repeat the rolling and dotting-with-fat process (using the last fat portion) followed by folding, sealing and resting.
7 Repeat the process again but without adding any fat and then chill for at least 2 hours, or preferably overnight, before use.
8 Roll out thinly and use as required but stand in a warm place for 15–20 minutes before baking in a very hot oven (230°C/450°F, Gas Mark 8).

Hot-Water-Crust Pastry

This is a special pastry used for raised pies. It is made by adding lard and boiling water to flour to form a strong dough which can be moulded or 'raised' to make a pie that will hold its shape during baking and cooling; the texture is not affected by the extra rolling and kneading involved. It can be either raised by hand or used in a cake tin or special hinged metal pie moulds.

450g/1lb plain flour
1½ level tsp salt
100g/4oz lard
200ml/7fl oz water or milk and water mixed

1 Sift the flour and salt into a bowl and make a well in the centre.
2 Put the lard and water into a saucepan and heat gently until the lard melts, then bring to the boil.
3 Pour the liquid into the well in the flour and mix quickly to form a fairly soft dough.
4 Turn onto a lightly floured surface and knead until smooth.
5 Use as required but quickly, for the pastry firms up as it cools. Keep reserved pastry in a bowl covered with a cloth to prevent hardening whilst waiting.
6 Bake in a fairly hot oven (200°C/400°F, Gas Mark 6) for 30 minutes then reduce to moderate (180°C/350°F, Gas Mark 4) for the remainder of the cooking time.

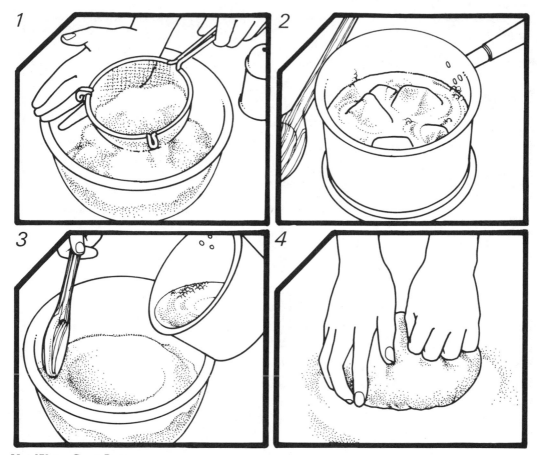

Hot-Water-Crust Pastry

TO RAISE A PIE USING A CAKE TIN OR MOULD

Grease a 15–20cm/6–8in round or square cake tin (preferably with a loose base) or a 900g/2lb loaf tin. Reserve one-third of the dough for the lid and keep covered in a bowl. Roll the larger piece to fit the cake tin (allowing about 10cm/4in larger than the tin) and carefully lower it into the tin and press to cover the base and sides evenly. Add the filling (see individual recipes) and then cover with a lid made from the reserved pastry, after damping the edges with water. Trim and crimp the edges and make a hole in the centre of the lid. Decorate with pastry trimmings then glaze and bake as stated in the recipe. Cool in the tin.

Line a pie mould in the same way, making sure the pastry is pressed well into the sides to show the patterns on the sides of the tin when baked.

TO RAISE A PIE BY HAND

Reserve a quarter to one-third of the dough and keep covered in a bowl. Use the remainder of the pastry to mould a cake tin or basin shape; the pastry firms up as it cools. Alternatively mould round the outside of a similar-shaped object and then lift it out carefully. Add the filling (see recipes) and cover with a lid made from the reserved pastry, damping the edges and pressing well together. Trim off any surplus pastry and crimp or decorate the edge. Make a hole in the centre and use the trimmings to decorate the top. Tie a wide double thickness band of greaseproof paper right round the pie to help it keep its shape during cooking. Bake as described in specific recipes. This method is good for small or individual pies.

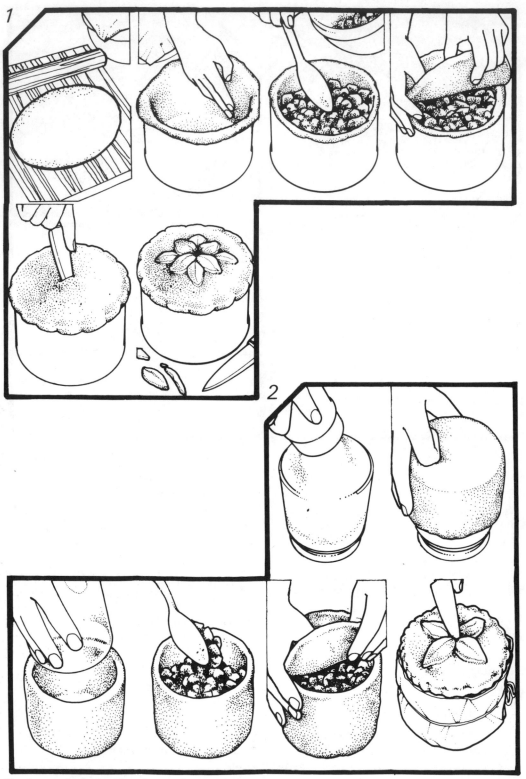

Shaping a raised pie: (1) using a cake tin; (2) by hand

Choux Pastry

Although called a pastry this is more of a paste for it needs to be piped or spooned into shape before baking. It is used for sweet and savoury dishes and can be baked and—for some dishes—deep fried. Eclairs, profiteroles, cream buns and aigrettes are well-known choux pastry recipes but care must be taken when making it to beat in as much air as possible with the eggs to achieve the characteristic lightness. It is also important to add the flour all at once and cook the paste until it forms a ball leaving the sides of the pan clean. Beware of sudden draughts if opening the oven door, for choux pastry sinks easily—it is best not to open the door until they are ready. Eclairs and profiteroles should be split open or pierced when cooked and returned to the oven to dry out. Use butter for the best flavour but a good margarine will also work well.

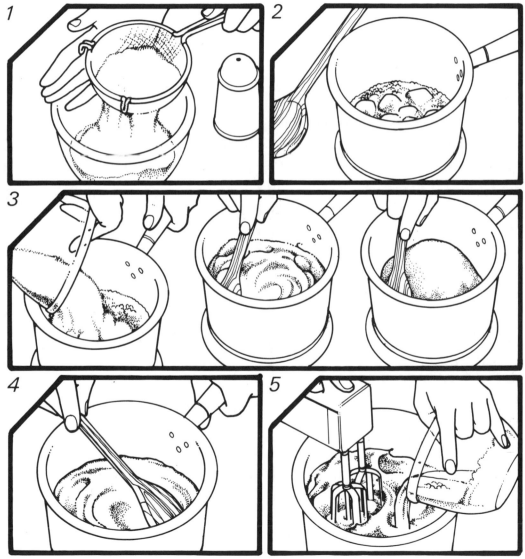

Choux Pastry

65g/2½oz plain flour
pinch salt
50g/2oz butter or margarine
150ml/¼pt water
2 eggs, beaten (size 3 or 4)

1 Sift the flour and salt into a bowl.
2 Put the fat and water into a saucepan and heat gently until the fat melts, then bring quickly to the boil.
3 Add the flour to the pan all at once and beat with a wooden spoon until smooth and the mixture forms a ball, leaving the sides of the pan clean.
4 Remove from the heat, spread the paste out over the base of the saucepan and leave to cool for a few minutes.
5 Beat the egg vigorously into the paste, a little at a time, to give a smooth and glossy paste. A hand-held electric mixer is best for

this as it helps incorporate the maximum amount of air required for a good rise. The pastry is now ready for use.
6 Bake in a hot oven (220°C/425°F, Gas Mark 7).

Note Choux balls can be piped and then frozen before baking (thaw completely when required to bake) or can be baked, cooled and then frozen for up to 3 months. Cooked choux balls are best refreshed in a warm oven after thawing and before filling.

How to Shape and use Pastry

Once the pastry has been made and usually chilled or rested for a short time it is ready for use. Pies, flans, vol-au-vents etc all call for a different method of shaping, covering or lining.

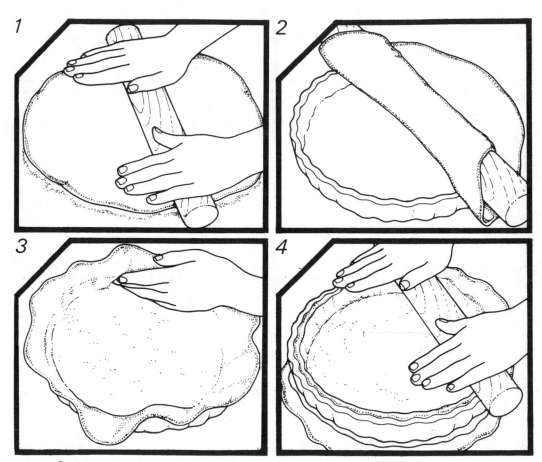

Lining a flan tin

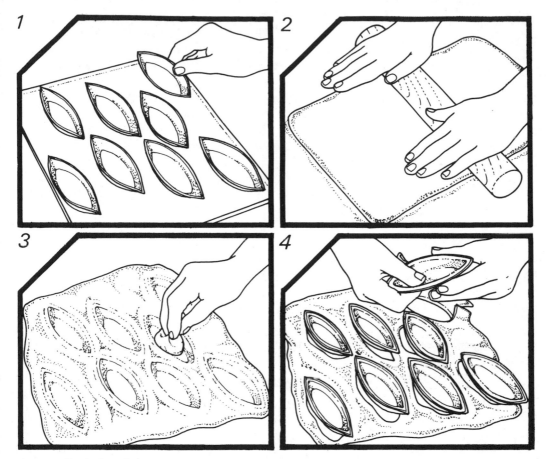

Lining individual tartlet tins

TO LINE A FLAN TIN, RING OR DISH

Choose a plain or fluted flan ring of the required size which should be placed on a flat baking sheet; a loose-based flan or sandwich (shallow) tin; or a china flan dish either round square or oval.

Measure the depth of the tin, double this and add to the diameter of the tin. Roll out the pastry to a little larger than this measurement but do not cut it to size. Using a rolling pin to lift the pastry, carefully lower it into the tin or fold the pastry carefully in half and position it in the tin. Lift the edges carefully and mould to the inside of the tin taking care not to stretch the pastry but taking it right to the corners. With fluted flans press your finger gently into each flute. With a plain ring, trim or cut off the surplus pastry a little over the edge and crimp or flute to decorate it; a fluted ring is trimmed by running the rolling pin across the top of the tin or dish when the surplus pastry will fall away.

INDIVIDUAL TARTLET TINS

Arrange the shallow tins close together on a baking sheet. Roll out the pastry to a rectangle larger than the baking sheet then carefully lay it loosely over the tins—like a blanket, but take care not to stretch the pastry. Use a small knob of dough or a clean cloth to press the dough into each tin then with a rolling pin roll across the tins and lift the surplus pastry carefully away. Reshape the pastry into the tins using your fingers. Deeper tartlet tins or sheets of tins have to be lined individually by cutting out circles or shapes of pastry a little larger than the tins and then lowering gently into the tins. The

31

edges can be left as they are or be lightly crimped.

BAKING BLIND

This process is often called for to part cook the pastry case before adding a cold or raw filling, or for complete cooking, or when the pastry case is to be stored for several days in an airtight container before use, or before freezing. It prevents the base rising up and the sides collapsing during cooking.

Line the flan tin as above then, if the pastry is to be completely cooked, prick all over the base with a fork. Cut a rough round of greaseproof paper about 5cm/2in larger than the tin. Grease lightly and place in the pastry-lined tin. Put a layer of uncooked beans (baking beans) or rice or pasta to cover the base evenly and then bake for 15–20 minutes or until the pastry is set and almost cooked.

Remove the paper and beans carefully (retain the beans for continuous future use) and return the flan to the oven for about 5 minutes or long enough to complete the cooking and dry out the pastry. If the pastry is to be part cooked before adding a liquid filling, it is best not to prick the base or the liquid will seep into the holes. Small tartlet tins can be baked blind by simply pricking the bases all over, no paper or beans being necessary; however if the sides are straight and as the tins get larger it is safer to use paper and beans. Fat wrappers can be used, greasy side down on the pastry.

COVERING A PIE DISH

Roll out the pastry to the thickness required and cut out 5cm/2in larger than the top of the dish using the empty inverted dish as a guide. Then cut a 2.5cm/1in strip off all

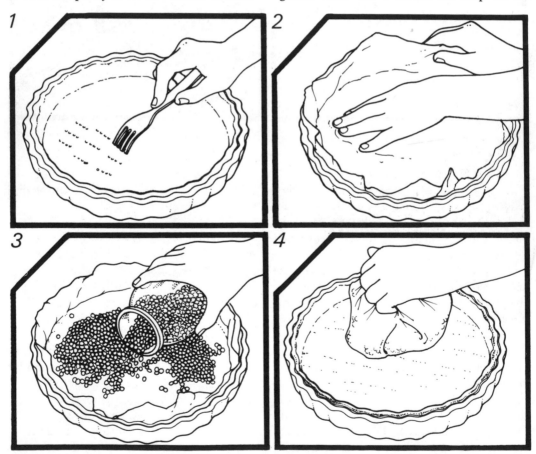

Baking blind

round the edge. Fill the pie dish so the filling is slightly rounded in the centre and up to the rim. With a very large dish, a very liquid filling or insufficient filling it is best to place a pie funnel in the centre of the dish which holds the pastry in place during cooking. Damp the rim of the dish with water and position the pastry strip on this rim; seal the join and brush the strip with water. Lift the pastry lid with the help of the rolling pin and position it over the filling. Press the lid firmly onto the pastry rim to seal it, and if a pie funnel is used press over the rim of the funnel to make a hole in the centre. Trim any excess pastry from the edge of the dish with a sharp knife held at an angle away from the dish. The best way to really seal the edges of the pastry is to 'knock up' or 'flake'. This is done by holding a sharp knife horizontally to the cut edge and making a series of shallow cuts into the pastry so it resembles the pages of a closed book, all the way round. This must be done when using flaked pastries but is optional with shortcrust but looks much better. A finish is then given by 'scalloping' the edge. Place your thumb or two fingers gently onto the edge of the pastry and with the back of a knife pull the edge up vertically at regular intervals to form a scallop each side of your fingers, then move your fingers on and repeat. This ensures an even distance between each scallop. Traditionally it is said that sweet pies have small scallops while those on savoury ones are much wider. Cut one or several slits in the top of the pie for the steam to escape during cooking and, if desired, use the pastry trimmings to make leaves for decoration, damping the undersides with water to make them adhere. Glaze the pastry with beaten egg or milk before baking.

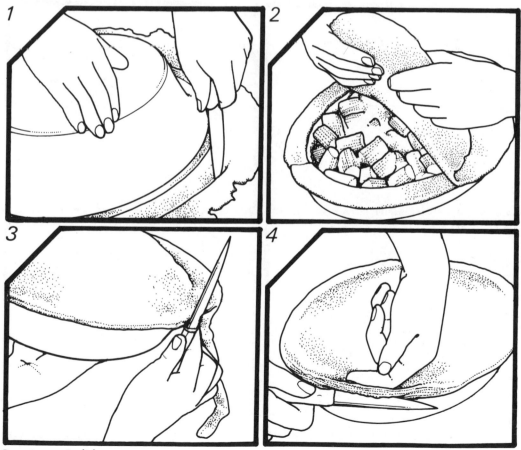

Covering a pie dish

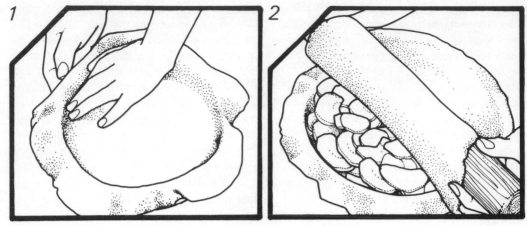

Making a double-crust pie

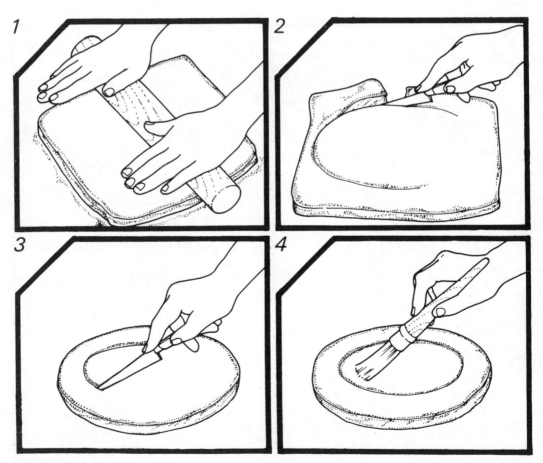

Large vol-au-vent

DOUBLE-CRUST PIE

This of course has a layer of pastry beneath and on top of the filling and care must be taken to ensure the base pastry is properly cooked through. It is a good idea to stand a baking sheet in the oven when you switch it on and then place the prepared pie on the very hot baking sheet in the preheated oven—this means the base of the pie begins to cook at the same time as the top.

Double-crust pies are usually made from shortcrust pastry or a short-pastry base with a flaked-pastry top. Flaked pastries do not cook well and cannot rise up with a filling on top of them in a pie but are fine when used in puffs and pasties etc. Divide the pastry in two, one part being a little larger than the other. Use the larger portion first and roll out to 2.5–5cm/1–2in larger than the top of the pie plate or tin. Ease into the tin, pressing gently to fit the corners and up over the rim. Do not stretch or leave any air bubbles under the pastry, also do not prick. Add the cold filling (hot fillings should not be used as they melt the pastry making it difficult to shape and also it cooks badly) keeping the surface of the filling slightly rounded in the centre. Roll out the reserved pastry to a size large enough to cover the top of the pie. Brush the rim of the pastry in the tin with water, position the lid carefully and press the edges well together. Trim as for covering a pie (see page 32) and then either knock up and crimp or pinch edges together between thumb and forefinger all the way round. Make one or two slits in the centre; if desired, decorate the top with leaves made from the pastry trimmings, damping the undersides with water to make them adhere; glaze with beaten egg or milk and bake.

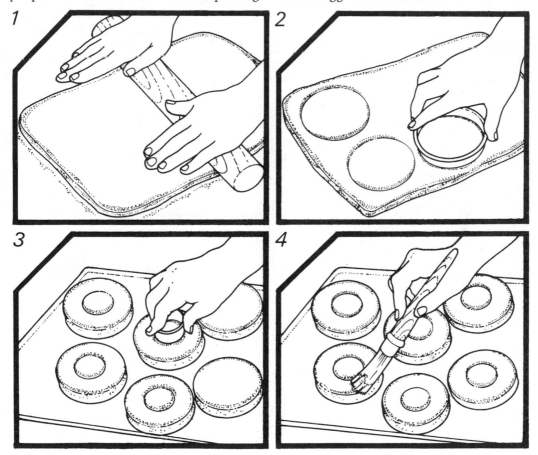

Small vol-au-vents

LARGE VOL-AU-VENT

Roll out the pastry to about 2.5cm/1in thick, place on a lightly greased baking sheet and cut out the size and shape of vol-au-vent you want—ie round or oval. Do not cut too near the edge of the pastry or the rise will be uneven. With a small sharp knife mark a smaller oval or round to correspond with the shape leaving about a 1–2.5cm/½–1in margin all round, then cut along this line to about halfway through the pastry—for the lid. Brush the top with beaten egg, chill for 10 minutes then bake for 30–35 minutes in a very hot oven (230–240°C/450–475°F, Gas Mark 8–9), covering with greaseproof paper when sufficiently browned. When cooked, carefully remove the lid and scoop out any soft pastry inside. Return to the oven for 5–10 minutes to dry out. Serve hot or cold. Cool on a wire rack.

SMALL VOL-AU-VENTS OR BOUCHÉES

Roll out the pastry to 1cm/⅓–½in thick and cut into rounds using a plain or fluted cutter. The size can vary from 2.5cm/1in up to 10–12.5cm/4–5in. Then take a smaller cutter and cut part way through the centre of each shape leaving about a 1cm/½in margin all round. Place on dampened baking sheets and glaze with beaten egg. Bake for 10–25 minutes depending on size in a hot to very hot oven (220–230°C/425–450°F, Gas Mark 7–8). Carefully remove the soft pastry from the centres and cool on a wire rack.

Pastry Edgings

There are several ways to decorate the edge of a pastry pie, flan or tart, some being very simple and others more complicated. The simple scallop is used for most pies, particularly those using a flaked pastry, but where the pastry lies on the rim of a pie tin there is much more scope for decoration.

SCALLOP

Place your thumb or forefinger on the pastry edge on the rim of the dish or tin, then with the back of a knife pull the pastry inwards to make an indentation. Move your thumb to the other side of the knife mark and repeat all the way round. The size of the scallops can be altered as desired. Traditionally sweet pies have small scallops whilst savoury ones are larger and wider apart. use this decoration for any type of pastry, short or flaked.

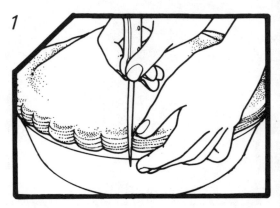

Scallop

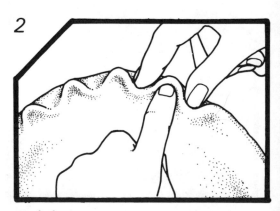

Pinched crimp

PINCHED CRIMP

Place the first finger of your right hand on the pastry edge on the rim of the dish or tin facing out from the filling. Then with the thumb and forefinger of the other hand, pinch the pastry around the finger into a point. Repeat all the way round. Not suitable for flaked pastries.

GABLE EDGE

Use for an open tart, flan or pie. Cut the pastry edging all round the rim at 1–2.5cm/½–1in intervals then fold every alternate piece inwards to lay over the filling or to fold over onto itself. Suitable for all pastries.

TRIANGULAR GABLE

Once again use for an open tart, flan or pie. Cut the pastry edging all round the rim at 1–2.5cm/½–1in intervals then fold each cut section in over itself diagonally taking the whole of the cut on the left side towards the centre of the pie and tapering it off to a point at the outer edge. Suitable for all pastries.

CIRCULAR OR LEAF EDGING

Cut a series of plain or fluted small circles of pastry (approx 1–2cm/½–¾in in diameter), damp the pastry rim and lay the circles evenly all round the rim just overlapping each one. An edging of leaves can also be made in the same way. Suitable for all pastries but flaked pastries should be cut a little larger to allow for shrinkage during baking.

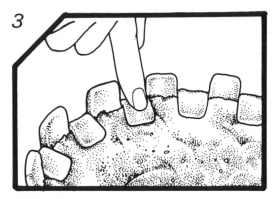

3

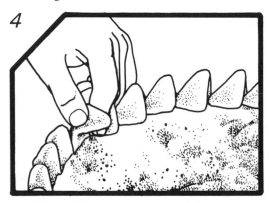

Gable edge

4

Triangular gable

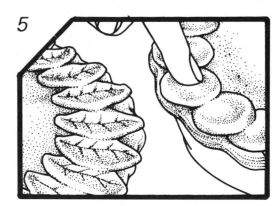

5

Circular or leaf edging

2
Main Dishes

2

Most types of pastry are suitable for savoury pies of one type or another. Puff, flaky and rough puff give the light crisp and airy pastry often preferred but it is best to use these as top crusts, plaits, envelopes and en croûte dishes for if used in a double-crust pie or flans the base pastry tends to become soggy and it cannot rise because of the weight of the filling. Shortcrust is also very popular with all types of pies, both single and double crust, and as this pastry does not rise there is no problem with the filling pressing down on it. However, sometimes the base does seem to be soggy for no apparent reason and a good way to avoid this is to place a baking sheet in the oven when you turn it on and then stand the pie on the hot baking sheet in the preheated oven so it immediately begins to cook from the base as well as the top; therefore the pastry base should cook before the filling has time to sink into it.

Pies of all types are favourites for main dishes as in fact are some savoury dishes which include pastry but are not true pies. Take for instance suet pastry—it makes a delicious steak and kidney pudding, the pastry being used to line the basin and the whole then boiled or steamed for several hours; or it can be used in the form of dumplings to bake on top of a casserole; or as a pie crust over a cooked filling. Then there is choux pastry, which is really a law unto itself for you can never roll it out, only spread or pipe it—but a gougère is delicious and looks most ambitious especially if made into a large ring, split and filled with an exotic filling. And of course the flaked pastries make crispy vol-au-vents, all the en croûte dishes as well as numerous pie toppings.

The fillings for single-crust pies are unlimited and can utilise any type of meat, poultry, game, fish, vegetables etc to suit your taste; in fact it is a good idea to convert your favourite casserole to a pie by simply adding a crust of one type of pastry or another. I prefer to precook the filling if the ingredients need more than an hour or so for, apart from hot-water-crust pastry, long cooking tends to spoil the texture of the pastry whilst trying to tenderise the filling. Also if you precook the filling it can be prepared the day before and chilled overnight, or stored in the freezer for 2–3 months. Then if a sudden meal is called for, the filling is there only requiring to be thawed, a pie crust is quickly added and hey presto, a meal fit for a king. Another reason for adding a pie crust is to stretch out a perhaps rather meagre amount of meat and no one will notice the shortage of filling. A pie with a precooked filling is cooked at one temperature only but with raw fillings it is best to start in a hot oven to set the pastry then reduce to moderate to allow time for the filling to cook.

It is not absolutely essential to glaze pies with beaten egg but it does produce the traditional golden glaze associated with pastry; milk does not give such a sheen but is a good second best, whilst egg white or egg yolk alone can also be used. When it comes to decorating the top with pastry trimmings this is not necessary either but it does make the pie look so much more 'finished' and uses up the scraps which would probably otherwise go to waste. Leaves are traditional, but flowers, circles and other shapes are often used and some pies can have quite elaborate and heavy decoration, especially the hot-water-crust raised pies. When making leaves from a flaked pastry remember to cut them a little larger than you want for they tend to shrink during cooking; also keep an eye on the pastry during cooking, for anything raised above the crust is likely to brown quicker. A sheet or small pieces of greaseproof paper in the appropriate place will help prevent over-browning. A china pie funnel is used in many pies to prevent the pastry sinking into the dish when there is insufficient filling and to raise the pastry up in the centre, particularly when the filling contains large pieces.

This section includes a good selection of pie fillings for flaked or shortcrust pastries (they can be intermixed as well). Also included are all the raised pies, which I have put in this chapter rather than in the section on picnics as they are really too elaborate for simple picnic fare, although ideal for the elegant hampers and cold buffets of today. There is also a selection of en croûte recipes which are fun to make, being really quite simple, but they do impress your guests and you can wrap more or less any piece of meat in pastry and cook it, provided the meat has been sealed or part-cooked first. Small items such as part-cooked steaks, chops etc can be wrapped in pastry and deep fried which is much quicker and prevents too much extra cooking after the pastry is added; they can be cooked conventionally in the oven too.

A word about freezing. Most types of pastry and pies freeze well, the main exception being hot-water-crust which is liable to crumble when thawed and cut. Double-crust pies freeze well and top-crust pies are also fine. Choux-pastry gougères also freeze but should not be filled first—they require refreshing in a warm oven before filling. Dumplings and suet puddings are best made and eaten when required although baked dumplings and scone-topped cobblers will freeze for a short time. Most dishes are all right for up to 2 months but if the filling is very spicy or contains fish then 3–4 weeks is long enough. I prefer to thaw before reheating but that is a matter of preference.

Steak and Kidney Pudding

Steak and kidney pudding was thought to have originated in Sussex but this well-loved savoury suet pudding has travelled the country and is now a real traditional British pudding. Oysters were often added but the long boiling necessary to tenderise the meat didn't improve the texture of the oysters and I prefer to omit them. Mushrooms are a good addition but again are a matter of preference.

1 recipe quantity suet-crust pastry (see page 25)
450g/1lb best braising or chuck steak
175g/6oz (approx) ox kidney
2 level tbsp well-seasoned flour
100g/4oz mushrooms, sliced or quartered
   (optional)
4tbsp (approx) stock, water or wine

1 Roll out three-quarters of the pastry and use to line a greased 1 litre/2pt pudding basin.
2 Cut the steak into approx 2cm/¾in cubes discarding any fat or gristle and cut the skinned and cored kidney into smaller pieces. Toss the meats in the seasoned flour.
3 Spoon the meat into the lined basin alternating with mushrooms and seasonings until almost full. Add the stock, water or wine.

4 Roll out the remaining pastry to form a lid, damp the edges and position, pressing edges firmly together.
5 Cover first with a layer of greased greaseproof paper with a pleat across the centre and then either a pudding cloth or a pleated foil lid, tying very securely under the rim of the basin.
6 Stand the basin either in a saucepan containing boiling water to reach halfway up the basin, or in the top of a steamer. Cover and simmer gently for about 4 hours, adding more boiling water to the saucepan as necessary.
7 To serve, remove the cloth or foil and greaseproof paper and either serve from the basin with a cloth tied round it or turn the pudding out carefully onto a warmed serving dish, hoping it will not split open or crack before serving.

Serves 4

VARIATIONS
Bacon and onion Add 1 level tsp dried mixed herbs or sage to the dry suet-crust mix and continue as above but using 675g/1½lb diced lean bacon, 2 large sliced onions, 4tbsp stock or water, and pepper only to season. Boil for 3–3½ hours.

Steak and Kidney Pudding

Chicken and ham Make as steak and kidney pudding but for the filling use 225g/8oz lean diced bacon, 350g/12oz chopped raw chicken meat, 1 chopped onion, 1 level tsp mixed herbs, 100g/4oz sliced mushrooms and 4tbsp stock or white wine. Boil for 3–3½ hours.

Veal and lemon Make as steak and kidney pudding but for the filling use 675g/1½lb lean diced pie veal, 1 chopped onion, 1 chopped carrot, grated rind of 1 lemon, 1tbsp freshly chopped parsley, 3tbsp stock and 1tbsp lemon juice.

Steak and Kidney Pie

One of the best-known and well-loved British recipes for a pie. Traditionally it has steak and kidney only for the filling but other ingredients have crept in and are favoured by some people. Onion I think is a must but whatever you add—be it mushrooms, oysters, aubergines or whatever—is a matter of personal preference. Most people prefer a puff or flaky pastry crust but shortcrust can also be used.

2tbsp oil or dripping
1 large onion, peeled and sliced
450g/1lb stewing steak, cut into 2cm/¾in
   cubes
100g/4oz ox kidney, chopped
1 level tbsp flour
1 meat extract cube or stock cube
1tsp Worcestershire sauce
1 level tbsp tomato purée (optional)
600ml/1pt water
salt and pepper
½ recipe quantity puff, rough puff or flaky pastry
   (see pages 21, 24)
beaten egg to glaze

1 Melt the dripping in a pan and fry the onion until soft. Add the steak and kidney and continue to cook until the meat is well sealed.

2 Stir in the flour and cook for 1 minute. Blend the stock cube, Worcestershire sauce and tomato purée with the water, gradually add to the pan and bring to the boil, stirring continuously. Season well.

3 Cover the pan and simmer gently for about 1½ hrs or until tender, stirring occasionally. Pour into a pie dish with a funnel in the centre and leave to cool. At this stage the meat can be refrigerated overnight.

4 Roll out the pastry and use to cover the pie dish (see page 32). Decorate with the pastry trimmings and glaze.

5 Cook in a hot oven (220°C/425°F, Gas Mark 7) for 25 minutes or until beginning to brown. Reduce the temperature to moderate (180°C/350°F, Gas Mark 4) and continue cooking for about 30 minutes or until the filling is piping hot and the crust well risen and browned. If the filling was taken straight from the refrigerator, increase the cooking time by 5–10 minutes.

Serves 4

VARIATIONS

Oyster Add 6–8 oysters, fresh or frozen, to the cooked meat.

Aubergine Add a diced small aubergine to the meat halfway through the initial cooking process.

Mushroom Add 100g/4oz halved or sliced mushrooms to the meat just before turning into the pie dish.

Chestnut Omit the kidney and add 175g/6oz lightly roasted or canned whole chestnuts to the meat halfway through the initial cooking process. 150ml/¼pt red wine can be used to replace some of the water.

Tomato and caper Add 4 peeled and chopped tomatoes and 2tbsp capers to the meat just before turning into the pie dish.

Beef and Tomato Pie

This is my version of a not so traditional Cornish pasty filling baked in a square cake tin to serve hot or cold.

450g/1lb raw minced beef
1 onion, peeled and finely chopped
1–2 carrots, peeled and finely chopped
1 clove garlic, crushed (optional)
salt and pepper
1tsp Worcestershire sauce

3–4 tomatoes, peeled and roughly chopped
1 recipe quantity shortcrust pastry (see page 16),
   or 2 recipe quantities quick-mix pastry (see
   page 25)
beaten egg or milk to glaze

1 Combine the beef, onion, carrots, garlic (if used), plenty of seasonings, Worcestershire sauce and tomatoes.
2 Roll out two-thirds of the pastry and use to line a shallow 20cm/8in square sandwich tin.
3 Spoon in the filling keeping well into the corners. Roll out the remaining pastry for a lid, damp the edges and position carefully pressing the edges firmly together. Trim the edges, crimp and make 2 or 3 holes in the top. Decorate with the pastry trimmings. Glaze with beaten egg or milk.
4 Bake in a fairly hot oven (200°C/400°F, Gas Mark 6) for 25–30 minutes. Reduce the temperature to moderate (180°C/350°F, Gas Mark 4) and continue cooking for 15–20 minutes. Serve hot or cold.

Serves 4

Cidered Beef with Dumplings

Dumplings have long been a sign of winter, giving something extra to a hearty casserole.

675g/1½lb chuck or braising steak
25g/1oz seasoned flour
3tbsp oil or dripping
1 large onion, peeled and sliced
1 clove garlic, crushed (optional)
300ml/½pt cider
300ml/½pt stock
2 large carrots, peeled and cut into sticks
3–4 sticks celery, sliced
1 level tsp French mustard
100g/4oz button mushrooms, halved
salt and pepper
½ recipe quantity suet-crust pastry (see page 25)
   with 1 level tsp mixed herbs added

1 Cut the meat into 2.5cm/1in cubes and toss in the seasoned flour.
2 Heat 2tbsp of oil or dripping in a pan and fry the meat until it is well sealed all over and then transfer to a casserole.
3 Add the remaining oil or dripping to the pan and fry the onion and garlic until lightly coloured.
4 Stir in any remaining seasoned flour then gradually add the cider and stock and bring to the boil.
5 Add the carrots, celery, mustard, mushrooms and plenty of seasonings and simmer for 2 minutes then add to the casserole and cover tightly.
6 Cook in a moderate oven (180°C/350°F, Gas Mark 4) for 1½ hrs, or until almost tender.
7 Make up the dumplings having added the herbs and divide into eight portions. Shape into even-sized balls. Remove the lid from the casserole, place the dumplings over the top and return to the oven without the lid. Cook for 25–30 minutes, until the dumplings are puffed up and lightly coloured.

Serves 4–5

Spiced Beef Pie

A beefy filling flavoured with tomatoes, onion and curry powder with a slight sweetness which comes from the jam.

675g/1½lb braising or stewing steak
2tbsp oil or dripping
4 onions, peeled and chopped
425g/15oz can tomatoes
1½ level tsp curry powder
2 level tbsp tomato purée
2tbsp wine vinegar
2 level tbsp apricot jam or redcurrant jelly
150ml/¼pt tomato juice
150ml/¼pt beef stock
salt and pepper
1 bay leaf
1 recipe quantity shortcrust pastry (see page 16),
   or 2 recipe quantities quick-mix pastry (see
   page 25)
beaten egg or milk to glaze

1 Cut the beef into narrow strips. Heat the oil or dripping in a pan and fry the meat until well sealed. Add the onions and continue to cook for 4–5 minutes.

2 Add the rest of the ingredients and bring to the boil, stirring frequently.

3 Transfer to a casserole, cover tightly and cook in a moderate oven (160°C/325°F, Gas Mark 3) for 2½–3 hours or until tender, adding a little boiling water if necessary. Turn into a pie dish with a funnel in the centre and allow to cool.

4 Roll out the pastry and use to cover the pie dish (see page 32) decorate with the pastry trimmings and glaze well.

5 Cook in a fairly hot oven (200°C/400°F, Gas Mark 6) for about 40 minutes until golden brown.

Serves 4–6

Steak and Pigeon Pie

Pigeons are now readily available and make a very tasty pie.

50g/2oz butter or margarine
2 large pigeons, jointed
225g/8oz braising steak, diced
1 onion, peeled and chopped
4 bacon rashers, derinded and chopped
1 clove garlic, crushed
40g/1½oz flour
450ml/¾pt stock
150ml/¼pt unsweetened orange juice
1tbsp tomato purée
1tbsp black treacle
100g/4oz mushrooms, quartered
½ recipe quantity flaky or rough puff pastry (see pages 21, 24)
beaten egg to glaze

1 Melt the fat and fry the pieces of pigeon until well browned. Remove from the pan and fry the steak in the same fat until well sealed. Add the onion, bacon and garlic and continue to cook for 2–3 minutes.

2 Sprinkle the flour into the pan, mix thoroughly then gradually add the stock and bring to the boil.

3 Place the pigeon pieces back in the pan, add the orange juice, tomato purée and black treacle. Cover tightly and simmer gently for about 1½ hours or until tender. Stir in the mushrooms, pour the whole into a pie dish

with a funnel in the centre and leave to cool.

4 Roll out the pastry and use to cover the pie dish (see page 32). Decorate with the pastry trimmings, glaze and cook in a fairly hot oven (200°C/400°F, Gas Mark 6) for about 40 minutes or until golden brown. Serve hot.

Serves 4

Beef Wellington

This is the en croûte recipe of all time. The fillet steak necessary is certainly not cheap but has no waste at all—but you must ask for the thick end of the fillet. I like a mushroom and onion stuffing around the meat but some prefer a layer of smooth pâté. However the choice is yours.

50g/2oz butter or margarine
675–900g/1½–2lb piece of fillet of beef (thick end)
2 onions, peeled and sliced
100g/4oz button mushrooms, sliced
1 level tbsp freshly chopped parsley
salt and pepper
pinch garlic powder (optional)
½ recipe quantity puff or flaky pastry (see pages 21–3)
beaten egg to glaze

1 Melt the fat in a frying pan and fry the fillet of beef on all sides until well sealed and browned—about 10 minutes. Remove the meat and allow to cool.

2 Fry the onions in the same fat until soft and lightly browned. Add the mushrooms and cook for 2–3 minutes. Remove from the heat and stir in the parsley, plenty of seasonings and a little garlic powder, if liked.

3 Roll out the pastry to a rectangle large enough to enclose the beef. Spread the mushroom mixture over the pastry and place the beef on top.

4 Wrap the beef in the pastry until completely enclosed, damping the edges to seal firmly. Place on a greased baking sheet with the pastry join underneath and decorate the top with a double row of pastry leaves made from the trimmings.

Beef Wellington

5 Glaze well and cook in a hot oven (220°C/425°F, Gas Mark 7) for about 1 hour until the pastry is well browned. If it is over-browning cover with a sheet of greaseproof paper. At this stage the beef should be pink inside. If a little more cooking is preferred reduce the temperature to moderate (180°C/350°F, Gas Mark 4) and leave for about 20 minutes when the beef will be medium done.

Serves 6–8

Note For a pâté stuffing, omit the onions, mushrooms and parsley and instead spread about 100g/4oz pâté (smooth or semi-coarse) over the pastry before adding the piece of beef.

Steak Parcels

Puff pastry can be deep fried as well as baked and when steak is the filling it is a good method for it does not overcook the steak.

40g/1½oz butter
100g/4oz mushrooms, chopped
2 rashers bacon, derinded and chopped

1 clove garlic, crushed
1 level tsp French mustard
1 level tbsp freshly chopped parsley
salt and pepper
4 minute steaks or rump or fillet steaks (approx 150–175g/5–6oz each)
½ recipe quantity puff pastry (see page 21)
beaten egg to glaze
fat or oil for deep frying
watercress and tomato to garnish

1 Melt half the butter in a small pan and fry the mushrooms, bacon and garlic until soft. Stir in the mustard, parsley and seasonings and leave to cool.
2 Season the steaks lightly and fry quickly in the remaining melted butter for 1–1½ minutes each side. Remove from the pan and leave to cool.
3 Roll the pastry out thinly and cut into circles large enough to enclose the steaks.
4 Spread each steak with the mushroom mixture and place on the pastry circles. Brush the edges with beaten egg and press together to enclose the steaks completely. Make sure the pastry is securely pinched together underneath.

5 Glaze the parcels all over and decorate tops with the pastry trimmings, then glaze again.
6 Heat the fat to about 180°C/350°F, or until a cube of bread browns in 30 seconds, and carefully lower the parcels into the fat, two at a time. Fry for about 5 minutes, turning over once, when the pastry should be golden brown. Drain on absorbent paper and keep warm whilst frying the remainder. Serve hot garnished with watercress and tomato.

Serves 4

Lamb Fillet en Croûte

A quickly prepared en croûte dish. The basic cooking and preparation can be carried out early in the day with the final cooking to be done when required. If taken straight from the refrigerator, increase the cooking time by 5–10 minutes.

2 large fillets of lamb
25g/1oz butter or margarine
1 medium onion, peeled and finely chopped
finely grated rind of ½ lemon
2tbsp freshly chopped parsley
salt and pepper
good pinch mixed spice
50g/2oz long-grain rice, cooked
200g/7oz can apricot halves
1 egg, beaten
⅓ recipe quantity puff or flaky pastry (see pages 21–3)

1 Trim the lamb fillets, fold the tail in and place one on top of the other, securing with fine string.
2 Fry in the melted fat for about 15 minutes until well sealed and browned all over. Remove from the pan and leave to cool.
3 Fry the onion in the same fat until soft then mix in the lemon rind, parsley, seasonings, spice and rice.
4 Drain the apricots (reserve the juice for making the gravy), chop and add to the stuffing mixture with about two-thirds of the beaten egg.
5 Roll out the pastry to a rectangle large enough to enclose the lamb. Untie the lamb and place one fillet on the pastry. Spread the stuffing over the lamb then top with the second piece of fillet.
6 Fold the pastry round the lamb to completely enclose it, damping the edges to seal firmly. Place on a greased baking sheet with the pastry join underneath and decorate the top with the pastry trimmings.
7 Glaze and cook in a hot oven (220°C/425°F, Gas Mark 7) for 20 minutes then reduce the temperature to moderate (180°C/350°F, Gas Mark 4) and continue cooking for 40–45 minutes. When the pastry is sufficiently browned cover with a sheet of greaseproof paper.

Serves 4–5

Minted Lamb Pie

This pie is topped with rough puff or quick puffy pastry, both quick and easy to make. Lamb is always enhanced by the flavour of mint as is shown here.

1tbsp dripping
450g/1lb lean lamb (from shoulder or top of leg)
1 onion, peeled and sliced
3 sticks celery, sliced
1 carrot, peeled and diced
300ml/½pt stock
1 level tbsp freshly chopped mint or 1–1½ level tsp dried mint
salt and pepper
1½ level tsp cornflour
6tbsp milk
3–4tbsp cream
75g/3oz cooked peas
½ recipe quantity rough puff pastry (see page 24), or 1 recipe quantity quick puffy pastry (see page 25)
beaten egg to glaze

1 Melt the dripping in a pan. Cut the lamb into small cubes and quickly fry in order to seal. Add the onion, celery and carrot and cook gently for about 10 minutes, stirring occasionally.
2 Stir in the stock, mint and seasonings and bring to the boil. Cover and simmer gently for about 20 minutes or until tender.

3 Blend the cornflour with the milk and cream and stir into the lamb mixture, bring back to the boil and simmer for 2 minutes. Stir in the peas, adjust the seasonings and pour the whole into a pie dish with a funnel in the centre.

4 Roll out the pastry and use to cover the pie (see page 32).

5 Glaze and cook in a fairly hot oven (220°C/425°F, Gas Mark 7) for 30–40 minutes or until well risen and golden brown. Serve hot.

Serves 4

Lamb and Orange Cobbler

The flavours of lamb, orange and apricots blend well and with the addition of a scone topping make a rather different meal.

2tbsp oil
1.25kg/2½lb (approx) neck of lamb, trimmed
2 onions, peeled and chopped
1 clove garlic, crushed
25g/1oz flour
450ml/¾pt stock
150ml/¼pt unsweetened orange juice
salt and pepper
1 bay leaf
175g/6oz dried apricots, soaked overnight

Scone topping
200g/8oz self-raising flour
pinch salt
50g/2oz butter or margarine
grated rind of 1 small orange
1 egg
milk to mix

1 Heat the oil in a pan and fry the meat until lightly browned. Transfer to an ovenproof casserole.

2 Fry the onions and garlic in the remaining oil until soft then add the flour and cook for a minute or so.

3 Add the stock and orange juice and bring to the boil, stirring frequently.

4 Season well, add the bay leaf and drained apricots then pour the whole over the lamb and cover the casserole.

5 Cook in a moderate oven (160°C/325°F, Gas Mark 3) for about 1¼ hours or until almost tender.

6 To make the topping, sift the flour and a pinch of salt into a bowl and rub in the fat until the mixture resembles fine breadcrumbs. Stir in the orange rind then add the egg and sufficient milk to mix to a softish dough.

7 Roll or pat out the dough to approx 1cm/½in thick and cut into 2.5–4cm/1½–2in rounds.

8 Remove the casserole from the oven and take off the lid. Discard the bay leaf and lay the scones in an overlapping circle all round the edge of the dish, brushing each with milk before adding the next one.

9 Increase the oven temperature to hot (220°C/425°F, Gas Mark 7) and return the uncovered casserole to the oven for about 15 minutes or until the scones are well risen, firm and golden brown. Serve hot.

Serves 4–5

Chicken and Ham Pie

The filling of chicken, ham, cheese and hard-boiled eggs makes this double-crust pie equally good to serve hot or cold.

1 large onion, peeled and chopped
50g/2oz butter or margarine
40g/1½oz flour
300ml/½pt milk
½ level tsp made mustard
pinch ground nutmeg
salt and pepper
75g/3oz mature Cheddar cheese, grated
100g/4oz cooked ham or bacon, chopped
225g/8oz cooked chicken (or turkey) meat, chopped
2 hard-boiled eggs, sliced
1 recipe quantity shortcrust pastry (see page 16)
beaten egg or milk to glaze

(*Clockwise*) Choux pastry, flaky pastry, shortcrust pastry lining a flan dish, puff pastry being cut for a vol-au-vent and wrapped around cream horn tins

1 Fry the onion gently in the fat until soft. Stir in the flour and cook for 1 minute then gradually add the milk and bring to the boil, stirring frequently.

2 Add the mustard and nutmeg and season well. Stir in the cheese until melted then add the ham and chicken meat. Leave to cool.

3 Roll out two-thirds of the pastry and use to line a shallow pie tin or plate measuring approx 20cm/8in; spoon in half the filling, cover with sliced eggs then add the remainder, levelling the top.

4 Use the remaining pastry to form a lid, position it, damp the edges and press firmly together. Trim, crimp the edges and decorate the top with the pastry trimmings.

5 Glaze and then cook in a fairly hot oven (200°C/400°F, Gas Mark 6) for 35–45 minutes or until golden brown. Cover with a sheet of greaseproof paper if over-browning. Serve hot or cold.

Serves 4–5

Colonial Goose in a Crust

This recipe has been handed around across the seas for some years supposedly originating in New Zealand. It is not at all what it sounds for it is in fact a leg of lamb with a rich stuffing of prunes and apples and was probably thought to be the nearest type of meat to goose flesh. It is worth the time necessary to bone the lamb, and when baked in a crust it is even better, I think, for all the juices are captured in the pastry.

2kg/4½lb leg of lamb
25g/1oz butter
1 small onion, peeled and chopped
100g/4oz prunes, soaked overnight
1 eating apple, peeled, cored and chopped
75g/3oz fresh breadcrumbs
salt and pepper

(*Clockwise*) Chicken and Ham Pudding, Colonial Goose en Croûte, Seafood Puff, Beef and Tomato Pie and Lamb and Orange Cobbler

1 level tsp rosemary (fresh or dried), chopped
1 egg, beaten
150ml/¼pt red wine
3tbsp oil
2 level tbsp flour
300ml/½pt stock
1tbsp redcurrant jelly
3–4tbsp soured cream
¾ recipe quantity puff or flaky pastry (see pages 21–3)
beaten egg to glaze
whole prunes and fresh rosemary to garnish

1 Bone out the leg of lamb—or ask the butcher to do it for you.

2 Melt the butter and fry the onion until soft. Chop and stone the prunes and add to the onion with the apple, breadcrumbs, seasonings and rosemary. Bind together with the egg and use to stuff the bone cavity.

3 Sew the joint back into shape if necessary with a trussing needle and fine string to enclose the stuffing, but not too tightly or the skin will split during roasting.

4 Place the lamb in a polythene bag with the wine and leave to marinate for about 6 hours, turning occasionally.

5 Remove the joint (reserving the marinade) and place it in a roasting tin with the oil, seasoning well. Roast in a moderate oven (180°C/350°F, Gas Mark 4) for 1½ hours, basting regularly. Remove the meat from the tin and allow to cool, then carefully take out the trussing string.

6 Pour off the excess fat from the pan juices and stir the flour into the residue. Cook for 1 minute then add the wine from the marinade, the stock and redcurrant jelly and bring to the boil for a minute or so. Season well, stir in the soured cream and leave to cool.

7 Roll out the pastry to a rectangle large enough to enclose the lamb. Place the joint in the centre, wrap up and seal the edges with water.

8 Place in a greased roasting tin with the pastry join underneath. Decorate the top with the pastry trimmings and glaze thoroughly.

9 Cook in a fairly hot oven (200°C/400°F, Gas Mark 6) for about 1 hour, covering with

a sheet of greaseproof paper when sufficiently browned. Serve hot with the reheated sauce and garnished with whole prunes and sprigs of rosemary.

Serves 6–8

Turkey and Artichoke Pie

Turkey casserole meat or thigh meat makes excellent pies and here it is teamed up with Jerusalem artichokes for an interesting flavour.

675g/1½lb turkey casserole meat or boneless thigh meat
75g/3oz butter or margarine
900ml/1½pt chicken stock
salt and pepper
1 bay leaf
450g/1lb Jerusalem artichokes
juice of ½ lemon
25g/1oz flour
1 level tbsp freshly chopped parsley
2–3tbsp cream
½ recipe quantity flaky or rough puff pastry (see pages 21, 24)
beaten egg to glaze

1 Cut the turkey into cubes measuring about 2.5cm/1in. Fry in 50g/2oz of the butter until well sealed then add the stock and bring to the boil.
2 Season well, add the bay leaf and cover the pan. Simmer gently for 30 minutes.
3 Peel the artichokes and place them in cold water, adding the lemon juice to prevent discoloration.
4 Add the artichokes to the pan, bring back to the boil and simmer for a further 30 minutes.
5 Discard the bay leaf, then transfer the turkey and artichokes to a pie dish using a slotted spoon.
6 Cream the remaining butter and the flour together then whisk this beurre manié in small pieces into the cooking liquor. Bring back to the boil, stirring continuously until the mixture has thickened. Adjust the seasonings, stir in the parsley and cream and pour into the pie dish. Leave to cool.

7 Roll out the pastry and use to cover the pie (see page 32). Decorate the top with the pastry trimmings, glaze and then bake in a fairly hot oven (200°C/400°F, Gas Mark 6) for about 40 minutes until golden brown. Serve hot.

Serves 5–6

Ham and Chicken Gougère

This method of making a gougère has the choux pastry spread round the edge of an dish with the filling baked in the centre.

50g/2oz butter or margarine
1 onion, peeled and chopped
1 green pepper, deseeded and chopped
100g/4oz mushrooms, sliced
25g/1oz flour
150ml/¼pt dry white wine or cider
200ml/8fl oz milk or stock
salt and pepper
½ level tsp dry mustard
175g/6oz cooked ham, cut into strips
225/8oz cooked chicken, diced
2 recipe quantities choux pastry (see page 29)
paprika to garnish

1 To prepare the filling, first melt the butter and then fry the onion and green pepper until soft; add the mushrooms and continue to cook for a minute or so.
2 Stir in the flour, cook for 1 minute then gradually add the wine or cider followed by the milk or stock and bring to the boil, stirring continuously. Simmer for 2 minutes, season well, then stir in the mustard, ham and chicken.
3 Grease a shallow ovenproof dish (approx 1.75 litres/3pt) and spread the choux pastry round the sides to make an even border.
4 Pour or spoon the filling into the centre of the dish (not over the choux pastry).
5 Cook in a fairly hot oven (200°C/400°F, Gas Mark 6) for 35–45 minutes or until the choux border is well risen, firm and golden brown. Sprinkle with paprika and serve at once.

Serves 4–5

Tarragon Chicken Pie

Tarragon and chicken go together so well and are used for this double-crust pie. If fresh tarragon is not available use the dried variety but you will not get the true flavour of tarragon.

50g/2oz butter or margarine
2 onions, peeled and sliced
40g/1½oz flour
450ml/¾pt chicken stock
salt and pepper
2tbsp freshly chopped tarragon, or 2tsp dried tarragon
350–450g/¾–1lb cooked chicken meat, cut into strips
2tbsp cream
1 recipe quantity shortcrust pastry (see page 16), or 2 recipe quantities quick mix pastry (see page 25)
milk to glaze
few sesame seeds

1 Melt the butter in a pan, fry the onions until soft but not coloured then stir in the flour and cook for 1 minute.
2 Gradually add the stock and bring to the boil, stirring frequently, and simmer for 2 minutes. Season well.
3 Stir in the tarragon, chicken and cream and leave to cool.
4 Roll out two-thirds of the pastry and use to line a 20cm/8in deep pie plate or tin. Spoon in the filling.
5 Use the remaining pastry to form a lid, damp the edges, position it and then trim. Crimp, decorate the top with the pastry trimmings and glaze.
6 Sprinkle with sesame seeds and cook in a fairly hot oven (200°C/400°F, Gas Mark 6) for about 40 minutes or until golden brown. Cover with a sheet of greaseproof paper if over-browning. Serve hot or cold.

Serves 4–5

Pheasant and Asparagus Parcels

When pheasants are available try this and the following pie recipe for two completely different recipes not even reminiscent of roast pheasant.

4 pheasant breasts (use remainder of birds for a casserole)
salt and pepper
40g/1½oz butter or margarine
1 large onion, peeled and thinly sliced
75–100g/3–4oz button mushrooms, sliced
grated rind of ½ lemon (optional)
1tbsp lemon juice
4 level tbsp fresh breadcrumbs
½ recipe quantity puff or flaky pastry (see pages 21–3)
350g/12oz can asparagus spears
beaten egg to glaze

Sauce
little stock or milk
40g/1½oz butter or margarine
40g/1½oz flour
salt and pepper
lemon slices and parsley to garnish

1 Carefully remove the breast of each pheasant from the carcass with a sharp knife.
2 Season the breasts and fry gently in the melted fat for 4–5 minutes each side or until almost cooked through. Remove from the pan and leave to cool.
3 Fry the onion in the remaining fat in the pan, then drain and cool.
4 Add the mushrooms, lemon rind and juice and breadcrumbs and season well.
5 Roll out the pastry thinly and cut into four pieces each large enough to enclose a piece of pheasant.
6 Drain the asparagus (reserving the liquor) and lay 3–4 spears on each piece of pastry. Spoon the stuffing on top and press a piece of pheasant into each.
7 Enclose the pheasant in the pastry, damping the edges to seal securely. Glaze and place on a greased baking sheet with the pastry joins underneath. Decorate with the pastry trimmings and glaze again.
8 Cook in a fairly hot oven (200°C/400°F,

Gas Mark 6) for 30–40 minutes or until a good golden brown.

9 To prepare the sauce, make the asparagus liquor up to 400ml/almost ¾pt with stock or milk. Melt the fat in a pan, stir in the flour and cook for 1 minute. Gradually add the liquor and bring to the boil, stirring frequently. Season well.

10 Chop the remaining asparagus and add to the sauce then simmer for 2 minutes. Serve in a sauce boat with the parcels garnished with lemon slices and parsley.

Serves 4

Note The parcels may also be served cold and make good elegant picnic fare.

Pheasant and Beef Pie

This recipe can use up the legs left over from the pheasants which were used for the previous recipe, or use a whole bird. Pheasant and other game is now readily available frozen from larger supermarkets.

225g/8oz raw minced beef
2 rashers bacon, derinded and chopped
1 onion, peeled and chopped
salt and pepper
25g/1oz butter or margarine
25g/1oz flour
300ml/½pt cider
cooked legs of 2 pheasants or 1 whole cooked
    pheasant
1 recipe quantity shortcrust pastry (see page 16)
beaten egg or milk to glaze

1 Cook the mince, bacon and onion gently in a saucepan with no extra fat added for 10 minutes, stirring frequently. Season well.

2 Melt the butter in a pan, stir in the flour and cook for 1 minute. Gradually add the cider and bring to the boil and simmer for 2 minutes. Season well and stir into the mince mixture.

3 Strip the flesh from the pheasant legs or whole bird, chop roughly and add to the mince. Pour the mixture into a pie dish and leave to cool.

4 Roll out the pastry and use to cover the pie

dish (see page 32). Decorate the top with the pastry trimmings, make a hole in the centre and glaze.

5 Cook in a fairly hot oven (200°C/400°F, Gas Mark 6) for about 40 minutes until the pastry is golden brown and the filling bubbling hot. Lay a sheet of greaseproof paper over the pastry if over-browning.

Serves 4–6

Creamy Pheasant Pie

An older pheasant is ideal for this pie as it has the necessary extra cooking to tenderise the meat before adding the pastry crust. The filling can even be made the day before it is required.

1 mature pheasant, oven ready
salt and pepper
40g/1½oz butter or margarine
2 onions, peeled and sliced
450ml/¾pt stock or water
1 bay leaf
1 level tbsp cornflour
150ml/¼pt single cream
100g/4oz mushrooms, sliced
2tbsp sherry (optional)
1 recipe quantity shortcrust pastry (see page 16),
    or 1 recipe quantity quick puffy pastry (see
    page 25)
beaten egg or milk to glaze

1 Cut the pheasant into four or eight portions. Season well and fry in a saucepan in the melted fat until well browned all over.

2 Add the onions, stock, bay leaf and seasonings and bring to the boil. Cover the pan and simmer very gently until almost tender (about 1 hour), adding a little extra stock if necessary during cooking.

3 Discard the bay leaf then thicken the juices with the cornflour blended with the cream and bring back to the boil for a minute or so. Stir in the mushrooms and sherry (if used) and adjust the seasonings. Pour into a pie dish with a funnel in the centre and leave to cool.

4 Roll out the pastry to form a lid and use to cover the pie (see page 32). Decorate with the

pastry trimmings, glaze and cook in a fairly hot oven (200°C/400°F, Gas Mark 6) for about 30 minutes or until well browned. Reduce the oven temperature to moderate (180°C/350°F, Gas Mark 4) and continue to cook for 15–20 minutes. Serve hot.

Serves 4

Farmhouse Game Pie

A mixture of game or just one kind can be used for the filling of this hot pie which is made in layers with forcemeat and baked under a shortcrust-pastry lid.

225g/8oz pork sausagemeat
100g/4oz fresh breadcrumbs
50g/2oz shredded suet
salt and pepper
1 onion, peeled and finely chopped
2tbsp freshly chopped parsley
2tsp freshly chopped thyme
1 egg, beaten
350g/¾lb cooked game, diced
200ml/8fl oz (approx) gravy or game stock
1 recipe quantity shortcrust pastry (see page 16)
beaten egg or milk to glaze

1 Mix together the sausagemeat, breadcrumbs, suet, seasonings, onion, parsley, thyme and egg. Put half this mixture into the base of a pie dish.
2 Cover with the chopped game and then a final layer of forcemeat.
3 Make a hole in the centre of the mixture and pour in some of the gravy or stock.
4 Roll out the pastry and cut a long strip about 2cm/¾in wide; lay this round the dampened rim of the dish.
5 Cut the rest of the pastry into circles 4–5cm/1½–2in in diameter and lay them, overlapping, all over the top of the pie to form a lid, brushing each with egg or milk before adding the next.
6 Glaze again and cook in a fairly hot oven (200°C/400°F, Gas Mark 6) for 15 minutes. Reduce the oven temperature to moderate (180°C/350°F, Gas Mark 4) and continue to cook for 45–50 minutes, covering the pastry

with a piece of greaseproof paper when sufficiently browned. Serve hot.

Serves 4–6

Breasts of Wild Duck en Croûte

This recipe can be prepared in advance and then takes only about half an hour to cook when required. It is also good served cold.

2 wild duck, oven ready
dripping or oil to roast
25g/1oz butter
1 onion, peeled and very finely chopped
2 duck livers (if available)
175g/6oz lean back bacon rashers, derinded and chopped
grated rind of ½ orange
8–10 stuffed olives, chopped
1tbsp brandy or port
1tbsp freshly chopped parsley
salt and pepper
⅓ recipe quantity puff pastry (see page 21)
beaten egg to glaze

1 Prepare the birds and roast in a hot oven (220°C/425°F, Gas Mark 7), using plenty of dripping and basting frequently, for about 40 minutes or until almost cooked. Remove and cool.
2 Carefully remove the breasts from the birds using a sharp knife.
3 Melt the butter and fry the onion until soft. Stir in the livers, bacon and orange rind and continue to cook for 3–4 minutes, mashing the livers as they cook. Stir in the olives, brandy or port, parsley and seasonings and leave to cool.
4 Roll out the pastry and cut into four squares, each large enough to enclose a piece of duck.
5 Divide the stuffing between the pastry squares, placing it in the centre and positioning a piece of duck on each. Damp the edges of the pastry with water and fold up to completely enclose the filling, sealing the edges firmly.
6 Place on lightly greased baking sheets with the pastry joins underneath. Glaze, decorate with the pastry trimmings and glaze again.

7 Cook in a fairly hot oven (220°C/425°F, Gas Mark 7) for about 30 minutes or until puffy and golden brown. Serve hot with gravy made from the pan juices from roasting the birds, stock flavoured with orange rind the juice, and—if liked—a little brandy.

Serves 4

Note Use the remaining meat from the duck carcasses for pâté, casseroles, a pie, potted duck etc, and the bones for soup.

Flaked Grouse Pie

An interesting mixture of minced meats and chopped grouse flavoured with oregano makes the filling for this pie.

225g/8oz lean pie veal
225g/8oz lean pork
100g/4oz salted belly pork
1 onion, peeled
salt and pepper
1 level tbsp freshly chopped parsley
½ level tsp dried marjoram or oregano
1 grouse, oven ready
100g/4oz lean collar bacon, derinded and diced
150ml/¼pt (approx) beef stock
½ recipe quantity flaky or rough puff pastry (see pages 21, 24)
beaten egg to glaze

1 Mince the veal, pork, salted pork and onion together. Season well and mix in the parsley and oregano.
2 Strip the meat off the grouse and cut into small pieces; mix into the minced meats with the bacon and sufficient stock to moisten. Place in a fairly shallow pie dish.
3 Roll out the pastry and use to cover the pie (see page 32); decorate, make a hole in the top and glaze.
4 Cook in a fairly hot oven (200°C/400°F, Gas Mark 6) for 30 minutes, reduce the temperature to moderate (180°C/350°F, Gas Mark 4) and continue to cook for about 45 minutes, covering the pastry with a sheet of greaseproof paper when sufficiently browned. Serve hot.

Serves 5–6

Venison en Croûte

My favourite way of serving venison when available, this makes a spectacular dish and a good alternative to turkey for Christmas.

2.25–2.75kg/5–6lb haunch of venison
1 onion, peeled and chopped
1 bay leaf
175g/6oz streaky bacon rashers, derinded
salt and pepper
4–5tbsp dripping or oil
3 level tbsp flour
5–6tbsp port
3 level tbsp redcurrant or cranberry jelly
2tsp lemon juice

Stuffing:
40g/1½oz butter or margarine
1 medium onion, peeled and chopped
175g/6oz mushrooms, chopped
40g/1½oz fresh breadcrumbs
1 level tsp French mustard
¾ level tsp dried basil
salt and pepper

¾ recipe quantity puff pastry (see page 21)
beaten egg to glaze
watercress to garnish

1 Bone the venison and make stock with the bones, 1.2–1.75 litres/2–3pt water, the onion and bay leaf. The boned venison should weigh between 1.75–2kg/4–4½lb.
2 Roll the venison into a neat joint, arrange the bacon rashers around it and secure with string. Season and spread all over with dripping or oil. Roast in a fairly hot oven (200°C/400°F, Gas Mark 6) for 1¼–1½ hours, basting several times. Remove to a plate and leave until cold.
3 Spoon off the excess fat from the pan drippings then stir the flour into the residue. Cook for 2–3 minutes then add 900ml/1½pt stock and bring to the boil, stirring frequently. Add the port, jelly, lemon juice and seasonings and boil until reduced to about 600ml/1pt. Leave to cool.
4 To prepare the stuffing, first melt butter in a pan and fry the onion gently until soft. Add the mushrooms and continue to cook for a minute or two. Remove from the heat, stir in

the breadcrumbs, mustard, basil and seasonings and leave to cool.

5 When the venison is cold roll out the pastry to a rectangle large enough to enclose the joint and spread the mushroom stuffing over the centre of it. Place the joint in the centre, after removing the string, and enclose in the pastry, sealing the edges with water.

6 Place in a lightly greased roasting tin with the pastry joins underneath and brush all over with beaten egg. Use the pastry trimmings to decorate with a flower and leaf design and glaze again. At this stage the dish can be kept in a cool place for several hours before proceeding.

7 Before baking glaze again with beaten egg and cook in a fairly hot oven (200°C/400°F, Gas Mark 6) for 30 minutes. Reduce the temperature to moderate (180°C/350°F, Gas Mark 4), lay a piece of greaseproof paper over the pastry, and cook for a further hour.

8 To serve, reheat the sauce and bring it to the boil for 2–3 minutes then pour into a sauce boat. Transfer the venison to a board or serving dish and garnish with watercress. Serve in fairly thick slices.

Serves 8

Venison Pie

Use any cut of venison suitable for a casserole —when flavoured with juniper berries and baked under a suet crust, the flavour is splendid.

675g/1½lb venison, cut into 2.5cm/1in cubes
25g/1oz seasoned flour
2tbsp oil or dripping
1 onion, peeled and chopped
100g/4oz streaky bacon, derinded and chopped
150ml/¼pt red wine
600ml/1pt stock
salt and pepper
6–8 juniper berries, crushed
2tbsp redcurrant or cranberry jelly
1 recipe quantity suet-crust pastry (see page 25)
beaten egg to glaze

1 Toss the venison in the seasoned flour then fry in the heated fat until well sealed. Add the onion and bacon and continue to cook for a few minutes.

2 Sprinkle in any remaining flour, mix well then add the wine and stock and bring to the boil. Season well, add the juniper berries and the redcurrant or cranberry jelly and cover the pan.

3 Simmer gently for about 1½ hours or until tender. Adjust the seasonings and pour into a pie dish with a funnel in the centre. Cool.

4 Roll out the pastry and use to cover the pie dish (see page 32). Use the pastry trimmings to make a fairly heavy decoration of leaves and glaze well with beaten egg.

5 Cook in a fairly hot oven (200°C/400°F, Gas Mark 6) for 35–45 minutes until the crust is a good golden brown and crisp.

Serves 4–5

Poacher's Pheasant en Croûte

A boned pheasant with a meaty stuffing roasted in a pastry crust.

1 plump pheasant, oven ready
350–450g/¾–1lb best sausagemeat
40g/1½oz fresh breadcrumbs
100g/4oz lean cooked ham, chopped
½ level tsp dried sage
100g/4oz mushrooms, chopped (optional)
salt and pepper
pinch garlic powder
few streaky bacon rashers, derinded
little butter or margarine
¾ recipe quantity puff or flaky pastry (see pages 21–3)
beaten egg to glaze

Sauce
2 level tbsp flour
1 level tbsp tomato purée
300ml/½pt good stock
150ml/¼pt red wine
2tbsp redcurrant or quince jelly
1 level tsp brown sugar
grated rind of ½ lemon (optional)
1tbsp lemon juice
salt and pepper

To garnish
watercress or parsley

1 Turn the pheasant onto its breast and make a cut right along its back bone. Gradually ease off the flesh from the carcass using a sharp pointed knife. At the wing, remove the top bone by scraping carefully; leave the rest of the wing as it is. Continue on to the leg and break at the socket joint. Ease out the thigh bone and continue carefully all round the rest of the bird until the whole carcass can be lifted out. Lay the pheasant meat on a flat surface skin side downwards.

2 Combine the sausagemeat, breadcrumbs, ham, sage, mushrooms (if used), seasonings and garlic powder; shape into a brick and place down the centre of the pheasant. Pull the edges together and the neck flap over to encase the stuffing and secure with fine skewers or sew together with fine string.

3 Turn the pheasant over and reshape the legs and remaining wing bones, securing with string. Lay the bacon over the breast, stand the pheasant in a roasting tin and spread with butter. Season well.

4 Roast in a moderate oven (180°C/350°F, Gas Mark 4) for about 1 hour. Leave to cool.

5 To prepare the sauce, spoon off the excess fat from the pan juices then stir in the flour and tomato purée and cook for 1–2 minutes. Gradually add the stock and wine, bring to the boil and simmer for 2 minutes. Strain into a clean pan, add the jelly, sugar, lemon rind and juice and seasonings to taste and simmer for 2 minutes. Leave to cool.

6 Roll out the pastry into a shape large enough to enclose the pheasant. Place the bird in the centre of it after removing the trussing string. Enclose the pheasant completely, damping the pastry edges with water to seal them.

7 Stand the pheasant in a greased roasting tin, glaze and decorate with the pastry trimmings. Glaze again and cook in a fairly hot oven (200°C/400°F, Gas Mark 6) for about 45 minutes until the pastry is a good golden brown, covering with a sheet of greaseproof paper if over-browning.

8 Reheat the sauce and serve with the pheasant which should be carved straight down across the breast in fairly thick slices so each portion receives pastry, pheasant meat and stuffing. Remove the legs and wings as you reach them. Garnish with watercress or parsley.

Serves 4–6

Note This dish is also good served cold in slices with salads; and the same recipe can be used with a chicken in place of the pheasant.

Rabbit Pie with Prunes

Young rabbit makes an excellent pie and can often be interchanged with chicken. Mature rabbits however require long slow cooking with plenty of flavourings added to prevent any toughness remaining. Some people believe that rabbit always has a strong flavour—this can be removed by soaking for 2 hours in cold water with 2tbsp vinegar or salt added; rinse under fresh cold water before cooking.

1 young rabbit (approx 900g/2lb), jointed
225g/8oz collar bacon in a piece, derinded and chopped
450ml/¾pt stock or water
1 large onion, peeled and sliced
2 carrots, peeled and chopped
1 bay leaf
juice of ½ lemon
salt and pepper
25g/1oz flour
1tbsp freshly chopped parsley
8–10 prunes, soaked overnight or use canned prunes
1 recipe quantity quick puffy pastry (see page 25)
beaten egg or milk to glaze

1 Soak the rabbit as described above then rinse and drain well.

2 Place in a saucepan with the bacon, stock, onion, carrots, bay leaf, lemon juice and seasonings. Bring to the boil, cover and simmer for ¾–1 hour until tender. Discard the bay leaf.

3 Remove the rabbit (retaining the cooking liquor) and strip the meat from the bones. Place the meat in a fairly shallow pie dish with a funnel in the centre.

4 Blend the flour with a little cold water, whisk this into the cooking liquor and bring back to the boil for a minute or so. Season well and stir in the parsley and prunes. Pour over the rabbit in the dish and leave to cool.
5 Roll out the pastry and use to cover the pie dish (see page 32) making a hole in the pastry over the hole in the funnel.
6 Glaze and bake in a fairly hot oven (220°C/425°F, Gas Mark 7) for about 40 minutes or until the pastry is well puffed up and golden brown. Serve hot.

Serves 4–6

Pork Fillet in a Crust

Many different foods can be cooked en croûte (in a pastry covering) but the tenderness and flavour of pork fillet make it an ideal choice.

3 pork fillets
2–3tbsp oil or dripping
1 onion, peeled and chopped
4 rashers bacon, derinded and chopped
75g/3oz mushrooms, chopped
grated rind of ½ orange
1 cooking apple, peeled, cored and coarsely grated
salt and pepper
½ recipe quantity puff pastry (see page 21)
beaten egg to glaze
orange slices and watercress to garnish

1 Cut the fillets into pieces approx 23cm/9in long, place all together (including the tail pieces) and tie into a neat shape.
2 Heat the oil or dripping in a pan and fry the pork roll gently on all sides for about 20 minutes or until well browned and partly cooked through. Leave to cool.
3 Fry the onion and bacon in the same fat until soft then drain off all excess fat and mix with the mushrooms, orange rind, apple and seasonings.
4 Roll out the pastry to a rectangle large enough to enclose the pork and spread the mushroom mixture down the centre of the pastry. Remove the string from the pork and place it on the filling.
5 Wrap the pastry round the pork to enclose

it completely, damping the pastry edges with water to seal.
6 Place in a lightly greased roasting tin with the pastry join underneath and glaze. Decorate with the pastry trimmings, make one or two holes in the top and glaze again.
7 Cook in a hot oven (220°C/425°F, Gas Mark 7) for 30 minutes. Reduce the temperature to moderate (180°C/350°F, Gas Mark 4) and continue to cook for 20–30 minutes. Cover with a sheet of greaseproof paper when sufficiently browned. Serve hot or cold, garnished with orange slices and watercress.

Serves 4–6

Veal and Mushroom Cobbler

Another variation of scone topping for a savoury dish.

1 large onion, peeled and sliced
25g/1oz butter or margarine
1tbsp oil
675g/1½lb pie veal, cubed
600ml/1pt stock
salt and pepper
finely grated rind of 1 lemon
1tbsp lemon juice
1 bay leaf
100g/4oz mushrooms, sliced
1 level tbsp cornflour

Scone topping
100g/4oz self-raising flour
100g/4oz wholemeal flour
1 level tsp baking powder
50g/2oz butter or margarine
milk to mix
little coarse salt
dried thyme

1 Fry the onion in a mixture of fat and oil until soft. Add the veal and continue to cook for 5 minutes, stirring occasionally.
2 Add the stock, seasonings, lemon rind, juice and bay leaf and bring to the boil. Cover and simmer for 1¼ hours or until tender.
3 Stir in the mushrooms and if necessary a little stock or water so the contents of the pan

are barely covered. Blend the cornflour with the minimum of cold water, stir into the pan and bring to the boil for a minute or so. Adjust the seasonings and pour the whole into a casserole.

4 To prepare the scone topping, put the flours, baking powder and a pinch of salt into a bowl and rub in the fat. Add sufficient milk to mix to a softish dough then roll out to 1cm/½in thick and cut into 2.5–4cm/ 1½–2in rounds.

5 Lay the scones in overlapping lines across the centre of the casserole, brushing each with milk before adding the next. Sprinkle the scones with coarse salt and dried thyme then cook in a hot oven (220°C/425°F, Gas Mark 7) for about 15 minutes or until the scones are well risen, firm to the touch and golden brown.

Serves 4

Quick Sausage and Kidney Pie

All the filling ingredients are quick to cook and the pastry is almost instant.

350g/¾lb chipolata sausages
1tbsp oil or dripping
12 streaky bacon rashers, derinded and rolled
6 lambs' kidneys, halved, skinned and cored
1 large onion, peeled and sliced
2 large carrots, peeled and sliced
100g/4oz mushrooms, sliced
300ml/½pt stock
150ml/¼pt red wine or cider
1 level tsp dried thyme
½tsp Worcestershire sauce
salt and pepper
1 level tbsp cornflour (optional)
4 tomatoes, peeled and quartered
1 recipe quantity quick puffy pastry (see page 25)
beaten egg or milk to glaze

1 Fry the chipolatas in the fat until lightly browned. Add the bacon rolls and kidneys and fry for a few minutes then add the onion and carrots and cook gently for 5 minutes.

2 Add the mushrooms, stock, wine or cider, thyme, Worcestershire sauce and seasonings and bring to the boil. Cover and simmer

gently for 15–20 minutes then thicken, if desired, using the cornflour blended with a little cold water. Add the tomatoes and pour the whole into a fairly shallow pie dish and leave to partly cool.

3 Roll out the pastry and use to cover the pie dish (see page 32). Decorate the top with the pastry trimmings and glaze.

4 Cook in a fairly hot oven (200°C/400°F, Gas Mark 6) for 30–40 minutes until the pastry is well puffed up and golden brown.

Serves 4

Stuffed Onion Dumplings

A good hearty meal for a cold day. By adding the centres of the onions to the sauce, they are not wasted whilst giving more space for the stuffing in the dumplings.

4 onions, peeled (approx 225g/8oz each)
salt and pepper
225g/8oz lamb's liver
25g/1oz butter or margarine
4 rashers bacon, derinded and chopped
50g/2oz mushrooms, chopped
¼–½ level tsp dried thyme
50g/2oz cooked rice
1½ recipe quantities shortcrust pastry (see page 16)
beaten egg or milk to glaze

Sauce
50g/2oz butter or margarine
25g/1oz flour
300ml/½pt stock or milk

1 Cook the onions in boiling salted water for 15–20 minutes then drain and cool.

2 Blanch the liver in boiling water for 1 minute then drain and chop finely.

3 Melt the 25g/1oz butter or margarine in a pan and fry the bacon and mushrooms together for 2–3 minutes. Add the liver, thyme, plenty of seasonings and the rice.

4 Using a small spoon scoop out the centres of the onions leaving an outer casing about 1cm/½in thick. Fill the onions with the liver mixture, pressing well down.

5 Roll out the pastry and cut into four

rounds each large enough to enclose an onion —approx 20cm/8in.

6 Stand the onions, filling end downwards on the pastry rounds, dampen the pastry edges of each round with water and wrap round to completely enclose each onion in pastry.

7 Stand on a greased baking sheet with the pastry joins underneath and decorate the tops with pastry leaves made from the trimmings.

8 Glaze and cook in a fairly hot oven (200°C/400°F, Gas Mark 6) for 20 minutes then reduce the temperature to moderate and continue to cook for a further 1–1¼ hours until the onions feel tender when pierced with a skewer.

9 Meanwhile chop the onion centres finely. Melt the 50g (2oz) butter or margarine in a pan and cook the onion for about 5 minutes. Stir in the flour, cook for 1 minute then gradually add the stock or milk and bring to the boil for 2 minutes. Season well and when the dumplings are cooked serve the sauce with them.

Serves 4

Note The filling can be changed as you please —try using minced cooked lamb in place of the liver.

Carrot and Bean Pie

For those who prefer meatless dishes; or as an accompaniment to a roast or casserole, this pie is hard to beat.

4 sticks celery, sliced
2 onions, peeled and sliced
2tbsp oil
450g/1lb carrots, peeled and sliced
425g/15oz can cannellini beans
150ml/¼pt stock
2 level tsp cornflour
salt and pepper
1 level tsp dried basil or marjoram
1 recipe quantity cheese pastry (see page 17)
50g/2oz mature Cheddar cheese, finely grated

1 Fry the celery and onions gently in the oil until soft but only lightly coloured.

2 Add the carrots, the liquor from the beans and the stock and bring to the boil. Cover and simmer for about 15 minutes or until tender.

3 Blend the cornflour with a little water, add to the saucepan and bring back to the boil, stirring continuously. Season well, stir in the beans and herbs and leave to cool.

4 Roll out two-thirds of the pastry and use to line a 20cm/8in shallow square cake tin or dish. Spoon in the filling.

5 Roll out the remaining pastry and cut into strips about 1cm/⅓in thick and long enough to reach across the pie dish. Arrange the strips to form a lattice pattern, attaching the ends with water.

6 Cook in a fairly hot oven (200°C/400°F, Gas Mark 6) for 20 minutes. Sprinkle with the cheese and return to the oven for a further 15–20 minutes until the pastry is cooked through. Serve hot.

Serves 4–5

Seafood Puff

There are several types of fish pie baked in a pastry crust, the best known being Russian fish pie and Koulibiaca. The filling here is rather more interesting than either of those and includes shellfish; also it is baked in an oblong rather than the traditional square envelope shape or plait.

225g/8oz cod or haddock fillet, skinned
3–4 scallops, quartered
1 small onion, peeled and chopped
150ml/¼pt dry white wine or milk
150ml/¼pt (approx) milk
salt and pepper
50g/2oz butter or margarine
50g/2oz flour
100g/4oz peeled prawns
1tbsp chopped capers
2 hard-boiled eggs, chopped
½ recipe quantity puff or flaky pastry (see pages 21–3)
beaten egg to glaze

1 Poach the white fish, scallops and onion in the wine or milk with added seasonings for 5

minutes. Drain; reserve the cooking liquor and make it up to 300ml/½pt with milk. Flake the fish.

2 Melt the butter in a pan, stir in the flour and cook for 1 minute. Gradually add the liquor and bring to the boil for 2 minutes. Adjust seasonings.

3 Stir in the flaked fish, scallops, prawns, capers and eggs and leave to cool.

4 Roll out the pastry and cut into two rectangles, one 30 × 20cm/12 × 8in and another 33 × 23cm/13 × 9in.

5 Place the smaller piece of pastry on a greased baking sheet and cover with the filling, leaving a 1cm/½in plain margin all round. Brush the margin with beaten egg and position the lid carefully on top to enclose the filling. Press the edges well together then flake and lightly scallop the edge.

6 Using a sharp knife lightly score the top of the pastry into diamonds and glaze well with the beaten egg.

7 Cook in a hot oven (220°C/425°F, Gas Mark 7) for 35–40 minutes or until well risen and golden brown. Serve hot or cold.

Serves 4

Salmon Gougère

There are two methods of making a gougère but both use choux pastry. This recipe makes a large gougère ring which is filled with the salmon mixture, or individual ones which are baked in little dishes.

1½ recipe quantities choux pastry (see page 29)
40g/1½oz butter or margarine
1 small onion, peeled and chopped
25g/1oz flour
300ml/½pt milk (or part milk and white wine)
½ level tsp made mustard
salt and pepper
2 hard-boiled eggs, chopped
350g/¾lb cooked salmon, flaked
2 large gherkins, chopped
2 level tbsp snipped chives or freshly chopped
    parsley
2tsp lemon juice

1 Put the choux pastry into a piping bag fitted with a 1cm/½in plain vegetable nozzle and pipe the mixture in two circles, one on top of the other, inside each of four individual 12.5–15cm/5–6in ovenproof dishes. Alternatively spread or pipe (using a 2.5cm/1in nozzle) the mixture into a fat ring about 20cm/8in in diameter on a greased baking sheet.

2 Bake in a hot oven (220°C/425°F, Gas Mark 7) allowing about 25 minutes for the individual gougères or 35–40 minutes for the large one, until well risen and golden brown.

3 Meanwhile make the filling. Melt the butter and fry the onion gently until soft. Stir in the flour and cook for 1 minute then gradually add the milk or milk and wine and bring to the boil, stirring continuously.

4 Add the mustard, season well and simmer for 2 minutes; then stir in the eggs, salmon, gherkins, chives or parsley, and lemon juice to sharpen then reheat gently.

5 Either spoon the fish mixture into the centre of the individual gougères, or cut a small ring-shaped 'lid' off the top of the large one, spoon the filling into the hollow pastry and replace the lid. Return to the oven for 5 minutes before serving hot.

Serves 4

Note Fresh or canned salmon may be used; or try 2 cans drained tuna fish with 4–6 chopped anchovy fillets; or white fish with 100g/4oz peeled prawns added.

Trout en Croûte

Fish baked in pastry is a special occasion dish which requires a little extra preparation prior to the actual cooking process. The bones and skin must be removed (to make for easy serving and eating), then the fish is re-assembled with butter, herbs and seasonings and enclosed in pastry. Individual trout, larger trout, sea trout or small salmon can all be cooked in this way. It is probably best served hot with Hollandaise sauce, but is also very good served cold with lemon mayonnaise.

900g – 1.3kg/2 – 3lb trout, sea trout, or salmon, cleaned
juice of ½ lemon
50g/2oz butter, softened
salt and pepper
1tbsp freshly chopped parsley
⅓ recipe quantity puff or flaky pastry (see page 21)
beaten egg to glaze

1 Cut off the head of the fish then fillet it using a sharp knife. To do this, slip the blade of the knife along the length of the backbone, cutting through the skin where necessary and remove the fillet. Turn the fish over and remove second fillet in the same way.
2 Lay each fillet, skin side down, on a flat surface and, using a sharp knife and beginning at the tail end, cut along the length of the fillet to remove the skin.
3 Sprinkle fillets with lemon juice. Beat butter, seasonings and parsley together and spread over one fillet, then cover with the second one to reassemble into a fish shape.
4 Roll out the pastry thinly and use to enclose the fish, damping the edges with water to seal. Turn the parcel over so that the seam is underneath and place on a greased baking sheet.
5 Glaze the parcel, decorate with pastry trimmings and glaze again. At this stage the fish may be chilled in the refrigerator for several hours—glaze again before cooking.
6 Bake in a hot oven (220°C/425°F, Gas Mark 7) for 30–40 minutes until the pastry is well puffed up and golden brown. Serve hot straight from the oven with Hollandaise sauce (see page 66) and vegetables; or leave until cold, garnish with salad and serve with lemon mayonnaise.

Serves 8 – 10

Note If fish are small, wrap each, after boning, in smaller pieces of pastry as above and serve as individual portions. Reduce the cooking time to about 25 minutes.

LEMON MAYONNAISE
2 egg yolks
½ level tsp dry mustard
salt and pepper
300ml/½pt oil
2tbsp lemon juice
approx ½ level tsp caster sugar
finely grated rind of ½ lemon

Put the egg yolks in a bowl with the mustard and seasonings and mix thoroughly. Add the oil drop by drop, whisking hard all the time, preferably using an electric hand-held mixer. When half the oil is added, beat in half of the lemon juice, then continue with the rest of the oil. Add the remaining lemon juice, sugar to taste and the lemon rind. Mayonnaise will keep in an airtight container in the refrigerator for up to 2 weeks.

Note All the ingredients must be at room temperature, for if at all cold the sauce is likely to curdle. If this should happen, place a fresh egg yolk in a warmed bowl, add first the curdled mixture drop by drop and then continue with the rest of the oil.

Somerset Fish Pie

Cider and apples come from Somerset and blend well with fish for a pie baked in cheese pastry.

450g/1lb cod or haddock fillet, skinned
300ml/½pt cider
salt and pepper
4 tomatoes, peeled, quartered and deseeded
2 eating apples, peeled, cored and sliced
25g/1oz butter
25g/1oz flour
1tbsp snipped chives or chopped parsley
1 recipe quantity cheese pastry (see page 17)
beaten egg or milk to glaze

1 Poach the fish in the cider with the seasonings for 8–10 minutes until tender. Drain the fish, reserving the liquor.
2 Flake the fish and place in a bowl with the tomatoes and apples.
3 Melt the butter in a pan, stir in the flour and cook for 1 minute. Gradually add the fish liquor and bring to the boil, stirring frequently. Season well, add the chives and pour the whole over the fish; leave to cool.
4 Roll out two thirds of the pastry and use to line a 20cm/8in deep pie plate or tin. Spoon in the filling.
5 Roll out the remaining pastry to form a lid. Damp the edges, position the lid and press edges firmly together. Trim the edge, crimp, and decorate the top with the pastry trimmings.
6 Glaze and cook in a fairly hot oven (200°C/400°F, Gas Mark 6) for about 40 minutes or until golden brown. Serve hot.

Serves 4–5

Raised Game Pie

Elizabethan banquets always had a large game pie amongst the huge spreads of elaborate foods of that age and they still make a good display on any buffet table as well as being an excellent addition to any picnic hamper, shooting lunch or hunt breakfast. This pie has one type of filling while the next recipe shows a different method, but both have an attractive appearance when cut open.

Raised pies are always served cold and should be made with hot-water-crust pastry.

225g/8oz pie veal
225g/8oz cooked ham
1 small onion, peeled
salt and pepper
good pinch ground mace or nutmeg
1 recipe quantity hot-water-crust pastry (see page 26)
350g/12oz (approx) any cooked game, diced
beaten egg to glaze
2 level tsp powdered gelatine
300ml/½pt game stock

1 Mince the veal, ham and onion and mix in plenty of seasonings and the mace or nutmeg.
2 Make up the pastry and use three-quarters of it to line a raised pie mould or an 18–20cm/7–8in round or square cake tin, preferably with a loose base. To raise the pie by hand, see the method on page 27. Keep the remaining pastry in a covered bowl.
3 Put half the minced meat mixture in the pie case and cover with the diced game, then add the remainder of the mince. Press lightly so that the surface is even.
4 Roll out the remaining pastry to form a lid; damp the edges, position the lid and press the edges well together. Trim the edges and crimp and then make a hole in the centre of the lid and decorate with pastry leaves.
5 Brush with the beaten egg and cook in a fairly hot oven (200°C/400°F, Gas Mark 6) for 30 minutes.
6 Glaze again and reduce the temperature to moderate (160°C/325°F, Gas Mark 3) and continue to cook for 1¼–1½ hours, covering with greaseproof paper when sufficiently browned.
7 Dissolve the gelatine in the stock and season well. As the pie cools pour the stock into the pie through a small funnel inserted into the central hole.
8 Chill until firm, preferably overnight, before removing from the tin. Serve in slices with salads.

Serves 8

Farmhouse Game Pie with Eggs

This version uses raw game for the filling and has hard-boiled eggs buried inside. As well as using a game pie mould or cake tin, a loaf tin or special oblong pie mould will suffice. Venison or hare may be used in place of the pheasant.

1 young pheasant
2 chicken portions, or 1 large turkey thigh
225g/8oz streaky bacon rashers, derinded
½ onion, peeled and finely chopped
salt and pepper
1 level tbsp freshly chopped parsley
pinch ground mace or nutmeg
1 recipe quantity hot-water-crust pastry (see
    page 26)
6 small eggs, hard boiled
beaten egg to glaze
2 level tsp powdered gelatine
300ml/½pt stock from pheasant and chicken or
    turkey bones

1 Strip all the meat off the pheasant and chicken or turkey portions and cut into very small pieces. Chop or mince the bacon and add to the pheasant and chicken or turkey with the onion, plenty of seasonings, parsley and mace or nutmeg.
2 Roll out three-quarters of the pastry and use to line a 20–23cm/8–9in cake tin or a 900g/2lb loaf tin. Keep the remaining pastry in a covered bowl.
3 Spoon in almost half of the filling and make six 'dents' in it for the eggs. Add these and use the remainder of the filling to mould round the eggs and completely cover them.
4 Roll out the remaining pastry to form a lid, damp the edges, position the lid and press the edges firmly together. Trim and crimp and make one or two holes in the top. Decorate with the pastry trimmings.
5 Glaze and then cook in a fairly hot oven (200°C/400°F, Gas Mark 6) for 30 minutes; glaze again and reduce the temperature to moderate (180°C/350°F, Gas Mark 4). Continue to cook for 1¼–1½ hours, covering the pie with greaseproof paper when sufficiently browned.

6 Meanwhile use the game and chicken or turkey bones to make a stock and dissolve the gelatine in 300ml/½pt of it. Season well and as the pie cools pour the stock into it through a funnel inserted in the holes in the lid.
7 Chill thoroughly until set before removing from the tin. Serve in slices with salads.

Serves 8

Raised Veal and Ham Pie

This is my version of the traditional pie sold in slices with an egg going right through the centre.

350g/12oz pie veal
225g/8oz cooked ham
225g/8oz raw collar bacon
1 small onion, peeled
salt and pepper
1 level tsp mixed herbs
1 recipe quantity hot-water-crust pastry (see
    page 26)
4 hard-boiled eggs (optional)
beaten egg to glaze
2 level tsp powdered gelatine
300ml/½pt stock

Make as for the Raised Game Pie (opposite) but finely chop the veal and ham and mince the bacon and onion before mixing all together with the salt, pepper and the herbs. If using hard-boiled eggs put half the meat in the pastry case then add the eggs and cover with remainder of the filling before adding the lid.

Raised Pork Pie

This is another traditional pie with a filling of pork and various flavouring. I like to chop half the pork and mince the remainder to give texture to the filling and use apples and onion for flavour.

675g/1½lb lean pork
1 sweet apple, peeled and cored
1 onion, peeled
salt and pepper
good pinch sage and thyme

1 recipe quantity hot-water-crust pastry (see page 26)
beaten egg to glaze
2 level tsp powdered gelatine
300ml/½pt stock

Make as for Raised Game Pie (page 64) but mince half the pork, the apple and onion; chop the remainder of the pork and add to the minced mixture with the seasonings and herbs.

Note This mixture can also be made into individual pork pies (see Little Picnic Pies—below).

Little Picnic Pies

This filling can be used equally well for a large pie or these little ones. To make a large pie follow the method for Raised Game Pie (page 64).

450g/1lb raw chicken or turkey meat, chopped
225g/8oz cooked ham or bacon, chopped
1 small onion, peeled and chopped
salt and pepper
225g/8oz sausagemeat
½ level tsp dried thyme
1 recipe quantity hot-water-crust pastry (see page 26)
beaten egg to glaze
2 level tsp powdered gelatine
300ml/½pt stock

1 Mix together the chicken, ham, onion, seasonings, sausagemeat and thyme.
2 Divide the pastry into six portions and keep warm in a covered bowl. Follow the method on page 27 for raising individual pies. Add the filling and the lids; glaze and make a hole in the centre of each lid then stand the pies on greased baking sheets.
3 Tie a strip of greased greaseproof paper round each pie if they look a little fragile or if they become misshapen during cooking.
4 Bake in a fairly hot oven (200°C/400°F, Gas Mark 6) for about 20 minutes then glaze again; reduce the temperature to moderate (180°C/350°F, Gas Mark 4) and continue to cook for about 30 minutes.

5 Dissolve the gelatine in the stock, season well and pour into the pies through a funnel in the central hole as they cool. Leave until cold and set.

Makes 6

Broccoli Hollandaise Vol-au-Vent

Large vol-au-vents are ideal for a main-course dish. The pastry can be cooked in advance and reheated when required or the whole thing can be prepared and cooked together. This filling has a combination of textures and makes a change from a meaty dish.

½ recipe quantity puff pastry (see page 21)
beaten egg to glaze
225g/8oz broccoli spears
salt and pepper
3 eggs

Hollandaise sauce
4tbsp wine vinegar
2tbsp water
8 peppercorns, crushed
4 egg yolks
175g/6oz butter
salt and pepper
squeeze lemon juice

1 Roll out the pastry to about 2.5cm/1in thick and use to cut an oval vol-au-vent shape (see page 36 for the method).
2 Glaze and then cook in a very hot oven (230°C/450°F, Gas Mark 8) as described, for 30–35 minutes.
3 Cook the broccoli in boiling salted water until just tender. Cook the eggs for 10 minutes until hard boiled.

———————————

(*Clockwise*) Raymond's Gâteau made from profiteroles, Orange Chiffon Pie, Flaky Raspberry Gâteau, French Apple Flan and Glazed Fruit Flans

4 To make the Hollandaise sauce, boil the vinegar, water and peppercorns in a small pan until reduced by half. Strain into a basin over a pan of simmering water or into the top of a double saucepan.

5 Gradually beat in the egg yolks then cook the mixture until it thickens, stirring continuously or it will curdle.

6 Beat in the butter, a small knob at a time, until a coating consistency is obtained. Season and add lemon juice to taste.

7 Drain the broccoli and place it in the base of the warm vol-au-vent; peel and quarter the eggs and place these on top of the broccoli; then coat with the sauce. Serve hot.

Serves 4

Chicken and Pineapple Vol-au-Vent

This vol-au-vent, served cold, has a spicy filling based on mayonnaise and curry powder.

1 baked vol-au-vent case (see previous recipe)

Filling
150ml/¼pt thick mayonnaise
1½ level tsp curry powder
good dash Worcestershire sauce
1tbsp apricot jam
salt and pepper
1–2tbsp lemon juice
4 spring onions, trimmed and sliced, or 1tbsp finely chopped onion
3–4 slices pineapple, chopped, or a drained can of crushed pineapple
225/8oz cooked chicken meat, diced
few toasted almonds

1 Place the vol-au-vent on a serving dish surrounded by salads.

2 Combine the mayonnaise, curry powder, Worcestershire sauce, jam, plenty of

(*Clockwise*) Danish Pastries, Raised Pie, Cornish Pasties and Steak and Kidney Pie

seasonings and sufficient lemon juice to give a thick coating consistency.

3 Add the onions, pineapple and chicken, mix well and leave to stand for 20 minutes.

4 Spoon the filling into the vol-au-vent, sprinkle with toasted almonds and serve.

Serves 4

Raised Turkey Pie

Turkey meat makes an excellent raised pie, particularly now that portions and joints of turkey are readily available. This one is flavoured with herbs and has a layer of chopped liver through the centre.

675g/1½lb raw boneless turkey meat (casserole meat, thigh or breast meat)
1 large onion, peeled
175g/6oz streaky bacon rashers, derinded
175g/6oz turkey livers, finely chopped
salt and pepper
good pinch ground nutmeg
1 level tsp oregano
6tbsp white wine or cider
1 recipe quantity hot-water-crust pastry (see page 26)
beaten egg to glaze
2 level tsp powdered gelatine
200ml/8fl oz chicken or turkey stock

1 Remove and discard any skin from the turkey meat and mince it with the onion and bacon. Divide the mixture into two equal portions in separate bowls.

2 Add the chopped liver, plenty of seasonings and nutmeg to one portion and mix well.

3 Season the other bowl of turkey meat, add the herbs and 2 tablespoons of wine or cider.

4 Roll out three-quarters of the pastry and use to line a 900g/2lb loaf tin. Keep the remaining pastry covered in the bowl.

5 Spoon half of the turkey and herb mixture into the base of the tin. Cover with the turkey and liver mixture and then finally the remainder of the herb mixture.

6 Roll out remaining pastry for a lid, damp the edges and place in position. Press firmly together, then trim and crimp.

7 Make three holes along the top of the pie and decorate them with leaves made from the pastry trimmings.

8 Glaze and cook in a fairly hot oven (200°C/400°F, Gas Mark 6) for 30 minutes. Glaze again, reduce temperature to moderate (180°C/350°F, Gas Mark 4) and continue for 1¼ hours, covering with greaseproof paper when sufficiently browned.

9 Dissolve the gelatine in the stock, add the remaining wine or cider and season well. As the pie cools, pour the stock into it through a funnel inserted in the holes in the lid.

10 Chill thoroughly until set before removing from the tin. Serve in slices with salads.

Serves 8 – 10

3
Puddings and Desserts

3

To follow a traditional Sunday roast there is nothing better than a steaming fruit pie, topped with crisp puff pastry or melting shortcrust, with lashings of cream or custard. Many people think that fruit pie is the *only* pudding and don't want to look any further: with a variety of fillings it completely satisfies their taste. But this is only one small corner of the pastry possibilities when it comes to puddings and desserts.

So many of the basic pastries can be used with sweet ingredients. In fact apart from the cheese pastries they can all be used in some way—even hot-water-crust, traditionally used for savoury raised pies, makes those splendid little gooseberry pies which originated in Oldbury in Gloucestershire many years ago (Chapter 7, Traditional Recipes).

Suet crust makes all the gooey, filling and fattening steamed puddings and roly-polys; flans and tarts are made with one of the shortcrusts, flan pastry or pâte sucrée, as the base; choux pastry is the basis for profiteroles and beignets as well as a selection of gâteaux, the best known being Gâteau St Honoré; and then come all the flaked pastries, which apart from pie crusts are used for jalousie, Gâteau Pithiviers and flaky gâteaux built up with layers of baked puff pastry, fruits and whipped cream. Other specialities include apple strudels which use their own particular sort of pastry, and baked cheesecakes which generally have a pastry or shortbread base.

It is the filling of the pie, flan or whatever that complements the pastry, and if you make a good decision on what to serve for pudding or dessert after a good main course (and do avoid two pastry dishes) you will certainly please your family and guests. For everyday eating try spotted Dick, cherry almond flan or treacle tart; complete a cool summery meal with gooseberry amber flan, French apple flan or apricot tart; keep the mince pies and Bakewell tart for the winter months; pecan pie, the famous American dessert, will delight the sweet-toothed members of the family. Elegant gâteaux and desserts for entertaining include profiteroles, Raymond's Gâteau (a pyramid of profiteroles assembled round a pillar of cream flavoured with chocolate and chestnuts, the whole thing drizzled with caramel), grape pastries (crisp pastry tartlets with rich creamy cheese filling topped with grapes in an apricot glaze) and strawberry shortcake which requires no explanation.

The pastry for many of the recipes is best made in advance. In some instances the pastry case or layers can be baked the day before and stored in airtight containers ready for last-minute assembly, which as some of the recipes suggest is an important stage if the very best results and appearance are to be achieved. Some of the cooked flans and tarts (without meringue or cream decoration) can be frozen for 4–8 weeks; mince pies, cherry almond flan, Bakewell tart, apple strudel, jalousie, French apple flan are some of those which do freeze well. They should be thawed out completely before serving either hot or cold; do not be tempted to heat up from frozen, for the pastry will more than likely turn soggy and spoil the result.

Apple and Apricot Pudding

Suet pastry can be used to line a pudding basin with the filling kept completely enclosed, but here it is arranged in layers, so everyone gets an equal share of the 'pud' and the filling.

1 recipe quantity suet-crust pastry (see page 25)
100g/4oz dried apricots, soaked overnight
350–450g/¾–1lb cooking apples, peeled, cored and sliced
175g/6oz demerara sugar
½ level tsp ground cinnamon (optional)

1 Divide the pastry into three portions making one very small and the other two progressively larger.
2 Grease a 1 litre/1½–2pt pudding basin thoroughly with butter, margarine or lard. Roll out the smallest piece of pastry and place in the base of the basin.
3 Drain the apricots, chop roughly and mix with the apples, sugar and cinnamon.
4 Spoon about one-third of the mixture over the suet pastry in the basin.
5 Roll out the middle-sized piece of pastry and lay it evenly in the basin over the fruit, but do not press down. Cover with the remaining fruit mixture.
6 Roll out the remaining suet pastry and lay it over the fruit, so it touches the sides of the basin. Level it but do not press down more than lightly.
7 Cover the basin first with greased grease-proof paper and then foil making a pleat across both to allow the pudding to rise, and tie securely round the rim of the basin with string. It is a good idea to make a string handle across the top to facilitate easy removal when the pudding is cooked.
8 Place in a large saucepan and add enough boiling water to reach halfway up the outside of the basin. Cover and simmer gently for 2–2½ hours, adding more boiling water to the pan as necessary.
9 Remove the basin from the saucepan and if possible allow to stand for 5 minutes before turning out the pudding onto a hot plate.
10 Serve with custard or cream.

Serves 6

VARIATIONS
Any mixture of fruit can be used allowing about 450g/1lb. Try apple and gooseberries; apple and blackcurrants; apple and blackberries; apple and rhubarb; apple and plums; apple and mixed dried fruit; apple and dates etc.

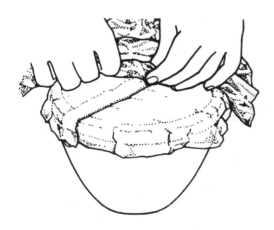

Covering a suet pudding ready for steaming

Steamed Blackcurrant and Apple Pudding

This is a true steamed suet pudding with fruit filling made in a basin. It can be served turned out onto a plate or straight from the basin.

1 recipe quantity suet-crust pastry (see page 25)
175–225g/6–8oz blackcurrants, fresh or frozen and thawed
350g/¾lb cooking apples, peeled, cored and sliced
100g/4oz sugar

73

1 Roll out three-quarters of the pastry carefully on a floured surface and use to line a well-greased 1 litre/1½–2pt pudding basin.
2 Combine the blackcurrants, apples and sugar and pack into the lined basin and add 1–2tbsp water.
3 Roll out the reserved pastry to fit the top of the basin, damp the edges and position for a lid. Press the edges very well together folding over if necessary to give a neat edge.
4 Cover first with a layer of greased grease-proof paper and then a layer of foil, both having a pleat across the top to allow the pudding to rise, and tie securely round the rim of the basin with string. It is a good idea to make a string handle across the top for easy removal of the basin when the pudding is cooked.
5 Place in a large saucepan and add boiling water to reach halfway up the outside of the basin. Cover and simmer gently for 2 hours, adding more boiling water to the pan as necessary.
6 Remove the basin from the saucepan, take off the coverings and either turn out carefully or serve straight from the basin.
7 Serve with cream or custard.

Serves 6

VARIATIONS
Use any types or mixtures of fruit as suggested for Apple and Apricot Pudding, page 73.

Delaware Roly-Poly

The old floured pudding cloth has now largely been replaced by greased foil making a roly-poly pudding much easier to prepare and handle.

¾ recipe quantity suet-crust pastry (see page 25)
1 cooking apple, peeled, cored and coarsely grated
1 level tsp mixed spice
good pinch ground nutmeg
50g/2oz mixed peel
100g/4oz currants or sultanas
75g/3oz demerara sugar
little milk

1 Make up the pastry and roll out carefully to a rectangle measuring approx 28 × 23cm/ 11 × 9in.
2 Combine the apple, spices, peel, dried fruit and sugar and spread over the pastry but leaving a 1cm/½in clear margin all round.
3 Brush the edges with milk and carefully roll up the pastry keeping it even, beginning from one of the short sides. Press well together at the ends and the final join.
4 Liberally grease a piece of foil measuring approx 33 × 23cm/13 × 9in with butter or oil and place the roll on the foil. Wrap up loosely (to allow for expansion during cooking) but make sure all edges and ends are securely pinched together to keep it water-tight.
5 Steam the roly-poly over a pan of rapidly boiling water for 1½–2 hours, replenishing the saucepan with boiling water as necessary.
6 Remove the pudding carefully from the foil and serve hot with custard or cream or a syrup sauce.

Serves 4–6

VARIATIONS
In place of Delaware filling try using 8tbsp mincemeat or 6–8tbsp thick chunky marmalade or jam.

Modern Spotted Dick

An old favourite from school days. Trad-itionally it contained only currants but I prefer the added fruit rind or spice and peel. It can also be steamed in a pudding basin instead of as a roll.

75g/3oz self-raising flour
pinch salt
75g/3oz fresh breadcrumbs
75g/3oz shredded suet
50g/2oz caster sugar (or soft brown sugar)
175g/6oz currants, raisins or sultanas
40g/1½oz mixed peel
grated rind of 1 orange or 1 lemon, or 1 level tsp
    ground cinnamon
4–6tbsp (approx) milk

1 Mix together the flour, salt, breadcrumbs, suet, sugar, dried fruit, peel and fruit rind or spice.

2 Either bind to a fairly soft dough with the milk and shape into a roll on a well-floured surface or mix to a soft dropping consistency by adding a little more milk and spoon the mixture into a well-greased 1 litre/1½–2pt pudding basin.

3 Wrap the roll loosely in well-greased greaseproof paper and then in foil securing ends and edges tightly. Cover the basin as for Apple and Apricot Pudding (see page 73) using greaseproof paper and foil.

4 Steam the long pudding over rapidly boiling water for 1½–2 hours or place the basin in a saucepan with boiling water reaching halfway up the outside of the basin and boil for the same length of time.

5 Unwrap or turn out the pudding and serve with custard.

Serves 4–6

Gooseberry Amber Flan

A variation on the apple-amber theme with a meringue topping.

1½ recipe quantities flan pastry (see page 19), or
¾ recipe quantity shortcrust pastry (see page 16)
425g/15oz can gooseberries
2 eggs, separated
25g/1oz butter, melted
50g/2oz caster sugar

1 Roll out the pastry and use to line a 20cm/8in flan ring, tin or dish. Trim and crimp.

2 Bake blind (see page 32) in a hot oven (220°C/425°F, Gas Mark 7) for 15 minutes. Remove flan and reduce oven temperature to moderate (180°C/350°F, Gas Mark 4).

3 Drain the gooseberries and either sieve or liquidise them. Beat in the egg yolks and melted butter.

4 Remove the paper and beans from the flan and pour in the gooseberry purée. Return the flan to the oven for about 15 minutes or until the filling is lightly set.

5 Whisk the egg whites until very stiff then whisk in the sugar a little at a time making sure the meringue is stiff again before adding further sugar.

6 Spread or pipe the meringue over the flan filling and return to the oven for about 10 minutes or until lightly browned. Serve hot or cold.

Serves 4–6

VARIATIONS
Use puréed apricots, plums, apple, rhubarb etc with sugar to taste if using raw fruit.

Cherry Almond Flan

This is equally good served at the tea table or for a dessert and may be eaten hot or cold.

1½ recipe quantities flan pastry (see page 19), or
¾ recipe quantity special shortcrust pastry (see page 19)
100g/4oz glacé cherries, halved, rinsed and dried
50g/2oz butter or margarine
50g/2oz caster sugar
1 egg (size 1 or 2)
25g/1oz self-raising flour
25g/1oz ground almonds
few drops almond essence
15g/½oz flaked almonds
icing sugar (optional)

1 Roll out the pastry and use to line a 20cm/8in shallow square sandwich tin.

2 Arrange the cherries evenly over the pastry base, cut side downwards.

3 To make the topping, cream the butter or margarine and sugar together until very light and fluffy then beat in the egg thoroughly.

4 Mix in the flour, followed by the ground almonds and a few drops of almond essence.

5 Spread carefully over the cherries in the pastry case and sprinkle with the flaked almonds.

6 Cook in a moderately hot oven (190°C/375°F, Gas Mark 5) for 30–40 minutes or until firm to the touch and golden brown.

7 Cool in the tin or cool for a few minutes then remove carefully.

8 Serve hot or cold dredged with icing sugar and accompanied by whipped cream or ice cream.

Serves 6

Note To serve at the tea table: allow the flan to get cold, dredge lightly with icing sugar and cut into 12–16 small fingers or small squares.

This flan will keep in the freezer for up to 2 months.

Bakewell Tart

The recipe for this traditional tart varies greatly and has been handed down through many families, each ending up with their own particular version. This one has a delicious moist filling and can be served hot or cold.

½ recipe quantity shortcrust pastry (see page 16), or special shortcrust pastry (see page 19)
3tbsp raspberry jam
50g/2oz butter or margarine
50g/2oz caster sugar
grated rind of ½ lemon or few drops almond essence
1 egg, beaten (size 1 or 2)
75g/3oz ground almonds
75g/3oz fine cake crumbs
1tbsp lemon juice or milk
little icing sugar

1 Roll out the pastry and use to line an 18–20cm/7–8in deep pie plate or tin. Trim and crimp the edge.
2 Spread the jam over the pastry base.
3 Cream the butter or margarine and sugar together until light and fluffy, add the lemon rind or almond essence then gradually beat in the egg.
4 Combine the almonds and cake crumbs and fold half into the mixture. Add lemon juice or milk together with the remaining almond mixture to give a dropping consistency then spread the mixture evenly over the jam.
5 Bake in a fairly hot oven (200°C/400°F, Gas Mark 6) for 20 minutes. Reduce the oven

temperature to moderate (180°C/350°F, Gas Mark 4) and continue to cook for a further 10–15 minutes or until the filling is firm to the touch.
6 Serve hot or cold sprinkled with icing sugar and accompanied by cream or custard.

Serves 4–6

This tart will keep in the freezer for up to 2 months.

Lemon Meringue Pie

A firm family favourite, so much better when made properly with fresh lemons.

1 recipe quantity pâte sucrée (see page 19), or 1½ recipe quantities flan pastry (see page 19), or ¾ recipe quantity shortcrust pastry (see page 16)
finely grated rind and juice of 2 large lemons
3 level tbsp cornflour
150ml/¼pt water
50–75g/2–3oz caster sugar
2 egg yolks
knob butter

Meringue
2 egg whites
75g/3oz caster sugar

1 Roll out the pastry and use to line an 18–20cm/7–8in shallow pie tin or flan ring, tin or dish and crimp the edge.
2 Bake blind (see page 32) in a moderately hot oven (190°C/375°F, Gas Mark 5) for 15–20 minutes, remove the paper and beans and return the flan to the oven for 5 minutes to dry out. Remove from the oven and leave to cool. Reduce the oven temperature to moderate (160°C/325°F, Gas Mark 3).
3 Make the fruit rind and juice up to 125ml/scant ¼pt with water then blend with the cornflour and the 150ml/¼pt water in a saucepan.
4 Bring slowly to the boil, stirring continuously until thickened and clear.
5 Stir in the sugar to taste then beat in the egg yolks followed by the butter. Pour the mixture into the pastry case.

6 Whisk the egg whites until stiff then whisk in the sugar a little at a time making sure the meringue is stiff again before adding further sugar.

7 Pipe or spread the meringue mixture over the filling and return to the cooler oven for about 15 minutes or until lightly browned. Serve hot or cold.

Serves 4–6

VARIATIONS

For Orange Meringue Pie use the grated rind of 2 oranges and the juice of 1–2 oranges and 1 lemon; for Grapefruit Meringue Pie use the rind and juice of 1 grapefruit; for Lime Meringue Pie use the rind and juice of 2 limes plus the juice of 1 lemon.

Fruit Cobbler

A 'cobbler' or scone topping to both sweet and savoury dishes has become very popular. It is probably a variation on dumplings which used to be boiled or baked on top of a stew, but to my mind is much tastier. The dough is rolled out, cut into circles and arranged in an overlapping circle all round the edge of the dish, with the centre left uncovered. Any fruit can be used and can be flavoured as you like, eg rhubarb with chopped stem ginger.

675g/1½lb stewed or part-stewed fruit, eg apples, rhubarb, gooseberries, plums, or apples and blackberries, apples and raspberries etc.

Scone topping
150g/6oz self-raising flour
40g/1½oz butter or margarine
25g/1oz caster or soft brown sugar
5–6tbsp (approx) milk
1 level tbsp demerara, granulated or coffee sugar crystals (optional)

1 Put the fruit into an ovenproof dish so that it is not more than two-thirds full. The fruit can be warm or cold.

2 Sift the flour into a bowl, rub in the fat until the mixture resembles fine breadcrumbs then stir in the sugar.

3 Add sufficient milk to mix to a fairly soft dough then turn onto a lightly floured surface.

4 Flatten out or roll to about 1cm/⅓in thick and cut into 2.5–4cm/1–1½in rounds— plain or fluted.

5 Brush the top of each scone with milk and arrange them in an overlapping circle around the edge of the dish over the fruit, leaving the centre uncovered.

6 Sprinkle the scones with sugar if liked and bake in a fairly hot oven (200°C/400°F, Gas Mark 6) for about 30 minutes or until the scones are well risen and golden brown. Serve fruit cobbler hot.

Serves 4–6

Note The scones may be flavoured with orange or lemon rind or any spice to complement the fruit used—cinnamon with apple, for example.

Fruit Cobbler

Apple Strudel

A famous dessert or teatime favourite from Austria and its surrounding countries often longed for by people who have been on holiday in those parts. The pastry is rather tedious to make but worth the effort in the end; however it is now possible to buy packets of strudel paste leaves from certain specialized delicatessens. This recipe will keep in the freezer for up to 3 months.

225g/8oz plain flour
good pinch salt
1 egg, beaten
2tbsp oil
4tbsp warm water
40g/1½oz raisins
40g/1½oz currants
75g/3oz caster sugar
½ level tsp ground cinnamon or mixed spice
1.1kg/2½lb cooking apples, peeled, cored and
    very thinly sliced
40g/1½oz melted butter
100g/4oz ground almonds
little icing sugar

1 Sift the flour and salt into a bowl. Make a well in the centre and add the egg, oil and water and mix to form a soft sticky dough.
2 Turn onto a floured surface and knead by hand for about 15 minutes or in a large electric mixer fitted with a dough hook for about 5 minutes or until smooth and even.
3 Shape into a ball, place in an oiled polythene bag and leave to rest in a warm place for about 1 hour.
4 Combine the dried fruits, sugar, spice and apples for the filling.
5 Spread out clean old cotton tablecloth or sheet and sprinkle with 1–2tbsp flour.
6 Place the dough in the centre and using a warmed rolling pin, roll it out carefully to a rectangle about 3mm/⅛in thick, lifting occasionally to prevent sticking.
7 Now gently stretch the dough using the backs of the hands underneath it and working from the centre outwards, until it is thin enough to read a newspaper through! Take care not to tear it. Rest it for 15 minutes.
8 Cut the pastry into strips approx 23 × 15cm/9 × 6in then place two at a time on a damp cloth and first brush with melted butter then sprinkle evenly with almonds.
9 Sprinkle apple mixture evenly over the dough leaving a 2.5cm/1in margin all round.
10 Fold these margins in over the filling then lift the corners of the cloth and carefully roll up to the strudels beginning at a narrow end, with the cloth as an aid.
11 Place on a greased baking sheet and complete the other strudels in the same way.
12 Brush all the tops with melted butter and then bake in a moderately hot oven (190°C/375°F, Gas Mark 5) for about 30 minutes or until golden brown.
13 Dust with icing sugar and serve hot, warm or cold with cream.

Makes 8–10

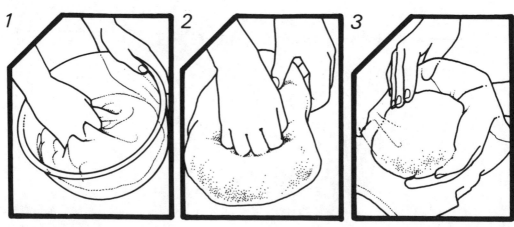

Apple Strudel (stages 1-3 and 6-12)

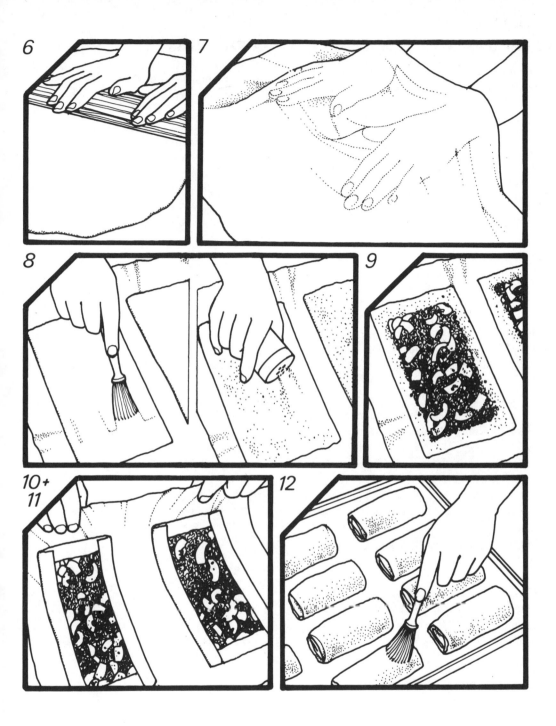

Treacle or Syrup Tart

The modern version is known as a treacle tart but is made with golden syrup. In the nineteenth century it was made with brown treacle, dried fruits, peel and spices and this must be where the name originated. We usually only add flavourings such as lemon, ginger or spice to the syrup and breadcrumb filling, but the extra ingredients sound a good idea.

½ recipe quantity shortcrust pastry (see page 16)
6–8tbsp golden syrup
finely grated rind of ½ lemon
50g/2oz fresh white breadcrumbs
few cornflakes, crushed (optional)

1 Roll out the pastry and use to line a shallow pie plate or tin measuring approx 18cm/7in, and crimp or decorate the edge.
2 Warm the syrup slightly and pour into the flan case.
3 Sprinkle first with lemon rind and then the breadcrumbs and leave to stand for a few minutes to allow the crumbs to begin to sink into the syrup.
4 If liked sprinkle a few crushed cornflakes on top.
5 Bake in a fairly hot oven (200°C/400°F, Gas Mark 6) for about 25 minutes or until the pastry is a light golden brown and the filling firm and golden. Serve hot or cold.

Serves 4–5

Note To measure syrup easily, brush the spoon or scale pan all over with oil before dipping into the syrup or pouring in the syrup and it will simply slide off.

This tart will keep in the freezer for up to 3 months.

APPLE PIES

There are many ways to make an apple pie and here are two versions, one with a single pastry top crust and the other a double-crusted pie. Remember that a fruit pie of any type needs plenty of filling if it is to be a good one. It is easy to recall the poor ones made with thick unappetising pastry and a meagre layer of fruit—but a real joy to remember the succulent ones with crisp light pastry and generous tasty filling.

Filling can be added raw, part-cooked or fully cooked, but should be cold before adding the pastry. The old manuscripts stated that puff pastry was used for fruit pies and that they were left undecorated and simply brushed with milk and dredged with sugar; but nowadays shortcrust is more often used, either alone or in combination with a flaked pastry, and some fruit pies have plenty of pastry decoration on top and no one complains.

Single Crust Apple Pie

675–900g/1½–2lb apples, peeled, cored and
    sliced
100g/4oz (approx) sugar
½ level tsp ground cinnamon, mixed spice or
    ginger; or a few whole cloves; or finely grated
    rind of ½ orange or lemon
2tbsp water
½ recipe quantity puff, flaky or rough puff pastry
    (see pages 21, 24), or 1 recipe quantity
    shortcrust pastry (see page 16)
beaten egg or milk to glaze

1 Mix the apples, sugar and chosen flavouring together and put into a 1 litre/1½–2pt pie dish and add the water.
2 Roll out the pastry on a floured surface to about 5cm/2in larger than the top of the dish and use to make a rim and to cover the pie as described on page 32.
3 Flake the edges and scallop them, and make one or two holes in the top. Use the pastry trimmings to make leaves and decorate around these holes in the pastry.
4 Brush the top with beaten egg or if

preferred brush the shortcrust pie with milk.
5 Bake puff, flaky or rough puff pies in a hot oven (220°C/425°F, Gas Mark 7) for 20 minutes then reduce the temperature to moderate (180°C/350°F, Gas Mark 4) and continue to cook for about 30–40 minutes until the pastry is golden brown and the fruit tender; bake a shortcrust pie in a fairly hot oven (200°C/400°F, Gas Mark 6) for about 20 minutes then reduce the temperature as above and continue to cook for a further 30 minutes or so.
6 Serve hot with cream or custard and if liked dredge the top lightly with caster sugar.

Serves 4–6

Note The filling may be part-cooked and cooled if preferred; in which case cut the cooking time by about 10 minutes.

Double-Crust Apple Pie

filling ingredients as above
1 recipe quantity shortcrust pastry (see page 16), or ½ recipe quantity shortcrust pastry and ¼ recipe quantity puff, flaky or rough puff pastry (see pages 21, 24)
beaten egg or milk to glaze

1 Roll out just over half the shortcrust pastry (or all the shortcrust if using two types) and use to line a deep pie plate or shallow pie tin—approx 18–21cm/7–8½in.
2 Peel, core and slice the apples and mix with the sugar and chosen flavouring and pack into the pastry case. Add water if liked, particularly if the apples are a dry variety.
3 Roll out the remaining shortcrust pastry (or puff pastry) and use to cover the pie as described on page 00.
4 Decorate the top with the pastry trimmings, make one or two slits in the top and glaze with milk or beaten egg.
5 Stand the pie on a hot baking sheet and bake in a hot oven (220°C/425°F, Gas Mark 7) for 20 minutes then reduce the temperature to moderate (180°C/350°F, Gas Mark 4) and continue to cook for about 30 minutes or until the pastry is lightly browned.

6 Serve hot or cold, sprinkled with sugar and accompanied, if liked, with cream, custard or ice cream.

Serves 4–6

VARIATIONS
Plums, blackcurrants, rhubarb, gooseberries, damsons, or a combination of fruits may be used for these pies. The filling may also be part-cooked and cooled before use, in which case reduce the cooking time by up to 10 minutes.

French Apple Flan

A true classic and hard to beat even if it does take a little time to arrange all the slices of apple neatly.

1 recipe quantity flan pastry or pâte sucrée (see page 19)
550g/1¼lb cooking apples
3tbsp water
sugar to taste
25g/1oz butter, melted
4tbsp apricot jam

1 Roll out the pastry and use to line an 18cm/7in deep pie plate or shallow pie tin and crimp the edges.
2 Bake blind (see page 32) in a moderately hot oven (190°C/375°F, Gas Mark 5) for 15 minutes, remove the paper and beans and return the flan case to the oven for about 5 minutes to set and dry out.
3 Meanwhile peel, core and slice all but two of the apples and cook gently in 2tbsp of the water until soft. Sweeten to taste, cool a little then spoon into the pastry case.
4 Peel, core and slice the remaining apples and arrange in overlapping slices in circles over the cooked apple. Brush with melted butter.
5 Protect the pastry edge with foil and place the flan under a moderate grill until the apples begin to brown. Remove at once.
6 Heat the jam and the remaining 1tbsp water together until melted then bring to the

French Apple Flan

boil. Sieve and brush carefully over the slices of apple.

7 Serve hot or cold with cream or ice cream.

Serves 4

Note For a larger flan double all the ingredients and use a 25cm/10in flan ring or dish.

Apple and Marmalade Jalousie

This recipe is borrowed from the French but becomes English with its filling of marmalade and apples. It is best made with puff pastry and care is needed with the folding and cutting of the special lid. You can vary the filling and serve it hot or cold.

½ recipe quantity puff pastry (see page 21)
175g/6oz chunky marmalade (any flavour)
450g/1lb cooking apples, peeled, cored and sliced
milk or egg white to glaze
25g/1oz (approx) caster sugar

1 Roll out the pastry and trim to a 30cm/12in square. Cut in half and place one piece on a dampened or lightly greased baking sheet.

2 Roll out the second piece of pastry until it measures 33 × 20cm/13 × 8in then fold in half lengthwise.

3 Using a sharp knife cut into the fold at 1cm/½in intervals to within 2.5cm/1in of the edges and ends.

4 Spread the marmalade over the pastry on the baking sheet leaving a 2.5cm/1in margin all round then cover with the sliced apple, forming it into a block.

5 Brush the pastry margin with milk or water and position the lid on top carefully unfolding it to completely enclose the filling, and so that the margins fit neatly together.

6 Press the margins well together then flake all round the sides with a sharp knife and scallop with the back of the knife.

7 Brush all the pastry with milk or egg white and dredge with the caster sugar to give an even covering.

8 Bake in a hot oven (220°C/425°F, Gas mark 7) for 25–30 minutes until the pastry is well risen and golden brown.

9 Serve hot or cold in slices with cream or ice cream.

Serves 4–6

This recipe will keep in the freezer for up to 3 months.

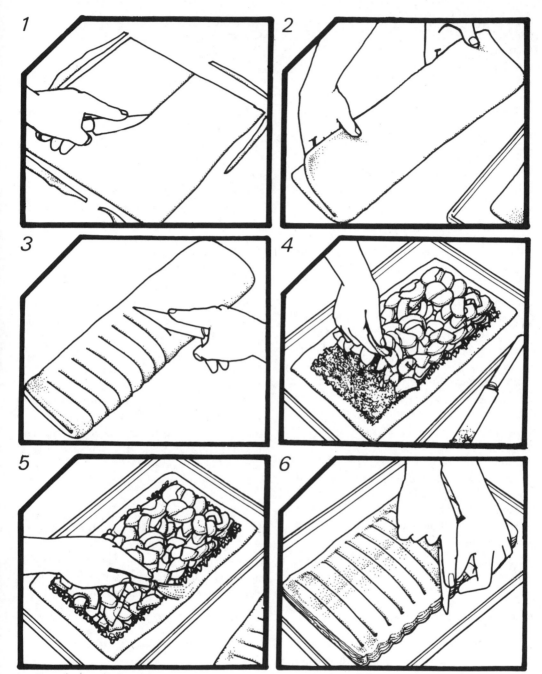

Apple and Marmalade Jalousie

Beignets with Apricot Sauce

Choux pastry is deep fried to produce crisp light puffs which are then tossed in spicy sugar and served with a tangy fruit sauce. It is best to prepare the pastry earlier in the day but do the cooking at the last minute and keep them hot for the minimum time possible.

1 recipe quantity choux pastry (see page 29)
oil for deep frying
25g/1oz caster sugar
½ level tsp ground cinnamon

Apricot sauce
225g/8oz can apricots
1½ level tsp arrowroot
2tbsp brandy
1 level tbsp brown sugar
pinch grated lemon rind
1tbsp lemon juice

1 To make the sauce, first take 1tbsp apricot juice and blend it with the arrowroot.
2 Sieve or liquidise the remaining apricots and their juice and put into a small pan with the brandy, sugar, lemon rind and juice and bring to the boil.
3 Stir in the slaked arrowroot and cook gently, stirring continuously until the mixture has thickened. Leave to cool.
4 Put the choux pastry into a piping bag fitted with a large star vegetable nozzle.
5 Heat the oil to about 180°C/350°F and when ready pipe lengths of choux mixture, measuring about 2.5cm/1in, into the fat cutting them off with a sharp knife. Do not overfill the pan or they will all join up and the oil will cool too rapidly to cook them.
6 Cook for about 5 minutes until well puffed up and browned—it may be necessary to turn them over during cooking.
7 Drain well on absorbent paper and toss them in a mixture of the sugar and cinnamon. Keep the beignets warm whilst frying the remainder.
8 Serve hot with the sauce which can be hot, warm or cold.

Serves 4–6

Orange Chiffon Pie

An American-style fluffy dessert using oranges for flavour but many other fruits, either fresh or canned, may also be used.

¾ recipe quantity shortcrust pastry (see page 16), or 1 recipe quantity flan pastry (see page 19)
3 large oranges
juice of 1 lemon
2 eggs, separated
75g/3oz caster sugar
2 level tsp powdered gelatine

To decorate
little whipped cream
jellied orange slices

1 Roll out the pastry and use to line a 20cm/8in fluted flan tin or ring.
2 Bake blind (see page 00) in a fairly hot oven (200°C/400°F, Gas Mark 6) for 15 minutes. Remove the paper and beans and return the flan case to the oven for 5 minutes to dry out and set.
3 Grate the rind finely from one of the oranges and put into a jug with the lemon juice and the juice from this orange. Make up to 150ml/¼pt with water.
4 Cut away the peel and pith from the other two oranges and carefully ease out the orange segments and reserve.
5 Put the juice and rind mixture into a heatproof basin over a pan of gently simmering water and beat in the egg yolks and sugar.
6 Cook gently, stirring fairly continuously until the mixture thickens then remove from the heat.
7 Dissolve the gelatine in 1tbsp water in a small basin over the pan of hot water, cool a little then stir into the orange and egg mixture. Cool until the consistency of unbeaten egg white.
8 Halve the orange segments and stir into the setting filling.
9 Whisk the egg whites stiffly and fold into the mixture then quickly pour the whole into the flan case. Chill until set.
10 To serve, remove the flan from the ring or tin and decorate with whirls of whipped cream topped with jellied orange slices.

Serves 4–6

(*Clockwise*) Chocolate Caramel Squares with Hazelnut Bars, Cream Puffs, Cream Horns, Macaroon Crisps, Meringue Tartlets with Apricot and Date Pies

Apricot Tart

An attractive tart with a crisp pastry case and a tangy fresh fruit and confectioner's custard filling.

2 recipe quantities pâte sucrée, or
    flan pastry (see page 19)
1 recipe quantity confectioner's custard (see
    page 89)
450–675g/1–1½lb fresh apricots
juice of 1 lemon
6tbsp water or half white wine and half water
50g/2oz caster sugar
¾ level tsp arrowroot

To decorate
little whipped cream
15g/½oz flaked almonds, toasted

1 Roll out the pastry thinly and use to line a 23cm/9in loose-based fluted flan ring, tin or flan dish.
2 Bake blind (see page 32) in a fairly hot oven (200°C/400°F, Gas Mark 6) for 15–20 minutes. Remove the paper and beans and return the pastry case to the oven for a few minutes to dry out and set. Cool in the tin or dish.
3 Meanwhile make up the confectioner's custard (see page 89) and when cool spread this into the flan case.
4 Halve the apricots, remove the stones and place the fruit in a frying pan, cut side downwards, with the lemon juice, water or water and wine mixture and the sugar sprinkled over all.
5 Cover the pan and bring the contents slowly to the boil, then simmer gently for about 5 minutes.
6 Using a slotted spoon drain the apricots and lay them on top of the filling in the tart.
7 Blend the arrowroot with the minimum of cold water, add to the juices in the pan and bring back to the boil, stirring continuously until the mixture has thickened and is clear.

(*Clockwise*) Cheese and Bacon Slices, Sausage Rolls with Salami Rolls, Military Pork Puffs, Quiche Lorraine, Armoured Cutlets and Drumsticks

8 Allow the glaze to cool a little then spoon the mixture over the apricots. When cold remove the tart from the tin and decorate with whipped cream and sprinkle with toasted almonds.

Serves 8

Note 2 × 425g/15oz cans apricots or peaches can be used when fresh apricots are unavailable. Use the juice in place of water but cut the amount of sugar to 25g/1oz. Fresh peaches may also be used but should be sliced not halved.

Mince Pies

These are traditional Christmas fare, but in my family they are made all year round and no one ever gets tired of them. I think it has something to do with the special lightness of the pastry. As the name implies they were once made with minced beef which was mixed with dried fruit and other spicy ingredients as a method of preserving the meat over the winter months for of course, in those days, there was no refrigeration; and it made a change from salting or smoking. Nowadays we use only shredded beef suet, not the beef, when making our mincemeat. To eke out the mincemeat and cut the ever-rising cost you can add a peeled and grated sweet apple to about 225g/8oz ready-made mincemeat. Mince pies can also be made from any other type of pastry and are equally good with a shortcrust base and a flaky top.

1 recipe quantity special shortcrust pastry (see
    page 19)
350–450g/¾–1lb mincemeat
little egg white, beaten lightly
caster sugar

1 Roll out almost two-thirds of the pastry on a lightly floured surface and cut into 18–20 plain or fluted rounds approx 7.5cm/3in in diameter. Place them in lightly greased or dampened patty tins.
2 Add about 2tsp mincemeat to each pastry case.

3 Roll out the remaining pastry and use to cut into a similar number of lids—plain or fluted—this time approx 6cm/2½in in diameter.

4 Damp the edges of the lids and position them over the mincemeat, pressing all edges well together to seal.

5 Brush the tops with egg white and dredge with sugar. Make one or two small slits in the tops for steam to escape.

6 Bake in a fairly hot oven (200°C/400°F, Gas Mark 6) for 20–25 minutes until golden brown and pastry is cooked through.

7 Cool on a wire rack and serve hot, warm or cold as they are or accompanied by whipped cream or brandy or rum butter.

Makes 18–20

These pies will keep in the freezer for up to 3 months but will also keep in an airtight container for up to 2 weeks.

Pecan Pie

This pie is a traditional American favourite often served at Thanksgiving to follow their enormous spread of roast turkey and everything else you can think of too. It is very sweet and sticky and ideal for anyone with a really sweet tooth. Pecans are available at most health food shops but are rather expensive; walnuts can be used instead.

1 recipe quantity flan pastry, or ¾ recipe quantity special short pastry (see page 19)
25g/1oz butter or soft margarine
175g/6oz soft brown sugar (light or dark)
3 eggs, well beaten
175g/6oz maple syrup
1tsp vanilla essence
good pinch salt
75–100g/3–4oz pecan halves

1 Roll out the pastry and use to line a 20cm/8in fluted flan ring, tin or dish.

2 Bake blind (see page 32) in a fairly hot oven (200°C/400°F, Gas Mark 6) for 10 minutes. Remove the paper and beans and return the pastry case to the oven for 5 minutes (it will not be completely cooked). Reduce the oven temperature to moderately hot (190°C/375°F, Gas Mark 5).

3 Combine the butter or margarine and the sugar then gradually beat in the eggs, followed by the maple syrup, vanilla essence and salt. The mixture looks a bit strange at this stage.

4 Arrange the pecans in the flan case, flat side downwards, then carefully pour in the filling.

5 Return the pie to the oven for 35–40 minutes. The filling will have risen rather dramatically but will fall on cooling.

6 Leave to cool and serve either slightly warm or cold with pouring cream. It is very rich so serve only small portions at first!

Serves 6–8

Pecan Pie

Flaky Raspberry Gâteau

A crisp and light dessert of layers of puff pastry filled with confectioner's custard, cream and fresh fruit.

½ recipe quantity puff pastry (see page 21)

Confectioner's custard
300ml/½pt milk
50g/2oz caster sugar
20g/¾oz plain flour
15g/½oz cornflour
1 egg
1 egg yolk
few drops vanilla essence
knob butter

Filling
300ml/½pt double cream
1tbsp any orange liqueur
350–450g/¾–1lb fresh raspberries or a mixture
  of any soft fruits

To decorate
little whipped cream
25g/1oz coarsely grated plain chocolate or
  chocolate curls

1 Roll out the pastry on a floured surface to a large rectangle and trim to 45 × 30cm/ 18 × 12in. Then cut into three strips measuring 30 × 15cm/12 × 6in.
2 Place each pastry strip on a baking sheet, leave to stand for 10 minutes then bake in a very hot oven (230°C/450°F, Gas Mark 8) for 15–20 minutes until well risen and golden brown. Cool on wire racks.

3 Meanwhile prepare the custard by first heating the milk gently in a pan.
4 Beat together the sugar, flour, cornflour, egg and egg yolk until smooth and creamy then beat in a little of the hot milk.
5 Whisk the mixture back into the rest of the milk and cook gently, stirring continuously until it thickens and comes to the boil. Boil for 1 minute.
6 Stir in a few drops of vanilla essence and the butter, cover the surface with a disc of wet greaseproof paper and leave until cold.
7 To prepare the filling, first reserve 16 raspberries for decoration. Whip the cream and the liqueur together until stiff. Fold half the mixture into the custard and put remainder into a piping bag fitted with a large star nozzle.
8 Not more than 30 minutes before required, assemble the gâteau. Place one pastry layer on a dish, spread half the custard cream over it and sprinkle with half the raspberries.
9 Cover with a second pastry layer followed by a layer each of custard cream and raspberries.
10 Top with the remaining pastry layer. Decorate the top with whipped cream and the reserved raspberries and sprinkle the grated chocolate over all. Chill until required.

Serves 8

Advanced preparation Bake the pastry layers and store in an airtight container with greaseproof paper between each; and make the confectioner's custard the day before.

Assembling the gâteau

Gâteau St Honoré

An old favourite combining a crisp pastry base, choux pastry and plenty of creamy filling.

1 recipe quantity pâte sucrée (see page 19)
1 recipe quantity choux pastry (see page 29)
beaten egg to glaze
300ml/½pt whipping cream
1½ recipe quantities confectioner's custard (see page 89)
grated rind of 1 small orange
225g/8oz granulated sugar
150ml/¼pt water
425g/15oz can apricot halves

To decorate
few blanched pistachio nuts or angelica strips

1 Roll out the pastry carefully to a 20cm/8in circle. Place on a greased baking sheet, crimp the edges and prick all over. Bake in a moderately hot oven (190°C/375°F, Gas Mark 5) for about 20 minutes or until golden brown and crisp. Cool on the baking sheet.
2 Put the choux pastry into a large piping bag fitted with a 1cm/½in plain nozzle and pipe a 19cm/7½in circle onto a greased baking sheet. Use the remaining paste to pipe 16–20 walnut-sized balls onto another greased baking sheet.
3. Glaze all the choux paste with beaten egg and bake in a hot oven (220°C/425°F, Gas Mark 7) allowing about 25 minutes or until well risen and firm to the touch.
4 Remove to a wire rack, pierce all the buns to allow steam to escape, and pierce the ring likewise in several places. Leave until cold.
5 Whip the cream and use half of it to fill the choux buns.
6 Beat half the remaining cream into the confectioner's custard with the orange rind and use some of it to fill the choux ring.
7 Place the pastry base on a flat plate.
8 Dissolve the sugar in the water, bring to the boil and boil rapidly without stirring until it turns a pale golden colour (127°C/260°F). Spread a little of this caramel mixture around the top edge of the pastry and stick the choux ring on top.
9 Dip the top of each choux bun quickly into the caramel mixture, add a dab to the base

Gâteau St Honoré

and stick the buns all round the top of the choux ring. Pour any extra caramel over all. Leave to set.

10 Chop half the apricots and mix into the custard then spoon the mixture into the centre of the choux ring. Arrange the remaining apricots on top and brush with apricot juice.

11 Decorate with whirls of the remaining whipped cream and pistachio nuts or angelica.

Serves 8–10

Advanced preparation Bake the pastry base and the choux ring and buns the day before. Store separately in airtight containers.

Profiteroles

Everyone's favourite and so easy to make, but do not fill with cream too far in advance or the choux buns will begin to go soft.

1 recipe quantity choux pastry (see page 29)
450ml/¾pt whipping cream
little icing sugar

Chocolate sauce
175g/6oz plain chocolate
small can evaporated milk
1tbsp rum (optional)

1 Put the choux pastry into a piping bag fitted with a 2cm/¾in plain nozzle and pipe walnut-sized balls onto greased baking sheets.

2 Bake in a hot oven (220°C/425°F, Gas Mark 7) for about 25 minutes until well puffed up, golden brown and firm to the touch. Remove from the oven, pierce each ball to allow steam to escape and cool on wire racks.

3 To make the sauce, first break up the chocolate and melt it gently in the top of a double saucepan or in a basin over a saucepan of gently simmering water, and stir until quite smooth.

4 Add the evaporated milk a little at a time stirring continuously until quite smooth

again. The chocolate becomes rather stiff at first but then melts again.

5 Stir in the rum if used, cover and leave until cool; then pour into a serving jug.

6 Whip the cream until stiff and put into a piping bag fitted with a 5mm/¼in plain nozzle.

7 Use the cream to fill the choux buns by inserting the nozzle into the hole pierced to let the steam out. Alternatively cut each bun in half and fill.

8 Arrange the buns carefully on a plate building up into a pyramid shape.

9 Dredge fairly thickly with icing sugar and serve with the chocolate sauce.

Serves 6

Advance preparation Make the choux buns the day before and store in an airtight container. Make the sauce the day before. Fill the buns just before required.

Raymond's Gâteau

Profiteroles with a difference, very rich and elegant enought to grace any table. A little patience is needed for the final assembly.

1½ recipe quantities choux pastry (see page 29)
568ml/1pt double cream
150ml/¼pt whipping cream
175g/6oz can chestnut spread (sweetened)
1tbsp rum
50g/2oz plain chocolate, coarsely grated

Caramel
225g/8oz granulated sugar
150ml/¼pt water

1 Put the choux pastry into a piping bag fitted with a 1cm/½in plain nozzle and pipe 40–45 walnut-sized balls onto greased baking sheets.

2 Bake in a hot oven (220°C/425°F, Gas Mark 7) for about 25 minutes or until golden brown and firm to the touch.

3 Pierce each bun to release the steam and cool on a wire rack.

4 Whip the creams together until stiff and use a little to part-fill the buns using a piping

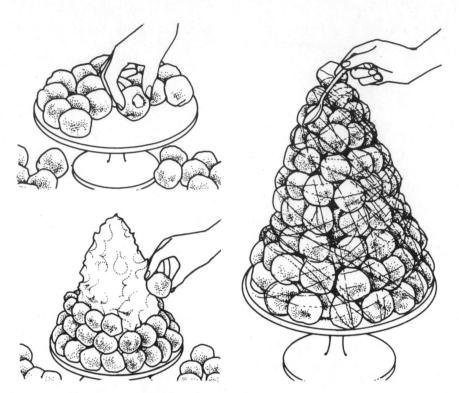

Raymond's Gâteau – profiteroles stuck to a pyramid of chestnut cream then drizzled with caramel

bag fitted with a plain 5mm/¼in nozzle—do not overfill.

5 Mash the chestnut spread until smooth then beat in the rum. Fold into the remaining cream followed by the grated chocolate.

6 Arrange a layer of buns on a serving dish to make about an 18cm/7in circle.

7 Spoon the chestnut cream onto these buns piling it right up into a pyramid.

8 Stick the buns in circles all round this pyramid, finishing with one at the top, and covering as much of the cream as possible.

9 To make the caramel, dissolve the sugar in the water then bring to the boil and boil rapidly without further stirring until the mixture becomes a light caramel colour (127°C/260°F). Cool until the caramel begins to thicken then drizzle the mixture carefully all over the pyramid. Leave to set.

Serves 8–12

Advance preparation Make the profiteroles the day before and store them in an airtight container.

Syllabub Tartlets

A short-textured pastry tartlet filled with fresh fruit and creamy syllabub. Delicious but not good for slimmers.

½ recipe quantity special short crust pastry (see page 19)
100g/4oz strawberries, sliced
1 orange, segmented and halved
1 large egg white
50g/2oz caster sugar
good pinch finely grated lemon rind
good pinch finely grated orange rind
2tsp lemon juice
4tbsp dry white wine or dry cider
150ml/¼pt double cream

To decorate
4 lemon slices

1 Roll out the pastry and use to line four individual Yorkshire pudding tins or tartlet tins (approx 11cm/4½in in diameter).

2 Crimp the pastry edges, prick the bases and bake blind (see page 32) in a fairly hot oven

(200°C/400°F, Gas Mark 6) for 15 minutes. Remove the paper and beans and bake for a further 5 minutes or until set and golden brown. Cool on a wire rack.

3 Mix the sliced strawberries and orange segments together.

4 Whip the egg until very stiff and then fold in the caster sugar and fruit rinds followed by the lemon juice and wine.

5 Whip the cream until very stiff and fold into the mixture.

6 Spoon the strawberry and orange mixture into the tartlet cases and spoon or pipe the syllabub on top.

7 Decorate with twisted lemon slices and chill for not more than 30 minutes before serving.

Serves 4

Advanced preparation Make the tartlet cases up to 3 days in advance and store in an airtight container.

Grape Pastries

A creamy cheese filling in a crisp pastry tartlet topped with glazed green grapes. Black grapes could be used too.

1 recipe quantity pâte sucrée (see page 19)

Filling
175g/6oz full fat soft cheese
grated rind of ½ lemon
25g/1oz caster sugar
2–3tsp lemon juice

Topping
225g/8oz green grapes
3tbsp apricot jam
1tbsp water

1 Roll out the pastry and use to line four individual Yorkshire pudding tins or tartlet tins (approx 11cm/4½in in diameter).

2 Crimp the pastry edges, prick the bases and bake blind (see page 32) in a moderately hot oven (190°C/375°F, Gas Mark 5) for about 20 minutes. Remove the paper and beans and

return the tartlets to the oven to dry out— about 5 minutes. Cool on a wire rack.

3 To make the filling, cream the cheese, lemon rind and sugar together until smooth then beat in sufficient lemon juice to taste and give a spreading consistency.

4 Divide the filling between the tartlet cases, levelling the tops.

5 Peel, halve and depip the grapes and arrange on top of the cheese filling in one or two layers.

6 Heat the apricot jam and water gently in a small pan until melted then bring to the boil for a minute or so. Sieve and cool.

7 Carefully brush or spoon the glaze over the grapes and chill before serving.

Serves 4

Note Other fruits such as strawberries, raspberries, mandarins etc may be used in place of grapes with an appropriate jam glaze.

Advance preparation Make the tartlet cases up to 3 days in advance and store in an airtight container.

Baked Lemon Cheesecake

A special type of pastry base is used for this cheesecake which can also be vanilla flavoured if preferred. Use fruit in season to decorate.

Pastry
100g/4oz self-raising flour
75g/3oz butter or margarine
50g/2oz icing sugar, sifted
1 egg beaten (size 3 or 4)

Filling
2 level tbsp cornflour
2tbsp natural yogurt
50g/2oz softened butter
2 eggs, separated
225g/8oz cream cheese
225g/8oz cottage cheese
50g/2oz caster sugar
grated rind of 1 lemon or ½tsp vanilla essence

To decorate
2 kiwi fruit or 175g/6oz strawberries, grapes or
    raspberries etc

1 To make the pastry base, put the flour, butter or margarine, sugar and egg into a bowl and beat together until smooth.

2 Spread the mixture into the bottom of a greased 23cm/9in loose-based round deep cake tin and bake in a moderately hot oven (190°C/375°F, Gas Mark 5) for 15 minutes.

3 Remove the tin from the oven and leave the base to cool in the tin.

4 Blend the cornflour and the yogurt together then beat in the butter, egg yolks, cheeses, sugar and lemon rind or vanilla essence until smooth.

5 Whisk the egg whites until stiff and fold evenly through the cheese mixture.

6 Spread the filling over the cooked pastry base and return it to the oven for about 25 minutes or until firm. Leave to cool.

7 Remove from the tin and decorate with slices of kiwi fruit or other types of fruit in season.

Serves 8–10

Strawberry Shortcake

A shortbread mixture made with brown sugar forms the base for this family favourite.

225g/9oz plain flour
150g/6oz butter
75g/3oz soft brown sugar, sifted
300ml/½pt double cream
2tbsp top of the milk or liqueur
450g/1lb strawberries

1 Sift the flour into a bowl and rub in the butter until the mixture resembles bread-crumbs.

2 Stir in the sugar and knead the mixture to form a pliable dough.

3 Divide the mixture into three and roll or press out each portion to fit a 20cm/8in flan ring, on baking sheets. Remove the ring, mark two of the circles into 8 with a knife, crimp the edges and prick well.

4 Cut the third round into 8 wedges and separate slightly. Crimp the edges and with a sharp knife mark each to represent a fan.

5 Bake in a moderate oven (180°C/350°F,

Gas Mark 4) allowing 25–30 minutes for the two circles and 15–20 minutes for the fans. Cool on the baking sheets.

6 Whip the cream and milk or liqueur together until stiff and put nearly half into a piping bag fitted with a star nozzle.

7 Spread half the remaining cream over one layer of shortbread on a serving plate.

8 Reserve 8 large strawberries for decoration and slice the remainder. Lay most of the sliced fruit over the cream and cover with the remaining cream.

9 Position the second layer of shortbread on the cream and pipe the reserved cream over this.

10 Decorate with the pastry fans, making a circle with the points in the centre and keeping them at a slight angle. Spoon the remaining sliced strawberries into the centre.

11 Complete the decoration with piped whirls of cream and the 8 whole strawberries.

Serves 8

Advance preparation Make the shortbread up to 3 days in advance and store in airtight containers.

Glazed Fruit Flans

These fruit-filled crisp pastry cases have a soured cream and sugar topping which is put under the grill until caramelised.

1 recipe quantity pâte sucrée (see page 19)
450g/1lb plums
1 large cooking apple, peeled, cored and sliced
75g/3oz (approx) sugar
½tsp cinnamon
300ml/½pt (approx) soured cream
100–175g/4–6oz demerara sugar

1 Roll out the pastry and use to line six fluted flan tins approx 11cm/4½in in diameter.

2 Bake blind (see page 32) in a moderately hot oven (190°C/375°F, Gas Mark 5) for 15 minutes. Remove the paper and beans and return the flan cases to the oven for about 5 minutes to dry out. Cool on a wire rack.

3 Meanwhile stew the plums and apple in the minimum of water until tender. Remove the plum stones and mash the fruits together, draining off some juice if very liquid. Beat in the sugar to taste and the cinnamon and leave to cool.

4 Stand the pastry cases on a baking sheet and fill with the fruit.

5 Beat the soured cream until smooth then spoon an even layer over the filling and sprinkle with demerara sugar.

6 Place under a hot grill until the sugar begins to caramelise. Serve at once or cool and chill.

Serves 6

Note Any type of stewed or canned fruits can be used for these flans but they should be semi-puréed.

Gâteau Pithiviers

Layers of puff pastry baked with an almond and rum filling.

½ recipe quantity puff pastry (see page 21)
175g/6oz ground almonds
100g/4oz caster sugar
2 eggs, beaten
50g/2oz butter cut into flakes
2tbsp rum
little caster sugar to glaze

1 Roll out the pastry and cut out two circles of 20cm/8in diameter.

2 Place one on a lightly greased baking sheet.

3 Mix the almonds and sugar together then gradually mix in almost all of the beaten egg mixture. Beat well and then beat in the butter and rum to give a spreading consistency.

4 Spread the mixture evenly over the pastry base leaving a 2cm/¾in plain margin all round the edge.

5 Damp the edges of the pastry and cover with the second piece, pressing well together. Flake the sides with a sharp knife.

6 Glaze the pastry with the remaining egg then mark the top into a fine criss-cross design with a sharp knife.

7 Bake in a hot oven (220°C/425°F, Gas Mark 7) for about 25 minutes until well risen and browned.

8 Sprinkle evenly with a little caster sugar and return the pastry to the oven for about 5 minutes to complete the cooking.

9 Serve hot or cold with cream.

Serves 6

Frangipan Fruit Flan

A good flan to serve in the winter months when soft fruits are unavailable except frozen. The dried fruit mixture blends well with the almond flavoured filling. In summer use a mixture of strawberries, raspberries and currants.

1 recipe quantity pâte sucrée (see page 19)

Filling
20g/¾oz cornflour
400ml/¾pt milk
4 egg yolks
25g/1oz caster sugar
75g/3oz ground almonds
few drops almond essence

Fruit topping
100g/4oz prunes, soaked overnight
100g/4oz dried apricots, soaked overnight
sugar to taste
2 oranges
1 large eating apple
little lemon juice
whipped cream (optional)

1 Roll out the pastry and use to line an 18–20cm/7–8in fluted flan ring, tin or dish.

2 Bake blind (see page 32) in a fairly hot oven (200°C/400°F, Gas Mark 6) for 15 minutes, remove the paper and beans and return the flan case to the oven for about 5 minutes to dry out.

3 To make the filling, first blend the cornflour with a little of the milk; heat the remainder of the milk in a small pan and pour onto the blended cornflour. Return the mixture to the saucepan and bring to the boil, stirring continuously.

95

4 Remove from the heat, beat in the egg yolks one at a time, followed by the sugar, ground almonds and essence.

5 Cook for a further minute or so, stirring continuously, until the mixture has thickened. Cover and leave to cool.

6 To make the topping, drain the prunes and apricots and put into a saucepan with water to barely cover and cook gently until tender. Add the sugar and heat until dissolved.

7 Meanwhile pare the rind thinly from one orange with a potato peeler and cut it into julienne strips. Cook in boiling water for 5 minutes until tender, then drain.

8 Cut the peel from the other orange and remove the pith from both the fruits, then remove the segments from between the membranes.

9 Core and thinly slice the apple, dip in lemon juice and add to the prunes and apricots with the orange segments.

10 Spread almond cream into the flan. Drain fruits and spoon on top.

11 Decorate with whipped cream if liked, and strew the julienne strips over all.

Serves 4–6

Hazelnut Galette

The nutty pastry is rather difficult to handle but the result is well worth any trouble it may cause. To make it easier roll it out between two sheets of polythene or non-stick paper.

75g/3oz shelled hazelnuts
110g/4½oz plain flour
pinch salt
75g/3oz butter
65g/2½oz caster sugar

Filling
300ml/½pt double cream
1–2tbsp coffee liqueur (optional)
225g/8oz raspberries or strawberries, or
    425g/15oz can black cherries, drained
little icing sugar

1 Toast the hazelnuts until browned, rub off the skins and grind them finely.

2 Sift the flour and salt into a pile on a working surface. Put the butter, cut into small pieces, in the centre and sprinkle the sugar and nuts over all.

3 Using the fingertips mix all the ingredients to a smooth paste. Wrap in foil or clingfilm and chill for 30 minutes.

4 Divide the pastry into three and carefully roll each portion out thinly to a circle approx 19cm/7½in in diameter. Transfer carefully onto greased baking sheets.

5 Bake in a moderate oven (180°C/350°F, Gas Mark 4) for about 20 minutes or until lightly browned. When firm transfer to a wire rack to cool.

6 Whip the cream and liqueur if used together until stiff. Fold in the whole raspberries, sliced strawberries or halved and stoned cherries. Use the mixture to sandwich the layers together.

7 Dredge the top with icing sugar sifting into an even layer and chill before serving.

Serves 6

Advance preparation Make the nutty pastry circles the day before required and store in an airtight container.

4
Teatime Fare

4

Teatime to me is an occasion that tends to be passed by, except for special occasions and feeding the children after school. We all remember childhood teas with bread and toast soldiers, jam tarts and light sponge cakes, easy to eat for little ones and tempting for mothers who would finish off the leftovers; and I often think of the Sunday teas which were a feature in the lives of our grandparents, when all the family regularly gathered round a large heavily decked table. If you are invited out to tea nowadays it is likely to consist of simply a cup of tea and perhaps a biscuit or piece of cake. I would like to remind everyone of the luscious and elaborate cakes and pastries which used to be served and were consumed in huge amounts—not the best thing for the figure, but much enjoyed and gloated over.

Pastry plays an important part in teatime cooking. So many cakes and tartlets are baked in pastry cases: the filling may be made with almonds, curd cheese, fruit, coconut, etc, and the pastry may be one of the shortcrusts, or flan or pâte sucrée, chosen to complement the filling. Then there is the range of choux-pastry favourites—chocolate and coffee éclairs, cream buns and others, all oozing with whipped cream; and the flaked pastries such as cream slices, cream horns, palmiers, Eccles cakes etc. Scones are always a favourite and can be made with unlimited flavourings and with both brown and white flours. Finally there are all the combinations which use shortbread, meringue, fruit fillings, dried fruit, nuts, chocolate, etc, used to make a wealth of pastries baked in large tins and cut to shape and size as required when cold.

When organising a tea party try to make sure there is an adequate selection of differing types of food. Not everyone likes the same thing, though almost everyone has a soft spot for something sweet. For around a dozen or so people, offer sandwiches and/or scones, some sort of large cake, something full of cream such as eclairs or cream horns, then a simple biscuit or cookie like shortbread or cherry nut pinwheels and one of the various types of pastry tart; this should be plenty to satisfy even the largest of appetites!

Cream Puffs

Choux pastry with a difference—these buns are cooked under tins in their own steam creating a crisp-textured bun which swells to about three times its original size. You need a deep tin with tight-fitting lid, or baking sheets with tins to invert over the buns.

1 recipe quantity choux pastry (see page 29)

Filling
300ml/½pt whipping cream, or 1 recipe quantity
    confectioner's custard (see page 89)

Topping
little apricot jam, warmed
50g/2oz flaked or nibbed almonds, toasted
few glacé cherries, chopped (optional)
icing sugar (optional)

1 Put the choux pastry into a piping bag fitted with a plain 1cm/½in nozzle and pipe buns about the size of a walnut onto greased baking sheets keeping well apart—3 to 4 per sheet is ample. Alternatively spoon teaspoons of the mixture on to the sheets.
2 Cover tightly with the lid or tins. If the fit is bad, seal with a flour and water paste.
3 Bake in a fairly hot oven (200°C/400°F, Gas Mark 6) for 40–50 minutes or until the buns move when the tin is gently shaken. *Do not remove the lid or tins during baking or the steam will escape and the buns will sink dramatically—and there is no cure!*
4 When ready cool the buns on wire racks.
5 Just before required fill the buns with whipped cream or confectioner's custard. Either cut the buns in half and fill, or pipe the filling in through a hole made in the side.
6 Either brush the tops with a little jam and sprinkle with nuts and/or chopped cherries; or simply dredge the filled buns with sifted icing sugar.

Makes 12–16

VARIATIONS
These buns can also be served as a dessert if filled extravagantly with whipped cream and fresh fruit, or cream flavoured with rum and chestnut spread; the lid should perch on top.

Chocolate Eclairs

This is the traditional well-loved choux pastry éclair filled with whipped cream and topped with chocolate—definitely not for slimmers!

1 recipe quantity choux pastry (see page 29)
200ml/8fl oz whipping cream
100g/4oz plain chocolate
25g/1oz butter

1 Put the choux pastry into a piping bag fitted with a plain 1cm/½in nozzle. Pipe the mixture onto greased baking sheets keeping a straight line and cutting the mixture off sharply to give approx 6cm/2½in éclairs. Keep well apart.
2 Bake in a hot oven (220°C/425°F, Gas Mark 7) for 20–25 minutes or until well risen, firm and pale golden brown. Make a slit in the side of each for steam to escape and return to the oven for a few minutes to dry out. Cool on a wire rack.
3 Just before serving, whip the cream until stiff and use to fill the éclairs either by spreading or by piping it in through the slit.
4 Melt the chocolate in a heatproof bowl over a pan of hot water until smooth, then stir in the butter until melted.
5 Cool until the chocolate begins to thicken then carefully dip the top of each éclair into the chocolate until well coated; or spread with a small spatula. Leave to set.

Makes 12–14

VARIATIONS
Coffee éclairs Top with coffee glacé icing made by mixing 100g/4oz sifted icing sugar with 1–2tsp coffee essence or strong black coffee and sufficient warm water to give a consistency that will coat the back of a spoon.

Note Eclairs can be made longer or smaller as desired by cutting off the mixture to the required lengths. Adjust baking times a little if necessary.

Choux Rings

Easier to eat than cream buns, these are a French favourite.

1 recipe quantity choux pastry (see page 29)
beaten egg to glaze
25g/1oz flaked almonds

Filling
100ml/4fl oz double or whipping cream
1 recipe quantity confectioner's custard (see page 89)
3–4tbsp apricot jam

Topping
icing sugar (optional)

1 Put the choux pastry into a piping bag fitted with a 1cm/½in plain nozzle. Pipe into 6–8 7.5cm/3in rings on greased baking sheets, keeping them well apart.
2 Brush with beaten egg and sprinkle with flaked almonds.
3 Bake in a hot oven (220°C/425°F, Gas Mark 7) for 15 minutes then reduce the temperature to moderately hot (190°C/375°F, Gas mark 5) and continue to cook for a further 15–20 minutes or until well risen, crisp and golden brown.
4 Slit with a sharp knife to allow the steam to escape and then cool the rings on a wire rack.
5 Whip the cream until stiff and fold evenly through the confectioner's custard.
6 Split the rings so a small amount of apricot jam can be spread in the base of each ring then fill with custard cream.
7 Reassemble the rings and if liked sprinkle with icing sugar.

Makes 6–8

VARIATIONS
Use 300ml/½pt whipped cream in place of the custard and mix in 25g/1oz grated chocolate, 25g/1oz sifted icing sugar and 1tbsp rum.

Coconut Tartlets

Another variation on the Bakewell tart theme; coconut lovers will fall for these munchy moist tartlets.

1 recipe quantity flan pastry (see page 19), or
    ¾ recipe quantity shortcrust pastry (see page 16)
apricot jam

Filling
50g/2oz butter or margarine
50g/2oz caster sugar
1 egg, beaten
50g/2oz desiccated coconut
3 level tbsp self-raising flour
little water

Topping
50g/2oz butter
100g/4oz icing sugar, sifted
little lemon juice
few strands or a little shredded coconut

1 Roll out the pastry and use to line 16–18 patty tins using a plain or fluted cutter.
2 Spread a little apricot jam in the bottom of each pastry case.
3 To make the filling, first cream the fat and sugar together until light and fluffy then beat in the egg.
4 Fold in the coconut followed by the flour and add a little water, if necessary, to give a soft dropping consistency.
5 Spread this mixture over the jam in each pastry case and bake in a moderately hot oven (190°C/375°F, Gas Mark 5) for 15–20 minutes or until golden brown and firm to the touch. Cool the tartlets on a wire rack.
6 To make the topping, cream the butter and the sugar together adding lemon juice to give a piping consistency. Either pipe a small whirl of icing onto each tartlet or spread with a small amount, then sprinkle with a few strands of coconut or a little shredded coconut.

Makes 16–18

Apricot and Date Pies

There are star-shaped peepholes in the lids of these fruit pies.

1 recipe quantity special shortcrust pastry (see page 19)
100g/4oz dried apricots, soaked overnight
75g/3oz dates, finely chopped
2tbsp thick honey
grated rind of ¼ lemon
3–4 level tbsp soft brown sugar
little demerara sugar

1 Stew the apricots in the minimum of water until soft then chop well and add the dates, honey, lemon rind and sugar; leave until cold.
2 Roll out the pastry and cut out 16–18 7.5cm/3in diameter circles and the same number of approx 6cm/2½in diameter.
3 Place the larger pastry circles in greased patty tins and divide the apricot mixture between them.
4 Cut a tiny star from the centre of each of the smaller rounds, using a cocktail cutter, damp the pastry edges and position these rounds as lids, pressing the edges together. (If no star cutter is available use a tiny round one or the wide end of a piping nozzle.)
5 Brush the tops with milk and sprinkle with a little demerara sugar. Bake in a fairly hot oven (200°C/400°F, Gas Mark 6) for 20–25 minutes or until golden brown. Cool on a wire rack.

Makes 16–18

Mincemeat Sponge Tarts

Sponge flavoured with mincemeat and walnuts is baked in pastry cases.

150g/6oz self-raising flour
50g/2oz soft margarine
150g/6oz soft brown sugar
1 egg
4tbsp mincemeat
25g/1oz walnuts, finely chopped
few drops vanilla essence
¾ recipe quantity shortcrust pastry (see page 16)
little icing sugar for topping

Eclairs, boats and tartlets

1 Put the flour, margarine, sugar, egg, mincemeat, walnuts and essence into a bowl and beat hard for 2 minutes or until well blended.

2 Roll out the pastry and use to line 16–18 patty tins, cutting the pastry with a 7.5cm/3in (approx) fluted cutter.

3 Divide the filling between the pastry cases so they are not more than two-thirds full.

4 Bake in a moderate oven (180°C/350°F, Gas Mark 4) for about 20 minutes or until well risen and firm to the touch.

5 Place the tarts on a wire rack to cool and sprinkle with icing sugar before serving. Serve fresh.

Makes 16–18

Mini Bakewell Tarts

Much easier to eat at the tea table than a slice from a whole large Bakewell tart—and simple to make too.

¾ recipe quantity shortcrust pastry (see page 16)
raspberry jam
50g/2oz butter or margarine
50g/2oz light soft brown sugar
1 egg, beaten
few drops almond essence
40g/1½oz self-raising flour
25g/1oz ground almonds
1–2tsp cold water

Topping
icing sugar

1 Roll out the pastry thinly and use to line 15–16 patty tins, cutting into approx 7.5cm/3in diameter fluted circles.

2 Spread a little raspberry jam in the bottom of each pastry case.

3 Cream the butter or margarine and the sugar until very light and fluffy then beat in the egg and essence.

4 Fold in the flour followed by the ground almonds and sufficient water to give a dropping consistency.

5 Spoon the filling into the tarts until just over half full.

6 Bake in a fairly hot oven (200°C/400°F, Gas Mark 6) for 15–20 minutes or until well risen and golden brown.

7 Cool the tarts on a wire rack then dredge with icing sugar.

Makes 15–16

These tarts will keep in the freezer for up to 2 months.

Meringue Tartlets

Quick to make and attractive to look at, these meringue-topped tartlets can be filled with fruit or lemon curd.

¾ recipe quantity shortcrust pastry (see page 16), or one recipe quantity one-stage shortcrust pastry (see page 21)
cherry or blackcurrant pie filling, or lemon or orange curd with 1tsp grated lemon or orange rind

Topping
1 egg white
50g/2oz caster sugar, or 25g/1oz each caster and sifted light soft brown sugar

1 Roll out the pastry and use to line 12–15 patty tins. Bake blind (see page 32) in a moderately hot oven (190°C/375°F, Gas Mark 5).

2 Divide the pie filling between the pastry cases, or if using lemon or orange curd, first mix in the appropriate fruit rind and then put into the cases.

3 To make the topping, whisk the egg white until stiff then beat in half the sugar a little at a time. Fold in the remaining sugar.

(*Top*) Avocado and Prawn Tartlets and Pissaladière; (*in basket*) Cheese Aigrettes; (*centre*) Cocktail Bouchées or Vol-au-Vents, Fleurons with pâté topping, and assorted Cocktail Canapés on shaped pastry bases; (*below left*) Pinwheel Puffs; (*with dip*) Anchovy Twists between Cheese Straws with and without sesame seeds

4 Put the meringue into a piping bag fitted with a plain or star vegetable nozzle and pipe a whirl on top of each tart to cover the filling and ending with a peak in the centre.
5 Reduce the oven temperature to moderate (160°C/325°F, Gas Mark 3) and bake the tartlets for 5–8 minutes or until lightly browned. Cool on a wire rack.

Makes 12–15

Note These tartlets may also be served hot and used as a dessert.

Curd Tarts

Curd cheese is popular in cheesecakes but also makes very tasty tarts for the tea table.

¾ recipe quantity shortcrust pastry (see page 16)
100g/4oz cottage or curd cheese
50g/2oz butter or margarine, softened
40g/1½oz caster sugar
grated rind of ½ lemon
15g/½oz self-raising flour
2 eggs, separated
25g/1oz currants or finely chopped dates
    (optional)

1 Roll out the pastry and use to line 16–18 patty tins, using a fluted cutter.
2 Beat the cheese and butter or margarine together then add the sugar, lemon rind, flour and egg yolks and beat well.
3 Whisk the egg whites until just stiff and fold evenly into the mixture followed by the currants or dates (if used).
4 Spoon the filling carefully into the cases and bake in a moderately hot oven (190°C/375°F, Gas Mark 5) for about 30 minutes or until set. Cool the tarts on a wire rack.

Makes 16–18

(*Clockwise*) Black Bun, Sussex Pond Pudding, Elizabethan Artichoke Pie, Coventry Godcakes and Huntingdon Fidget Pie

Chestnut Tartlets

A rich creamy filling flavoured with chestnuts and rum. The tarts can be made larger to serve as a dessert.

1 recipe quantity pâte sucrée (see page 19), or
    1 recipe quantity flan pastry (see page 19)

Filling
225g/8oz (approx) can chestnut spread
    (sweetened)
1–2tbsp rum
150ml/¼pt double cream

To decorate
few pieces marron glacé, or glacé cherries and
    angelica, or chocolate curls

1 Roll out the pastry and use to line 12–14 patty tins, using a 7.5cm/3in fluted pastry cutter.
2 Bake blind (see page 32) in a moderately hot oven (190°C/375°F, Gas Mark 5) for about 15 minutes or until set. Cool the pastry cases on a wire rack.
3 To make the filling, first beat the chestnut spread and the rum together.
4 Whip the cream until stiff and fold evenly through the chestnut mixture.
5 Put the filling mixture into a piping bag fitted with a large star vegetable nozzle and pipe whirls of the mixture into the pastry cases finishing with a peak in the centre of each tartlet.
6 Decorate either with a piece of marron glacé, half a cherry with two or three angelica leaves, or a few chocolate curls.
7 Chill until ready to serve.

Makes 12–14

Pineapple Streusel Tarts

The slightly sharp flavour of the pineapple makes these crunchy topped tarts very popular.

1 recipe quantity flan pastry (see page 19), or
    1 recipe quantity pâte sucrée (see page 19)
1 can crushed pineapple, drained

Topping
100g/4oz butter or margarine
75g/3oz light soft brown sugar
2 level tsp ground cinnamon
2 level tbsp plain flour
40g/1½oz walnuts, chopped
little whipped cream to decorate (optional)

1 Roll out the pastry and use to line 16–18 patty tins.
2 Divide the crushed pineapple between the pastry cases.
3 To make the topping, melt the butter or margarine in a pan then stir in all the other ingredients (except the cream) until well blended.
4 Spoon a little of the topping into each pastry case over the pineapple and bake in a fairly hot oven (200°C/400°F, Gas Mark 6) for 20–25 minutes or until the topping is browned. Cool the tarts on a wire rack.
5 Serve plain or topped with a whirl of whipped cream.

Makes 16–18

PASTRY BOATS

These are borrowed from the famous French pâtisserie which covers a wide selection of individual and large flans and tarts with various fillings, but all use pâte sucrée to give a crisp but melting texture to the pastry cases. Many French pastries are baked in boat-shaped tins and these are available from good kitchen equipment stores in varying sizes—11cm/4½in is a good average. The following have my own favourite fillings.

Fruit Boats

½ recipe quantity pâte sucrée (see page 19)
4tbsp apricot jam
1tbsp water
grapes, mandarin oranges, cherries etc (either fresh, frozen or canned)
little whipped cream to decorate

1 Roll out the pastry thinly and use to line nine pastry-boat tins. Bake blind but without adding any beans, in a moderately hot oven (190°C/375°F, Gas Mark 5) for 7–10 minutes or until lightly tinged brown. Cool the boats on a wire rack.
2 Melt the jam and water in a pan. Sieve.
3 Brush the inside of the pastry cases with the glaze then fill with fruit; glaze the fruit.
4 Just before serving decorate with small stars of whipped cream.

Florentine Boats

40g/1½oz butter
50g/2oz caster sugar
50g/2oz flaked almonds, toasted and chopped
25g/1oz raisins, chopped
25g/1oz chopped mixed peel
40g/1½oz glacé cherries, chopped
finely grated rind of 1 lemon
1–2tsp rum (optional)
9 baked pâte sucrée boats (see Fruit Boats)
50g/2oz plain chocolate to decorate

1 Melt the butter in a pan, stir in the sugar and when dissolved boil for 1–2 minutes.
2 Remove from the heat and stir in the almonds, raisins, peel, cherries and lemon rind and the rum (if used).
3 Divide the filling evenly between the pastry boats and leave to set.
4 Melt the chocolate in a basin over a pan of hot water, stir until smooth then put into a paper icing bag.
5 Cut the tip off the bag and drizzle the chocolate backwards and forwards over the filling in the pastry cases. Chill until set.

Coffee Walnut Boats

75g/3oz shelled walnuts
50g/2oz butter
50g/2oz caster sugar
1tbsp coffee essence or strong black coffee
6–8tbsp cake crumbs
9 baked pâte sucrée boats (see Fruit Boats)
150g/6oz icing sugar, sifted
1tsp coffee essence
2tbsp (approx) warm water

1 Reserve 9 walnut halves for decoration and cut each in half carefully. Chop the remainder.
2 Cream the butter and sugar together until light and fluffy then beat in the coffee essence or strong black coffee.
3 Gradually work in the chopped nuts and cake crumbs to give a fairly stiff consistency. A little milk or water may be required.
4 Spoon the filling into the pastry boats.
5 To make up the glacé icing, put the icing sugar into a bowl, add the coffee essence and sufficient water to mix to a coating consistency.
6 Coat the filling in the boats with glacé icing, top each with 2 pieces of walnut and leave to set.

Cream Slices

Individual cream slices can be filled with confectioner's custard or whipped cream along with the jam. A large mille-feuille makes an excellent dessert when layered up with whipped cream and fresh fruit.

¼ recipe quantity puff pastry (see page 21)

Glacé icing
100g/4oz icing sugar, sifted
1–2tbsp warm water or lemon juice
few toasted hazelnuts, chopped, to decorate

Filling
6tbsp raspberry (or other) jam
150ml/¼pt double cream, whipped, or ½ recipe quantity confectioner's custard (see page 89)

1 Roll out the pastry to a rectangle and trim to 30 × 25cm/12 × 10in. Cut in half lengthwise then cut each into strips measuring 12.5 × 5cm/5 × 2in.
2 Place the pastry strips on lightly greased or dampened baking sheets and leave to rest for 10 minutes.
3 Bake in a very hot oven (230°C/450°F, Gas Mark 8) for about 15 minutes or until well puffed up and golden brown. Cool on wire racks.
4 To make the glacé icing, sift the icing sugar into a bowl and beat in sufficient warm water or lemon juice to give a thick coating consistency.
5 Quickly spread the icing over the six best pieces of pastry, sprinkle with the nuts and leave to set.
6 To assemble, spread the remaining pastry bases first with jam and then with whipped cream or confectioner's custard and position the iced layers on top, pressing gently to give an even shape.

Makes 6

Note For a large mille-feuille bake the two rectangles of pastry (30 × 12.5cm/12 × 5in) for 15–20 minutes then cover one layer with icing and nuts and leave to set. Assemble with jam and cream when required.

Cream Horns

A favourite tea-time delicacy made from puff pastry with a sweetened cream and jam filling. A simple egg glaze can be added for traditional glazed horns, or a glaze of egg white and sugar if preferred.

¼ recipe quantity puff or flaky pastry (see page 21)
1 egg, beaten or 1 egg white, lightly beaten
little caster sugar (optional)
lemon curd, raspberry jam or bramble jelly
200ml/8fl oz whipping cream, whipped
icing sugar (optional)

1 Lightly grease eight metal cream horn tins.
2 Roll out the pastry thinly to a strip measuring approx 63 × 11cm/25 × 4½in and cut into eight long strips approx 1cm/½in wide.
3 Brush the strips with either beaten egg or egg white and then wind one strip of pastry carefully around each horn tin beginning at the tip, keeping the glazed side outwards and overlapping slightly each time.
4 Place the horns on a greased baking sheet keeping the pastry join underneath. Glaze again and sprinkle the egg-white-glazed horns with caster sugar.

5 Bake in a hot oven (220°C/425°F, Gas Mark 7) for about 10 minutes or until well puffed up and golden brown. Cool for a few minutes when the pastry should begin to shrink slightly and allow the horn tins to slip out easily. Cool the pastries on a wire rack.
6 When cold put 1tsp lemon curd or jam in the tip of each horn and then fill up with whipped cream. Glazed horns can be dredged with icing sugar before serving.

Makes 8

Note See Chapter 6 for Savoury Horns.

Palmiers

Crisp puff or flaky pastry biscuits made by folding the sugar dredged pastry in a special way so that when cut and baked they open out to give butterfly shapes. They can be served plain or filled with cream and/or jam.

¼ recipe quantity puff or flaky pastry (see page 21)
caster sugar
mixed spice or ground cinnamon

Filling
whipped cream
raspberry or apricot jam

1 Roll the pastry out thinly and evenly to a rectangle measuring approx 30 × 25cm/ 12 × 10in.
2 Sprinkle liberally with caster sugar and then with a little mixed spice or cinnamon.
3 Fold the long sides halfway to the centre; dredge again with sugar and mixed spice or cinnamon.
4 Fold the folded sides right to the centre and dredge with sugar and mixed spice or cinnamon again.
5 Fold in half lengthwise to hide all the other folds and press lightly together.
6 Cut through the roll to give twelve even-sized slices then place the palmiers on greased baking sheets keeping them well apart.
7 Open the top of each out a little and flatten slightly with a round-bladed knife, then dredge with a little more sugar.
8 Bake in a hot oven (220°C/425°F, Gas Mark 7) for about 7 minutes or until golden brown. Turn over carefully and continue baking for a further 4–5 minutes or until golden brown. Cool the palmiers on a wire rack.
9 Fill the palmiers by spreading cream over six of them and, if used, jam over the remainder. Sandwich together. They may be lightly dredged with icing sugar.

Makes 12, or 6 filled pairs

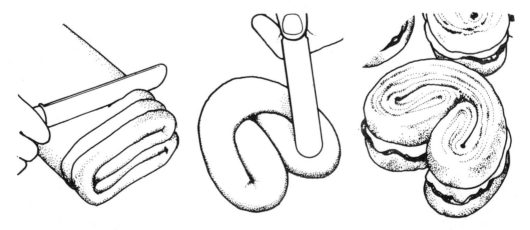

To make Palmiers, fold and slice as described, then slightly open out and flatten each slice with a round-bladed knife

Eccles Cakes

The Eccles and Banbury cakes we know today are very similar apart from the shape. Traditionally Eccles produced round cakes whilst Banbury preferred them oval. The filling is of spiced dried fruit—the pastry should be rolled thinly enough so the fruit shows through—and they are sugar crusted.

As far back as the eighteenth century a Banbury tart was made with a spicy fruit filling similar to a black bun cake but much shallower and often of yeast pastry. It isn't known why or when the cakes became smaller and why the pastry changed to flaky but they are very crisp, light and tasty. A Banbury tart can still be made using dried fruits, spices and a little sugar syrup or honey and it should be baked in shortcrust pastry as a double-crust plate pie.

¼ recipe quantity puff or flaky pastry (see page 21)
beaten egg white
caster sugar

Filling
25g/1oz butter, softened
25g/1oz soft brown sugar (light or dark)
25g/1oz mixed peel
50g/2oz currants
½ level tsp mixed spice

1 Roll out the pastry thinly and cut into 10cm/4in plain rounds.
2 Beat all the filling ingredients together, then place a small teaspoonful of the mixture in the centre of each pastry round.
3 Moisten the edges of the pastry with water and draw them all together in the centre, enclosing the filling. Press well together.
4 Turn over so the pastry join is underneath and roll out carefully until the currants just show through the pastry, to a circle about 1cm/⅓in thick.
5 Place the cakes on greased baking sheets and stand in a cool place for 10 minutes.
6 Brush with lightly beaten egg white, dredge with caster sugar and then make three slits in the top of each cake.
7 Bake in a very hot oven (230°C/450°F, Gas mark 8) for about 15 minutes or until golden brown and crisp. Cool on a wire rack.

Makes 8–10

These cakes will keep in the freezer for up to 2 months.

Sacristans

These are knots, twists, circles and other shapes of puff or flaky pastry coated in nuts and spices. As they do not require the extra rise found in the first rolling, it is a good recipe for using up trimmings and leftovers of pastry.

¼ recipe quantity (approx) puff or flaky pastry (see page 21) or the equivalent in pastry trimmings
1 egg white, lightly beaten
25g/1oz blanched almonds, hazelnuts or walnuts, finely chopped
25g/1oz caster or light soft brown sugar
1–1½ level tsp ground cinnamon or mixed spice

1 If using pastry trimmings knead lightly together then roll the pastry to a rectangle measuring approx 35 × 10cm/14 × 4in.
2 Brush all over with beaten egg white then sprinkle first with the nuts, then the sugar and finally the spice.
3 Cut into strips measuring about 1–2cm/ ½–¾in wide and place on greased baking sheets as they are, or twisted, tied in knots, shaped into circles etc.
4 Bake in a hot oven (220°C/425°F, Gas Mark 7) for about 10 minutes or until puffy and browned. Cool on a wire rack.

Makes about 25

VARIATION
For savoury sacristans, in place of the nuts, caster sugar and spice, sprinkle first with 1–2 level tsp dried mixed herbs and then with 75g/3oz finely grated Cheddar cheese or 2–3tbsp Parmesan cheese. A little powdered garlic may also be used.

Shortbread

Famous in Scotland but well loved the world over. The two basic methods of making shortbread are by rubbing in or by creaming; the basic amount of flour can be broken down to include ground rice, semolina, cornflour etc, which are all family secrets of how to make the best shortbread. Butter must be used to obtain the right flavour.

150g/6oz plain flour, or 125g/5oz plain flour and 25g/1oz ground rice, rice flour, cornflour or semolina
100g/4oz butter
50g/2oz caster sugar
caster sugar for dredging.

Method 1
1 Sift the flour or combination of flours into a bowl and rub in the butter until the mixture resembles breadcrumbs.
2 Mix in the sugar and knead the mixture until it forms a pliable dough.
3 Either press the mixture into an 18–20cm/7–8in greased sandwich tin (round or square) or roll out into a 20cm/8in round and place on a baking sheet (a flan ring helps).
4 Prick the top and mark into 8–10 wedges; mark a square into fingers; crimp the edges.
5 Bake in a moderate oven (180°C/350°F, Gas Mark 4) for about 40 minutes or until a pale brown.
6 If baked on a baking sheet, dredge with sugar, re-mark the cuts and leave until cold. If baked in a tin, allow to firm up then carefully remove from the tin before dredging with sugar; leave to cool.

Method 2
1 Cream the butter and sugar together until very light and fluffy.
2 Sift the flour or combination of flours together and gradually work into the butter and sugar to give a smooth pliable dough; then proceed as for Method 1.

VARIATIONS
These are not traditional but make a nice change. Replace the caster sugar with sifted icing sugar or light soft brown sugar. Add 1 level tsp ground mixed spice or cinnamon or grated lemon or orange rind to the flour. For a crunchy top sprinkle the shortbread with demerara or granulated sugar before baking.

Note Shortbread pastry can also be rolled out and cut to any shape for biscuits. Keep it fairly thin, approx 5mm/¼in, and bake for 20–25 minutes. Store in an airtight container.

Chocolate Caramel Squares

The layers of shortbread, caramel and chocolate in these munchy squares make them hard to resist, especially by children.

125g/5oz plain flour
pinch salt
100g/4oz butter
50g/2oz caster sugar

Caramel
100g/4oz butter or margarine
100g/4oz light soft brown sugar
2tbsp golden syrup
1 small or ½ large can condensed milk
vanilla essence
25g/1oz walnuts, finely chopped (optional)

Topping
100g/4oz plain chocolate

1 Sift the flour and salt into a bowl. Add the butter and sugar and rub in until the mixture resembles breadcrumbs, then knead to a pliable dough.
2 Press the mixture evenly into a greased (and foil lined, if liked) 18cm/7in shallow square cake tin.
3 Bake in a moderate oven (180°C/350°F, Gas Mark 4) for about 25 minutes or until pale golden brown and just firm. Leave to cool in the tin.
4 To make the caramel, first put the fat and sugar into a saucepan with the syrup and condensed milk. Heat gently until melted then bring to the boil and cook gently for 7–8 minutes, stirring occasionally. Remove from the heat.

5 Add a few drops of vanilla essence and the nuts (if used) and beat well until smooth and beginning to thicken.

6 Pour the caramel mixture over the shortbread base, smooth if necessary, cool and then chill.

7 Melt the chocolate in a basin over a pan of hot water, stir until smooth then spread evenly over the caramel. As it begins to set swirl with a knife to give an attractive top.

8 Leave until completely set then cut into 16 squares and remove from the tin.

Makes 16

Shortbread Sponge Fancies

Attractive cakes with a crisp shortbread base.

½ recipe quantity shortbread (see opposite)

Sponge
50g/2oz soft margarine
50g/2oz caster or light soft brown sugar
1 egg
50g/2oz self-raising flour, sifted
½ level tsp baking powder
grated rind of ½ orange (optional)

Decoration
3–4tbsp apricot jam
75g/3oz butter or margarine
150g/6oz icing sugar, sifted
little orange juice
orange food colouring (optional)
25g/1oz (approx) flaked almonds, toasted
few tiny jellied orange slices

1 Roll out the pastry and cut into 10–12 rounds of about 7.5cm/3in diameter. Place on greased baking sheets, prick and then bake in a moderate oven (180°C/350°F, Gas Mark 4) for about 20 minutes or until pale brown and firm. Cool on a wire rack.

2 Put all the ingredients for the sponge into a bowl and beat hard for about 2 minutes or until the mixture is smooth and evenly blended.

3 Grease 10–12 patty tins and two-thirds fill each one with sponge mixture. Bake in a moderate oven (160°C/325°F, Gas Mark 3)

for 20–25 minutes or until well risen and firm to the touch. Cool on a wire rack.

4 Spread each shortbread base lightly with jam and invert a sponge bun on top.

5 Cream the butter and icing sugar together adding sufficient orange juice (and a few drops of orange colouring, if liked) to give a smooth spreading consistency.

6 Use the mixture to spread over the buns—but not the bases.

7 Stick a few toasted almonds all over the butter cream and complete with one or two mini jellied orange slices standing up on top.

Makes 10–12

Apple Crunch

Slices of glazed apple are baked on an almond and sugar-covered shortbread pastry.

150g/6oz self-raising flour
pinch salt
1 level tbsp light soft brown or caster sugar
75g/3oz butter
2 eggs
75g/3oz ground almonds
75g/3oz demerara sugar
1½ level tsp mixed spice or ground cinnamon
3 eating apples, peeled, cored and sliced
2tbsp apricot jam
1tsp water

1 Sift the flour, salt and sugar into a bowl then rub in the butter until the mixture resembles fine breadcrumbs.

2 Add one beaten egg and mix to a firm pliable dough.

3 Press out the pastry to fit the base of a greased rectangular tin (approx 28 × 18 × 4cm/11 × 7 × 1½in) keeping as even as possible.

4 Beat the second egg and use all of it to glaze the pastry.

5 Combine the almonds, demerara sugar and spice and sprinkle over the egg glaze.

6 Arrange the apple slices in overlapping rows across the sugar topping, leaving about 2.5cm/1in between the rows.

7 Heat the jam and water together until

melted and brush over the apples.

8 Bake in a moderate oven (180°C/350°F, Gas Mark 4) for about 1 hour.

9 Leave to cool in the tin for about 10 minutes then cut into squares. Leave until quite cold before removing from the tin.

Makes about 18

Mincemeat Squares

Short-textured sweet pastry is used to sandwich a layer of mincemeat which bakes into munchy squares.

200g/8oz self-raising flour
100g/4oz butter or margarine
100g/4oz caster or light soft brown sugar
1 egg, beaten
2–3tbsp milk
5–6tbsp mincemeat
2 level tbsp demerara sugar

1 Sift the flour into a bowl and rub in the fat until the mixture resembles fine breadcrumbs then stir in the sugar.

2 Add the egg and sufficient milk to mix to a fairly soft dough.

3 Halve the pastry and press one half into the base of a greased 20cm/8in shallow square tin.

4 Spread with the mincemeat, leaving a small plain margin all round.

5 Roll out the remaining pastry and lay over the mincemeat, pressing the edges together firmly and the top lightly so it is quite even.

6 Brush lightly with milk and sprinkle with demerara sugar.

7 Bake in a moderately hot oven (190°C/375°F, Gas Mark 5) for 35–40 minutes or until well risen and firm to the touch.

8 Cool in the tin and when cold cut into squares.

Makes 12–16

VARIATIONS
In place of the mincemeat use 1 grated apple mixed with 3–4tbsp chunky marmalade; or

50g/2oz chopped glacé cherries mixed with 25g/1oz chopped stem or preserved ginger and 25g/1oz currants mixed with 1tbsp clear honey.

Danish Pastries

These are made with a special soft-textured yeasted pastry and for the best results it is advisable to use ordinary plain flour, not the strong flour usually preferred for yeast cooking. Fillings can be added to suit your taste.

25g/1oz fresh yeast, or 1 level tbsp dried yeast and
    1 level tsp caster sugar
150ml/¼pt warm water (43°C/110°F)
450g/1lb plain flour
1 level tsp salt
50g/2oz lard
25g/1oz caster sugar
2 eggs, beaten
275g/10oz butter
beaten egg to glaze

1 Blend the fresh yeast with the water; or for dried yeast, dissolve the sugar in the water, sprinkle the yeast on top and leave in a warm place for about 10 minutes or until frothy.

2 Sift the flour and salt into a bowl, rub in the lard then mix in the sugar.

3 Add the yeast liquid and the beaten eggs and mix to form a soft elastic dough, adding a little more water if necessary.

4 Turn the dough onto a lightly floured surface and knead by hand until smooth—about 3–4 minutes.

5 Put the dough into an oiled polythene bag and chill for 10 minutes.

6 Soften the butter until it can be shaped into an oblong measuring approx 25 × 10cm/10 × 4in.

7 Remove the dough from the bag and roll it out to a 28cm/11in square and spread the butter down the centre of it.

8 Enclose the butter by folding the flaps of dough to overlap in the middle, seal the top and bottom with the rolling pin, then roll out to a strip three times as long as it is wide.

9 Fold the bottom one-third of the strip

upwards and the top one-third downwards to make a neat parcel and then seal the edges. Return to the polythene bag and chill for 10 minutes.

10 Repeat the rolling, folding and chilling process three more times, giving the pastry a quarter turn each time so that the fold is always at the right-hand side.

11 Chill for 30 minutes and the pastry is ready for use (see overleaf). It can be frozen at this stage and kept in the freezer for up to 4 months.

FILLINGS

Spiced nut Toast 50g/2oz hazelnuts or almonds and chop roughly. Mix with 25g/1oz each butter and soft brown sugar and ½ level tsp ground mixed spice.

Ginger Cream 25g/1oz caster sugar with 25g/1oz butter, ½ level tsp ground ginger and 40–50g/1½–2oz finely chopped crystallized, preserved or stem ginger.

Apple Peel, core and slice 2 cooking apples and cook in the minimum of water to a pulp, then beat until smooth and stir in a knob of butter and sugar to taste. Flavour with a pinch of ground cinnamon or mixed spice, if liked, or add a few currants, raisins or sultanas.

Marzipan Mix together 50g/2oz each ground almonds and caster sugar and bind to a pliable paste with a few drops of almond essence and beaten egg. Alternatively use a commercial marzipan.

Mixed fruit Cream 25g/1oz soft brown sugar with 25g/1oz butter and beat in a pinch of ground allspice or cinnamon and 25g/1oz each currants, sultanas and chopped mixed peel.

Confectioner's custard See page 89.

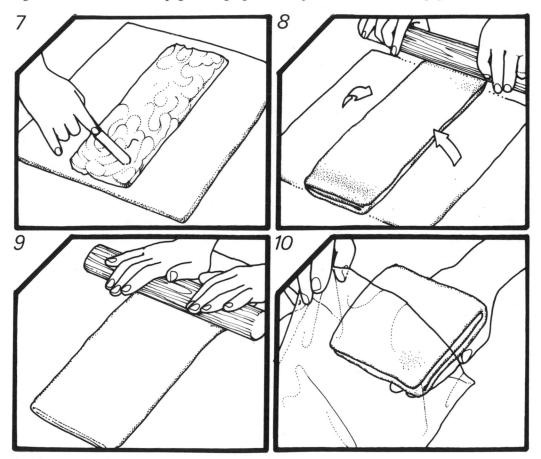

Danish Pastries – the basic rolling, folding and chilling process (stages 7-10)

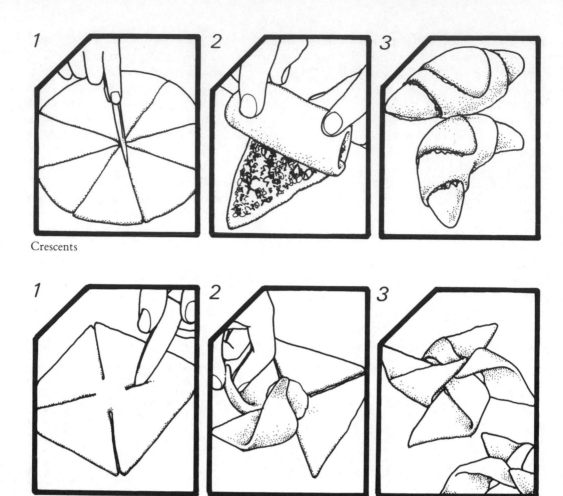

Crescents

Windmills and Imperial Stars

Use toasted or plain almonds, flaked, nibbed, split or chopped; chopped or sliced glacé cherries, chopped angelica; toasted hazelnuts, roughly chopped; pieces of chopped ginger; clear honey, apricot jam, glacé icing.
Glacé icing Sift 100g/4oz icing sugar into a bowl. Add 1–2tbsp warm water or lemon juice to give a smooth coating consistency that will coat the back of a spoon thickly.

CRESCENTS
1 Roll out a quarter of the dough to a 23cm/9in diameter circle and cut into six even-sized wedges.
2 Put 1tsp marzipan, confectioner's custard or stewed apple at the wide base of each wedge and roll up towards the point.

3 Curve into a crescent shape and place on a greased baking sheet. Cover lightly with oiled polythene and put to rise in a warm place for 20–30 minutes or until puffy.
4 Brush with beaten egg and bake in a hot oven (220°C/425°F, Gas Mark 7) for 10–15 minutes or until a light golden brown.
5 Remove to a wire rack and whilst still warm coat with a little glacé icing and sprinkle with nuts and/or cherries, ginger etc. Leave until cold.

Makes 6

WINDMILLS AND IMPERIAL STARS
1 Roll out a quarter of the dough thinly and cut into 7.5cm/3in squares. Make diagonal cuts from each corner to within 1cm/½in of the centre.

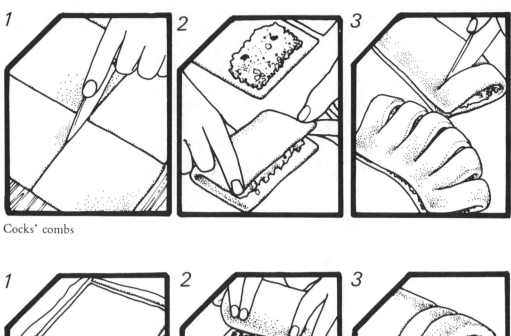

Cocks' combs

Pinwheels

2 Put a small piece of marzipan in the centre then fold one corner of each cut to the centre to make a windmill, and seal with beaten egg.

3 Place on greased baking sheets and cover with oiled polythene.

4 Put to rise, then glaze and bake as for the Crescents for about 20 minutes.

5 Whilst still warm partly cover with glacé icing or brush with honey or apricot jam. For Windmills sprinkle with toasted nuts and/or cherries etc; for Imperial Stars add glacé icing to the projections and a spoonful of confectioner's custard and a halved glacé cherry to the centre. Leave until cold.

Makes 6–8

COCKS' COMBS

1 Roll out a quarter of the dough thinly and cut into strips measuring 11×12.5cm/$4\frac{1}{2} \times 5$in.

2 Spread half the width of each strip with any one of the fillings, fold over the other half to enclose the filling. Seal with egg.

3 Make four or five cuts into the folded edge and place the pastries on greased baking sheets curving each one a little to open out the comb.

4 Put to rise, then glaze and bake as for the Crescents for about 20 minutes.

5 Brush with honey or jam or spread with glacé icing and sprinkle with nuts and/or cherries whilst still warm. Leave until cold.

Makes 6–8

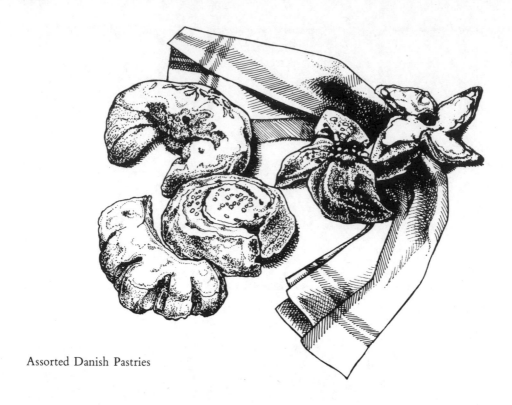

Assorted Danish Pastries

PINWHEELS

1 Roll out a quarter of the dough thinly and cut into a rectangle measuring 30 × 20cm/ 12 × 8in.

2 Spread all over with mixed fruit or ginger filling. Roll up like a Swiss roll, beginning at the narrow end; seal with beaten egg.

3 Cut into 2.5cm/1in slices and place these on a greased baking sheet. Flatten slightly.

4 Put to rise, then glaze and bake as for the Crescents for 15–20 minutes.

5 Remove to a wire rack and ice or brush with honey or jam and sprinkle with nuts and/or cherries, etc. Leave until cold.

Makes 8

Sultana Bars

A pastry-based cake with a layer of jam and a special moist sponge topping full of fruit.

1 recipe quantity shortcrust pastry (see page 16)
4–5 level tbsp jam (raspberry, apricot, black-
    currant etc)
100g/4oz soft margarine
175g/6oz can condensed milk (small can size)
½tsp vanilla essence
2 eggs
100g/4oz self-raising flour
175g/6oz sultanas or mixed dried fruit
100g/4oz icing sugar, sifted
little warm water

1 Roll out the pastry and use to line a shallow rectangular tin (approx 28 × 18 × 2.5cm/11 × 7 × 1in). Crimp the edges and spread the jam over the pastry base.

2 Put the margarine, condensed milk, essence, eggs, flour and sultanas or mixed dried fruit into a bowl and beat hard for 2 minutes or until thoroughly blended.

3 Spread the sponge mixture over the jam, levelling the top.
4 Bake in a moderately hot oven (190°C/375°F, Gas Mark 5) for 30–35 minutes or until the sponge is well risen, firm to the touch and golden brown. Cool in the tin.
5 Blend a little warm water with the icing sugar to give a piping consistency then put into a greaseproof icing bag. Cut off the tip and drizzle lines of glacé icing all over the sponge.
6 When the icing is set cut into bars or into small squares.

Makes 16

VARIATION
Replace the vanilla essence with almond essence and replace 50g/2oz dried fruit with chopped flaked almonds.

Shoofly Tart

A friend in Georgia suggested I tried this speciality from the Deep South. It is rather sweet but quite delicious, with a crumbly topping.

½ recipe quantity shortcrust pastry (see page 16), or 1 recipe quantity flan pastry (see page 19)
100g/4oz dates, chopped
50g/2oz light soft brown sugar
3tbsp hot water
good pinch bicarbonate of soda
100g/4oz plain flour
½ level tsp ground cinnamon
¼ level tsp ground ginger
¼ level tsp allspice or nutmeg
50g/2oz butter or margarine
50g/2oz light soft brown sugar

1 Roll out the pastry and use it to line an 18–20cm/7–8in pie plate or tin, crimping the edge.
2 Sprinkle the dates into the pastry case.
3 Mix the sugar and water together, add the bicarbonate of soda and pour over the dates.
4 Sift the flour and spices into a bowl and rub in the fat until the mixture resembles fine breadcrumbs.

5 Stir in the sugar and spoon the mixture over the dates in the pastry case.
6 Bake in a moderately hot oven (190°C/375°F, Gas Mark 5) for 30–35 minutes or until a pale brown. Leave to cool.
7 Serve cut into wedges.

Makes 8–10 slices

Note This tart can be served warm as a dessert with custard or cream.

Honey Cheese Slices

A rich pastry base is used for these spicy honey-flavoured slices.

1 recipe quantity flan pastry (see page 19)
25g/1oz thick honey
100g/4oz full fat soft cheese
25g/1oz caster or soft brown sugar
½ level tsp ground cinnamon
2 eggs, beaten
little caster sugar and cinnamon for sprinkling

1 Roll out the pastry thinly and use to line a small Swiss roll tin (approx 28 × 18 × 2cm/ 11 × 7 × ¾in).
2 Cream the honey and cheese together until smooth then beat in the sugar, cinnamon and eggs.
3 Pour the mixture into the pastry case and sprinkle lightly with caster sugar and cinnamon.
4 Bake in a moderate oven (180°C/350°F, Gas mark 4) for 30–35 minutes until set.
5 Cool in the tin then cut into slices.

Makes 14–16

Hazelnut Bars

A chewy filling with a crunchy nut topping forms these rich pastry bars.

1 recipe quantity flan pastry (see page 19)
1 egg white
100g/4oz icing sugar
100g/4oz toasted hazelnuts, finely chopped

1 Roll out the pastry and use it to line a shallow 20cm/8in square tin; crimp the edges.
2 Whisk the egg white until stiff then fold in the sifted icing sugar and half the chopped nuts.
3 Spread this mixture over the pastry base and sprinkle with the remaining nuts.
4 Bake in a moderate oven (180°C/350°F, Gas Mark 4) for about 20 minutes until the pastry is cooked and the filling set firm.
5 Cool in the tin then cut into fingers.

Makes 10–12

Note Walnuts, pecans or almonds may be used in place of hazelnuts.

Macaroon Crisps

Crisp sweet pastry bases with a circle of macaroon and a jam filling.

1 recipe quantity pâte sucrée (see page 19)
1 egg white
75g/3oz caster sugar
50g/2oz ground almonds
almond essence
little apricot or raspberry jam, sieved

1 Roll out the pastry fairly thinly and cut into 5cm/2in rounds. Place these on a greased baking sheet.
2 Whisk the egg white until stiff then fold in the sugar, ground almonds and a few drops of almond essence.
3 Put the mixture into a piping bag fitted with a small plain vegetable nozzle (approx 5mm/¼in) and pipe a ring round the top edge of the biscuits.
4 Bake in a moderate oven (180°C/350°F,

Gas Mark 4) for 15–20 minutes until lightly browned with crisp bases. Cool on a rack.
5 Before serving fill the centre of each with a little sieved jam.

Makes 20

Cherry Nut Pinwheels

A special sweetened self-raising shortcrust pastry is used for these crunchy biscuits which are best eaten fresh. They can also be made with a flaked pastry but the filling can fall out without very careful rolling-up.

150g/6oz self-raising flour
25g/1oz caster sugar
75g/3oz butter or margarine
1 egg, beaten

Filling
50g/2oz ground almonds
50g/2oz glacé cherries, roughly chopped
50g/2oz dark soft brown sugar
2 pieces stem or preserved ginger, chopped
15g/½oz angelica, chopped
1 egg yolk

1 Sift the flour into a bowl, add the sugar then rub in the fat until the mixture resembles fine breadcrumbs. Add the egg and mix to form a pliable dough.
2 Knead lightly then roll out the pastry on a floured sheet of greaseproof or non-stick paper to a rectangle about 3mm/⅛in thick.
3 Mix together the ground almonds, cherries, sugar, ginger and angelica, then add the egg yolk and mix well.
4 Spread the filling evenly over the pastry taking it right to the edges.
5 Beginning at a long edge, carefully roll up the dough using the paper as an aid. Damp the edge with water to seal.
6 Cut the roll carefully into slices about 5mm/¼in thick and place these on greased baking sheets cut side upwards.
7 Bake in a fairly hot oven (200°C/400°F, Gas Mark 6) for about 20 minutes until golden brown. Cool on a wire rack.

Makes 20–24

Rich Floury Scones

Scones are halfway between pastry and cake but are made in the same way as short pastry so I feel they have a place in a pastry book. Scones are best made and eaten fresh; and with sour milk—you can easily sour fresh milk by adding 1tsp lemon juice to 4–5tbsp milk.

200g/8oz self-raising flour
pinch salt
50g/2oz butter or margarine
50g/1oz caster or light soft brown sugar
40g/1½oz sultanas (optional)
1 egg, beaten
4–5tbsp milk (preferably sour)
flour for dredging

1 Sift the flour and salt into a bowl and rub in the fat until the mixture resembles fine breadcrumbs.
2 Stir in the sugar and sultanas (if used).
3 Add the egg and sufficient milk to mix to a fairly soft dough.
4 Turn onto a floured surface, knead lightly just into shape then pat out or lightly roll to about 2–2.5cm/¾–1in thick.

5 Cut into 4–5cm/1½–2in circles or triangles or squares and dredge fairly thickly with flour.
6 Place the scones on greased baking sheets and bake in a very hot oven (230°C/450°F, Gas Mark 8) for 12–15 minutes or until well risen, lightly browned and just firm.
7 Turn onto a wire rack covered with a clean cloth, wrap up and leave to cool. Serve warm or cold but fresh, split and buttered, and with jam or honey if liked.

Makes 10

Note For a scone round, pat the dough into a flattish circle 18–20cm/7–8in in diameter and place on the baking sheet. Mark deeply into 8–10 wedges and bake for 15–20 minutes.

The tops of the scones may be brushed with beaten egg or milk instead of dredging with flour and for a crunchy top sprinkle with demerara or granulated sugar.

VARIATIONS
Wholemeal Replace 100g/4oz flour with wholemeal flour and add 1 level tsp baking powder.

Scones, Eccles Cakes and Mince Pies

Honey and walnut Replace sultanas with chopped walnuts and 1tbsp milk with clear honey.

Lemon and date Add the freshly grated rind of 1 lemon (or orange) and finely chopped dates in place of the sultanas.

Spicy Use soft brown sugar and add 1 level tsp ground cinnamon or mixed spice to the dry ingredients.

Ginger Add ½–1 level tsp ground ginger and use 25g/1oz finely chopped preserved or stem ginger in place of sultanas.

Cheese Omit the sugar and sultanas and add ½ level tsp dry mustard and 50g/2oz finely grated mature Cheddar cheese or 1–1½ level tbsp grated Parmesan cheese. Sprinkle the tops with a little grated cheese.

Herby Omit sugar and sultanas and add 1tbsp freshly chopped herbs (any variety) or 1–1½ level tsp dried herbs.

Anchovy Omit sugar and sultanas and add ½ can anchovies, drained and finely chopped. Use the remaining anchovies blended with butter to spread inside the cooked scones.

Freezing All scones freeze well and will keep in the freezer for up to 4 months, except the highly spiced varieties and those containing herbs and anchovies which are best used within 2 months.

Plain Scones

200g/8oz self-raising flour
pinch salt
50g/2oz butter or margarine
milk to mix (preferably soured)

1 Sift the flour and salt into a bowl and rub in the fat until the mixture resembles fine breadcrumbs.
2 Add sufficient milk to mix to a softish dough.
3 Knead lightly and pat out or roll to about 2.5cm/1in thick.
4 Cut into 4–5cm/1½–2in rounds and place on a greased baking sheet.
5 Brush the tops with milk and bake in a very hot oven (230°C/450°F, Gas Mark 8) for about 12–15 minutes until well risen and golden brown. Cool on a wire rack.

Makes 8

VARIATIONS
Fruit Add 40g/1½oz sultanas to the dry mixture.
Cheese Add 50g/2oz finely grated mature Cheddar cheese to the dry mixture.
Herby Add 1tbsp freshly chopped or 1 level tsp dried herbs to the dry mixture.

5
Suppers and Picnics

5

The same kinds of pastry dishes are often suitable for either suppers or picnics. For supper, as opposed to dinner, we usually want something uncomplicated, which can be served hot or cold but must satisfy a certain amount of hunger. A typical picnic demands something filling, interesting, easy to eat and transportable—and although with today's sophisticated picnic equipment almost any food can become portable, pastry is a sure winner. Foods fully or partly encased in pastry are suitable for all appetites, from tots to teens to grannies; and the ways the pastry can be shaped, and the types and varieties of fillings, are unending. As well as quiches and flans you can try plenty of pasties and individual pies, sausage rolls and their relatives, and a host of pizzas.

Cold pies, quiches and pasties, etc, make excellent picnic fare, requiring only to be covered in foil or clingfilm before packing up. Some people prefer to 'plate' their picnic meals first, rather than take a lot of separate containers. You can buy plastic trays with moulded hollows for main course, pudding, roll and glass, ready to fill as required; some simply require a knife and fork added, and a sheet of foil over each one; others come complete with cutlery and plastic snap-on lid. For really elegant picnics to be held in the garden, before the theatre, for shooting parties or point-to-points, or some other special occasion, as well as using the recipes in this section try borrowing the raised game and other hot-water-crust pies from the chapter on Main Dishes; these will surely grace any spread.

For packed lunches for school, the office or to feed outdoor workers, something baked in pastry or a slice cut off a pastry roll with savoury filling such as Poacher's Roll or Cheese and Bacon Slice, are much more popular and nutritious than the perennial everlasting sandwich.

For suppers, too, a slice of quiche with salad makes an excellent summer meal; and in the depths of winter a hot pizza or a slice of hot Smoked Mackerel Plate Pie with peas will give a warm and ·satisfied feeling. For many of us supper is the secondary meal of the day, not necessarily requiring a plate full of vegetables to accompany it or a filling pudding; we like a lighter meal with just a salad or one simple vegetable, followed by a piece of fresh fruit, yogurt or cheese and biscuits. But however you want to organise your suppers or picnics, I hope some of the following recipes will supply some new and interesting thoughts.

QUICHES

The quiche has become a firm family favourite with its unending list of fillings baked into a savoury custard with a crisp pastry casing. A good idea borrowed from the French, it is quite at home whether served at the table, in the garden or on a picnic for it is easy to transport. It is so versatile; serve it hot or cold, chill in the refrigerator for several days, or freeze for 1–2 months; vary the pastry from shortcrust to one-stage, cheese, wholemeal or quick mix. All the following quiches are baked in a 20cm/8in tin and will serve 4–5 persons.

Basic Quiche Lorraine

See page 19 for amounts of pastry to fit other sized tins

¾ recipe quantity shortcrust pastry (see page 16) using 150g/6oz flour etc
175g/6oz bacon rashers, derinded and chopped
1 small onion, peeled and chopped (optional)
2 eggs, beaten
150ml/¼pt single cream (or milk)
150ml/¼pt milk
salt and pepper
pinch ground nutmeg
75g/3oz Cheddar or Emmental cheese, grated

1 Roll out the pastry and use to line a 20cm/8in flan tin, ring or dish.
2 Fry the bacon in its own fat for a few minutes then add the onion (if using) and continue to cook for 2–3 minutes more.
3 Drain the bacon and onion thoroughly and put into the flan case.
4 Beat the eggs thoroughly with the cream and milk and add plenty of seasoning and the nutmeg. Pour the mixture into the flan case.
5 Sprinkle with the grated cheese.
6 Stand the flan on a hot baking sheet and bake in a hot oven (220°C/425°F, Gas Mark 7) for 15–20 minutes. Reduce the temperature to moderate (180°C/350°F, Gas Mark 4) and continue to cook for 30–35 minutes until the filling is set and golden brown.

MUSHROOM AND HERB QUICHE

Fry 175g/6oz sliced mushrooms in 2tbsp oil for 2–3 minutes, drain well and use in place of the bacon and onions. Add 1 level tsp mixed herbs to the egg custard.

CHEESE AND ONION QUICHE

Fry 2 large sliced onions gently in 2tbsp oil until soft—about 15 minutes. Drain well and use in place of the bacon and onion. Increase the amount of cheese to 100–125g/4–5oz.

STILTON QUICHE

Fry 1 sliced or chopped onion in 1tbsp oil until golden brown. Add to the flan with 100g/4oz crumbled Stilton cheese and 50g/2oz grated Cheddar cheese in place of the bacon and onion. Add 1tbsp freshly chopped parsley to the egg custard.

TUNAFISH QUICHE

Fry 1 chopped onion in 1tbsp oil until soft. Add to the flan with a 200g/7oz can tunafish, drained and flaked, in place of the bacon and onion. Add 1 level tsp dried basil or marjoram to the egg custard.

SAUSAGE AND TOMATO QUICHE

Cook 225g/8oz chipolata sausages and lay them in the flan case. Cover with 3 peeled and sliced tomatoes and the cheese in place of the bacon and onion. Add 1 level tsp mixed herbs to the egg custard, if liked.

SPINACH QUICHE

Cook and thoroughly drain a 225g/8oz packet frozen leaf spinach and lay it in the flan case. Cover with 75g/3oz grated Cheddar cheese. Beat 2 eggs with 150ml/¼pt single cream, 4tbsp milk, plenty of seasonings, good pinch ground nutmeg and 2tbsp grated Parmesan cheese and pour into the flan case.

FLANS

Again a good idea for home or picnic eating. The pastry case can be baked in advance with the filling added as and when required. Serve it hot or cold or chilled with a jellied filling. Flans are ideal for using up leftovers of this and that or stretching something which can be added to a sauce to make a quick but satisfying meal. On the other hand attractive ingredients can be arranged in pastry cases— large or small—and be set with gelatine or aspic for elegant outdoor eating. Pastries of all sorts can be used—either short or flaked.

20cm/8in baked pastry case (shortcrust, wholemeal, one-stage, puff, flaky etc)

CRAB AND EGG FLAN
Make 300ml/½pt white sauce and season well. Mix in 2tbsp freshly chopped parsley, 2 peeled and chopped tomatoes, 200g/7oz can crab meat, drained and flaked, 2 hard-boiled eggs (sliced or chopped) and 1tbsp capers. Use to fill the flan case and serve hot or cold.

CHICKEN AND SWEETCORN FLAN
Fry 1 sliced onion in 1tbsp oil until golden brown, add a can condensed chicken soup, 4tbsp milk, small can drained Mexicorn, 175g/6oz diced cooked chicken or turkey, and plenty of seasonings. Mix well and use to fill flan case; serve hot or cold.

HAM AND ASPARAGUS FLAN
Finely chop 100g/4oz ham or cooked bacon and add it to 300ml/½pt well-seasoned white sauce (use asparagus liquor from can, if liked). Reserve 8 asparagus spears from 350g/12oz can, chop the remainder and add to the sauce. Spoon the filling into the flan case, top with a wheel of asparagus spears and serve hot or cold.

CURRIED TURKEY AND GRAPE FLAN
Combine 150ml/¼pt thick mayonnaise, 4tbsp cream, 2tbsp apricot jam, 1tbsp lemon juice, 1 level tsp curry powder, 1–3 chopped spring onions (optional) and plenty of seasonings. Fold in 225g/8oz cooked turkey or chicken, cut into strips, and 50–75g/2–3oz halved and depipped green grapes. Pile into the flan case and serve cold.

MINTED TOMATO AND SAUSAGE FLAN
Peel, quarter and deseed 450g/1lb tomatoes and put into a bowl with 1–2tsp finely chopped fresh mint. Add 3–4 thinly sliced cooked sausages and 1 carton natural yogurt mixed with 2–3tbsp salad cream or mayonnaise. Toss well, pile into the flan case and serve cold.

JELLIED VEGETABLE AND EGG FLAN
Chop 2 spring onions, mix with 100g/4oz each cooked diced carrots, peas and—if liked—asparagus. Slice 3 hard-boiled eggs and arrange them in the flan case with the vegetables and 2 peeled and sliced tomatoes. Dissolve 2 level tsp powdered gelatine in part of 300g/10oz can consommé, mix in the remainder of the consommé and pour the whole over the vegetables. Chill until set then decorate with piped whirls of thick mayonnaise and anchovy fillets.

PASTIES

The Cornish pasty is thought to have originated as a packed lunch for the miners. Although it is now traditionally savoury, at one time it was dual purpose, having a savoury filling at one end and a sweet filling at the other to provide a complete meal. It is said that a true Cornish pasty can only be made by a Cornish woman although they are available all over the country—or at least in some form. To achieve the best, use the best; finely chop the best lean beef and vegetables and make a good shortcrust pastry. Not so traditional but also very good are pasties made with a flaked pastry.

175g/6oz best raw minced beef or finely chopped
    rump or flank steak
1 onion, peeled and very finely chopped
1 small carrot, very finely chopped (optional)

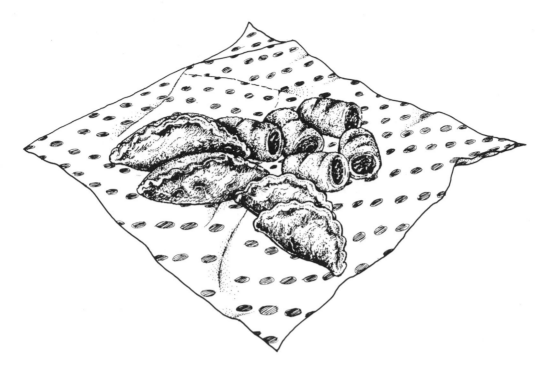

Cornish Pasties (left), Venison Pasties and Sausage Rolls

100g/4oz peeled potato, very finely chopped
salt and pepper
1 recipe quantity shortcrust pastry (see page 16), or ⅓ recipe quantity puff or flaky pastry (see page 21)
beaten egg or milk to glaze

1 Combine the meat, onion, carrot (if used), potato and plenty of seasonings.
2 Roll out the pastry and cut into four 18cm/7in rounds.
3 Divide the filling into four and place one portion in the centre of each round.
4 Damp the edges of the pastry and bring together at the top. Press firmly together and crimp.
5 Place the pasties on lightly greased baking sheets and glaze with beaten egg or milk.
6 Bake in a hot oven (220°C/425°F, Gas Mark 7) for about 30 minutes or until golden brown. Serve hot, warm or cold.

Makes 4

These pasties will keep in the freezer for up to 2 months.

LEEK AND BACON PASTIES
Thinly slice 2 leeks and blanch in boiling water for 2 minutes; drain well. Mix with 4–6 chopped lean bacon rashers, plenty of seasonings and 1tbsp top of the milk or cream; continue as for Cornish pasty.

RABBIT PASTIES
Mince 100g/4oz raw rabbit with 50g/2oz streaky bacon rashers. Mix with 1 finely chopped onion, 1 chopped carrot, 1 chopped raw potato, 1tbsp freshly chopped parsley and plenty of seasonings. A few crushed juniper berries may also be added; continue as for Cornish pasty.

CHEESE AND ONION PASTIES
Mince 225g/8oz onion and mix with 175g/6oz grated Cheddar cheese, plenty of seasonings and 1tsp Worcestershire sauce; continue as for Cornish pasty.

CHICKEN AND MUSHROOM PASTIES
Mince 175g/6oz raw chicken and mix with 1 finely chopped onion, 75g/3oz finely

chopped mushrooms, plenty of seasonings, 2tbsp thick mayonnaise and pinch dried tarragon; continue as for Cornish pasty.

EGG AND ANCHOVY PASTIES

Make 150ml/¼pt thick white sauce and leave to cool. Mix in plenty of seasonings, 2tbsp finely chopped onion, 3 chopped hard-boiled eggs and ½ can anchovies, drained and chopped; continue as for Cornish pasty.

BACON AND TOMATO PASTIES

Mix together 1 finely chopped onion, 2–3 peeled, deseeded and chopped tomatoes, 175g/6oz chopped lean bacon, ½ level tsp mixed herbs, and seasonings; continue as for Cornish pasty.

'Armoured' Foods

Ideal for suppers and picnics are mini en croûte dishes or, as I prefer to call them, 'armoured' food. Chicken drumsticks and thighs, small turkey drumsticks, lamb cutlets and sausages are a few which take kindly to this method of cooking. Some pre-cooking of the meat is necessary and flavourings can be spread or wound round the food before it is enclosed in either a flaked or a short pastry. Once cooked they can be served hot or cold and will freeze well for up to 1 month, if required. Try them for a packed lunch.

6–8 lamb cutlets, or 6–8 chicken or small turkey
    drumsticks, or 6–8 sausages
salt and pepper
little chutney, mint jelly, horseradish etc
    (optional)
1 recipe quantity shortcrust pastry (see page 16),
    or ½ recipe quantity puff, flaky or rough puff
    pastry (see pages 21, 24)
beaten egg to glaze

1 Either fry or grill the cutlets, drumsticks or sausages with a little added fat until well browned all over and almost cooked through. Remove to a plate, sprinkle with salt and pepper and leave until cold.
2 Roll out the pastry thinly and cut into long strips 2.5cm/1in wide and brush with beaten egg.
3 Spread a little chutney, mint jelly, horseradish etc over one side of the meat, if liked.
4 Carefully wind strips of pastry around each cutlet or drumstick etc, keeping the glazed side outwards and overlapping a little as you go until the meat is completely enclosed. Add another strip of pastry as necessary.
5 Place the 'parcels' on greased baking sheets and glaze again.
6 Bake in a hot oven (220°C/425°F, Gas Mark 7) for flaked pastries or a fairly hot oven (200°C/400°F, Gas Mark 6) for shortcrust, for about 20 minutes or until the pastry is well browned and crisp. Cool on a wire rack if to be served cold, or serve immediately with vegetables.

Makes 6–8

PIZZAS

A true Italian pizza is made with a special yeasted pastry dough but there are many other versions which are called pizza. Plain bread dough, rolled very thinly, and brushed with oil before adding the topping is one; yeast pastry is another; a scone dough or enriched scone dough with added egg both provide excellent quick bases; another type of pastry made with oil can be fried in a frying pan, then have a topping added which is immediately browned under the grill, the pizza not going near an oven at all. The pizza has really arrived now, with pizza restaurants springing up all over the place; the toppings they offer are unlimited and in many of them you can even choose your own combination of ingredients for the topping. This is getting rather far away from the traditional tomato and cheese topping from Italy but shows there is great scope for dreaming up and making your own favourites.

15g/½oz fresh yeast or 1½ level tsp dried yeast
    and 1 level tsp sugar
150ml/¼pt (approx) warm water (43°C/110°F)

225g/8oz strong plain flour (white or a
    combination of white and brown)
1 level tsp salt
15g/½oz lard or margarine
oil
topping (see below)

1 Blend the fresh yeast with the water; for
dried yeast dissolve the sugar in the water,
sprinkle the yeast on top and leave in a warm
place until frothy—about 10 minutes.
2 Sift the flour and salt into a bowl (don't
sift brown flour) and rub in the fat.
3 Add the yeast liquid and mix to form a
fairly stiff dough. Knead until smooth and
elastic—about 10 minutes by hand or 3–4
minutes in an electric mixer fitted with a
dough hook.
4 Shape the dough into a ball, place in a
lightly oiled polythene bag and put to rise in
a warm place until doubled in size—about
1 hour, or longer in cooler conditions.
5 Remove the dough, knead until smooth
and roll out to a long narrow strip. Brush all
over with oil and roll up like a swiss roll.
6 Repeat the rolling process again but
without the oil.
7 For one large pizza roll out the dough and
use to fit a 30cm/12in greased plain flan ring
on a greased baking sheet; or for two smaller
pizza, halve the dough and roll out each piece
to fit a 20cm/8in flan ring.
8 Brush the dough all over with oil, add the
topping of your choice and put to rise in a
warm place for 15 minutes.
9 Bake in a hot oven (220°C/425°F, Gas
Mark 7) for about 20–25 minutes then reduce
the temperature to moderate (180°C/350°F,
Gas Mark 4) and continue to cook for 15–20
minutes for the large pizza or 10–15 minutes
for the smaller ones. Remove the flan rings
and serve hot, warm or cold.

Yeast Pastry Pizza

½–1 recipe quantity yeast pastry (see
    page 26)
oil
topping (see below)

Roll out pastry and use to line flan rings as
above. Brush with oil, add toppings, (see
below) and leave to stand in a warm place for
15–20 minutes before baking as above.

Scone Pizza

150g/6oz self-raising flour
½ level tsp salt
40g/1½oz butter, margarine or lard
1 egg, beaten (optional)
milk to mix
topping (see below)

1 Sift the flour and salt into a bowl and rub
in the fat until the mixture resembles fine
breadcrumbs.
2 For an enriched dough add the egg and a
little milk, if necessary, to mix to a fairly soft
dough. For ordinary scone dough omit the
egg and add sufficient milk to mix to a fairly
soft dough.
3 Knead the dough lightly then pat out or
roll lightly to fit a 20–23cm/8–9in flan ring
on a greased baking sheet.
4 Add the topping of your choice (see below)
and bake in a hot oven (220°C/425°F, Gas
Mark 7) for 25–30 minutes until the scone
base is cooked through and the topping well
browned.

Serves 4–5

Note For a 30cm/12in pizza use double the
recipe quantity; 1 level tsp any herbs may be
added to the dry ingredients, if liked.

Cheese and Tomato Pizza

30cm/12in pizza base or two 20cm/8in bases
350g/12oz onions, peeled and sliced
1–2 cloves garlic, crushed
2tbsp oil
450g/1lb tomatoes, peeled and sliced, or
    825g/1lb 13oz can tomatoes
salt and pepper
1–2 level tsp oregano or basil
175g/6oz thinly sliced cheese (Mozzarella,
    Bel Paese or Gouda)
1 can anchovy fillets, drained
few black or stuffed green olives

1 Fry the onions and garlic gently in the oil until soft but only lightly coloured.

2 Add the fresh tomatoes or partly drained canned tomatoes and cook for about 10 minutes or until thick, stirring from time to time. Season well.

3 Spread the mixture over the pizza base, sprinkle with the herbs and then cover with cheese.

4 Arrange the anchovies on the top in a lattice design and fill in the gaps with olives. Bake as on page 127.

Mushroom and Pepper Pizza

20cm/8in pizza base
1 red pepper, deseeded and sliced
1 green pepper, deseeded and sliced
1 onion, peeled and chopped
2tbsp oil
1 clove garlic, crushed (optional)
100g/4oz mushrooms, thinly sliced
2–3 tomatoes, sliced
salt and pepper
175g/6oz grated cheese (Cheddar, Gouda, Emmental or Gruyère)

1 Fry the peppers and onion gently in the oil with the garlic (if used) for about 5 minutes or until soft.

2 Add the mushrooms and continue to cook for a few minutes then add the tomatoes and season well.

3 Spoon the mixture over the pizza base and sprinkle with cheese. Bake as on page 127.

Tuna and Tomato Pizza

20cm/8in pizza base
2 onions, peeled and sliced
2tbsp oil
200g/7oz can tuna fish, drained and flaked
4 tomatoes, sliced
salt and pepper
½ level tsp dried tarragon
100g/4oz Mozzarella cheese, thinly sliced

1 Fry the onion in the oil until soft and lightly browned. Spread over the pizza base.

2 Sprinkle the flaked tunafish over the onion then cover with the tomatoes.

3 Season well, sprinkle first with herbs and then cover with cheese; bake as on page 127.

Sardine and Tomato Pizza

20cm/8in pizza base
1 onion, peeled and chopped
1 clove garlic, crushed
1tbsp oil
425g/15oz can tomatoes
1tbsp tomato purée
salt and pepper
2 cans sardines in oil, drained
1 level tsp mixed herbs (optional)
100g/4oz Cheddar cheese, grated

1 Fry the onion and garlic in the oil until soft. Add the tomatoes, tomato purée and plenty of seasonings and cook until fairly thick, about 10 minutes, stirring from time to time.

2 Spread the tomato mixture over the pizza base then arrange the sardines in a wheel shape on top, keeping the tails to the centre.

3 Sprinkle with herbs (if used) and then the cheese; bake as on page 127.

Bacon and Mushroom Pizza

20cm/8in pizza base
175g/6oz streaky bacon rashers, derinded and roughly chopped
1 onion, peeled and sliced
100g/4oz button mushrooms, sliced
salt and pepper
2tbsp cream
100g/4oz Cheddar cheese, grated
12 stuffed green or black olives

1 Cook the bacon gently in a pan until the fat begins to run. Add the onion and cook for about 5 minutes until soft.

2 Add the mushrooms and cook for 1–2 minutes then season and stir in the cream.

3 Spread the mixture over the pizza base, sprinkle with cheese and dot with the olives; bake as on page 127.

Poacher's Roll

One of my favourites for a picnic and so easy to transport. The flavouring of sage can be changed to stuffed olives, pickled walnuts or salami. It sounds like a game pie but in fact is based on sausagemeat.

450g/1lb sausagemeat
225g/8oz lean bacon rashers, derinded and chopped
1 small onion, peeled and finely chopped
100g/4oz button mushrooms, chopped
salt and pepper
1 level tsp dried sage
½ recipe quantity puff or flaky pastry (see page 21)
beaten egg to glaze

1 Combine the sausagemeat, bacon, onion, mushrooms, seasonings and sage and form into a brick shape.
2 Roll out the pastry and trim to a square approx 30cm/12in.
3 Lay the sausagemeat down the centre of the pastry. Brush the edges with beaten egg and fold the pastry over to enclose the filling.
4 Trim off any surplus pastry from the ends, brush with egg and fold up to enclose the filling completely.
5 Turn the roll over so the pastry join is underneath and place on a greased baking sheet. Decorate the top with leaves made from the pastry trimmings and make 2 or 3 slits in between.
6 Glaze with beaten egg and bake in a hot oven (220°C/425°F, Gas Mark 7) for 20 minutes. Reduce the temperature to moderately hot (190°C/375°F, Gas Mark 5) and continue to cook for 30–40 minutes until well browned. Lay a sheet of greaseproof paper over the roll if there is over-browning.
7 Leave to get cold and serve in slices.

Serves 6–8

VARIATIONS
In place of the dried sage use 6–8 finely chopped stuffed green olives, or 3 chopped pickled walnuts; or omit the sage and replace 75g/3oz bacon with chopped salami.

Cheese and Bacon Slice

A cross between a pastry and a scone mixture with a bacon and onion filling.

1 onion, peeled and sliced
100g/4oz streaky bacon rashers, derinded and chopped
50g/2oz butter or margarine
200g/8oz self-raising flour
salt and pepper
125g/5oz Cheddar cheese, grated
1 egg, beaten
little milk
½–1 level tsp dried sage
little grated Parmesan cheese (optional)

1 Fry the onion and bacon together gently until the fat from the bacon begins to run then increase the heat and continue to cook until lightly browned. Drain off any excess fat.
2 Rub the butter or margarine into the flour until the mixture resembles fine breadcrumbs then stir in plenty of seasonings and 75g/3oz grated cheese.
3 Add the egg and sufficient milk to mix to a fairly soft dough.
4 Divide the dough in half and roll each piece out to a 20cm/8in square on a floured surface.
5 Place one piece on a greased baking sheet. Cover with the onion and bacon mixture and sprinkle with herbs and a little pepper.
6 Damp the edges of the pastry and cover with the second piece, pressing the edges firmly together.
7 Brush with milk and sprinkle with the remaining grated cheese and a little Parmesan, if liked.
8 Bake in a fairly hot oven (200°C/400°F, Gas Mark 6) for 20–25 minutes or until crisp and golden brown. Serve hot or cold cut into fingers or squares.

Serves 4–6

VARIATIONS
Fry the onion in 1tbsp oil until soft. Omit the bacon and instead use a can of sardines in oil, drained and mashed.

Smoked Mackerel Plate Pie

Any smoked fish can be used for this recipe but mackerel is the easiest to prepare (kippers have so many bones to remove and cod or haddock need to be cooked first). The filling can also be enclosed in a pasty shape or in small pies cooked in Yorkshire pudding tins.

1 recipe quantity shortcrust or wholemeal pastry
    (see pages 16–17)
25g/1oz butter or margarine
1 onion, peeled and chopped
25g/1oz flour
150ml/¼pt milk
3tbsp cream
grated rind of ¼ lemon
1tbsp lemon juice
2tbsp freshly chopped parsley
2 hard-boiled eggs, chopped
6 stuffed olives, chopped
350g/12oz smoked mackerel fillets, skinned and
    flaked
salt and pepper
beaten egg or milk to glaze

1 Melt the butter or margarine in a small pan and fry the onion gently until soft. Stir in the flour, cook for 1 minute then gradually add the milk and bring to the boil for a minute or so.
2 Remove from the heat, beat in the cream, lemon rind and juice, parsley, eggs, olives, mackerel and seasonings to taste. Leave until cold.
3 Roll out two-thirds of the pastry and use to line a deep pie plate or tin measuring approx 21cm/8½in.
4 Spoon in the filling, and cover with a lid made from the remaining pastry after damping the edges.
5 Cut a cross in the centre of the lid approx 7.5cm/3in wide and fold back the flaps to give an open top to the pie. Press the edges of the pie well together and scallop them.
6 Glaze with beaten egg and bake in a fairly hot oven (200°C/400°F, Gas Mark 6) for about 30 minutes or until golden brown. Serve hot or cold.

Serves 4–6

Sausage Rolls

Always a favourite, they can be made any size you like from cocktail snack to hearty working man's lunch rolls. Sausagemeat with a touch of onion is the traditional filling but try some of the variations given below as well. Use a flaked pastry, shortcrust, cheese or yeast pastry for variety. Sausage rolls can be frozen raw or cooked, whichever you prefer.

450g/1lb sausagemeat, pork or beef and with or
    without herbs
1 small onion, peeled and very finely chopped or
    minced
salt and pepper
½ recipe quantity puff or flaky pastry (see
    page 21), or 1 recipe quantity shortcrust or
    cheese pastry (see pages 16–17), or ½ recipe
    quantity yeast pastry (see page 26)
beaten egg to glaze

1 Combine the sausagemeat, onion and seasonings.
2 Roll out the pastry thinly and cut it into two squares of approx 25cm/10in. Then cut each square into two strips 25 × 12.5cm/ 10 × 5in.
3 Divide the sausage mixture into four and roll each into a long sausage to fit the strips of pastry; place to one side of centre on the pastry strips.
4 Damp the edges of the pastry and fold over to enclose the filling; press the edges firmly together and flake with a sharp knife.
5 Cut into 6cm/2½in lengths and place on lightly greased or dampened baking sheets.
6 Glaze with beaten egg, make two or three cuts along the top and bake in a hot oven (220°C/425°F, Gas Mark 7) for flaked pastry, or a fairly hot oven (200°/400°F, Gas Mark 6) for short pastry, allowing about 20 minutes cooking time or until the pastry is golden brown. With yeast pastry allow to stand for 15–20 minutes before baking in a very hot oven (230°C/450°F, Gas Mark 8) for 15–20 minutes. Serve hot or cold.

Makes 16

Note These rolls can be cut to any size from 2.5cm/1in for cocktail snacks, to 12.5cm/5in for large ones. The strips can be cut 10cm/4in wide for cocktail rolls to make a neater shape.

VARIATIONS

Salami and sausage rolls Add 75g/3oz minced salami to the raw sausagemeat.

Garlic Add either 2 crushed cloves garlic or 75g/3oz minced garlic sausage to the raw sausagemeat.

Cheese and olive rolls Use cheese pastry and add 1–2 level tbsp grated Parmesan cheese and 6–8 finely chopped stuffed olives to the raw sausagemeat.

Military rolls Add 50g/2oz finely chopped bacon and 2tbsp Military pickle to the raw sausagemeat.

Sausage and Tomato Tart

Another tart which is as nice hot as when served cold. A slice wrapped in foil goes well in a school lunch box; the whole tart disappears hastily from the back of my car at a gymkhana.

8 chipolata sausages
1 recipe quantity shortcrust or wholemeal pastry
   (see pages 16–17)
225g/½lb tomatoes, peeled and sliced
½ level tsp mixed herbs (optional)
1 large egg, beaten
150ml/¼pt milk
salt and pepper
pinch garlic powder
50g/2oz Cheddar cheese, grated

1 Fry or grill the chipolatas lightly until browned. Leave to cool.
2 Roll out two-thirds of the pastry and use to line a 20cm/8in flan ring, tin or dish.
3 Lay half the tomatoes in the base, cover with chipolatas and fill in the gaps with the remaining tomatoes. Sprinkle with herbs if used.
4 Beat the egg and milk together with the seasonings and garlic powder and pour the mixture into the pastry case. Sprinkle with cheese.

5 Roll out the remaining pastry, cut into narrow strips and arrange in a lattice pattern over the filling, attaching the ends carefully to the edge of the flan.
6 Bake in a hot oven (220°C/425°F, Gas Mark 7) for 15 minutes then reduce the temperature to moderate (180°C/350°F, Gas Mark 4) and continue to cook for 30–35 minutes until the filling is firm to the touch and golden brown. Serve hot or cold.

Serves 4–6

Beef and Horseradish Pielets

Tangy pies with a 'bite' to the filling.

225g/8oz raw minced beef
1 onion, peeled and finely chopped
1 carrot, peeled and coarsely grated
1 stick celery, finely chopped
salt and pepper
1tbsp creamed horseradish
1 recipe quantity shortcrust or wholemeal pastry
   (see pages 16–17)
beaten egg or milk to glaze

1 Combine the minced beef, onion, carrot and celery with plenty of seasonings and the creamed horseradish.
2 Roll out two-thirds of the pastry and line four individual Yorkshire pudding tins.
3 Add the meat filling to the pastry cases keeping the tops level.
4 Use the remaining pastry to form lids; damp the edges, position each lid and press the edges well together.
5 Crimp the edges, decorate the tops with pastry trimmings and make a slit in the top of each pielet.
6 Brush with beaten egg and bake in a hot oven (220°C/425°F, Gas Mark 7) for 15 minutes. Reduce the temperature to moderate (180°C/350°F, Gas Mark 4) and continue to cook for 25–30 minutes until golden brown. Serve hot or cold.

Makes 4

Military Pork Puffs

Military pickle has a very distinctive taste which is used to flavour the filling for these puffs. As the meat is precooked the baking can be done at one temperature only.

25g/1oz butter or margarine
1 small onion, peeled and chopped
25g/1oz flour
150ml/¼pt stock
4tbsp milk, single cream or natural yogurt
salt and pepper
1½–2tbsp Military pickle or other chunky pickle
175g/6oz cooked lean pork, minced
½ recipe quantity puff or flaky pastry (see page 21)
beaten egg to glaze

1 Melt the butter or margarine in a small pan and fry the onion until soft. Stir in the flour, cook for 1 minute then gradually add the stock and bring to the boil for a minute or so.
2 Remove from the heat, stir in the milk, cream or yogurt followed by plenty of seasonings, the pickle and the pork. Leave until cold.
3 Roll out one-third of the pastry and cut into four 12.5cm/5in circles. Place on a greased baking sheet.
4 Spoon the filling onto the pastry rounds leaving a 1cm/½in plain margin all round.
5 Roll out the remaining pastry and cut into four 15–17cm/6–6½in rounds. Damp the edges and position carefully over the filling on each portion of pastry.
6 Press all the edges firmly together, flake and scallop (see page 36). Decorate the tops with the pastry trimmings and make a hole in the centre of each one.
7 Glaze with beaten egg and bake in a hot oven (220°C/425°F, Gas Mark 7) for 30–35 minutes or until well puffed up and golden brown. Serve hot or cold.

Makes 4

Curried Chicken and Egg Pies

Hidden in the centre of these pies you will find a whole hard-boiled egg. The curry flavour can be changed to herb or horseradish or omitted altogether, if preferred.

25g/1oz butter or margarine
25g/1oz flour
200ml/7fl oz milk or stock
salt and pepper
¾–1 level tsp curry powder
225g/8oz cooked chicken meat, diced
4 hard-boiled eggs
1–1½ recipe quantities shortcrust pastry (see page 16)
beaten egg or milk to glaze

1 Melt the butter or margarine in a pan, stir in the flour and cook for 1 minute. Gradually add the milk or stock and bring to the boil for 1 minute.
2 Remove from the heat and stir in plenty of seasonings, the curry powder and the cooked chicken. Leave until cold.
3 Roll out the pastry and cut into four 12.5cm/5in rounds and four 17–18cm/6½–7in rounds.
4 Place the four small rounds on a greased baking sheet and divide the filling between them leaving a plain margin all round the edge of each one. Bury a hard-boiled egg in each mound of filling.
5 Dampen the edges of the pastry with water and position a large round of pastry over each of the smaller ones. Carefully mould to cover the filling, pressing the edges firmly together, then crimp.
6 Decorate the tops with pastry trimmings, make a hole in the centre of each and glaze with beaten egg.
7 Bake in a hot oven (220°C/425°F, Gas Mark 7) for about 35 minutes until golden brown. Serve hot or cold.

Makes 4

VARIATIONS
Replace the curry powder with either 1–2 tsp creamed horseradish or 1 level tsp dried tarragon, thyme or sage.

Venison Pasties

An old-fashioned favourite, these are now easier to make again as venison becomes more plentiful. Take them on a special picnic or to a shooting-party lunch and watch them disappear. If venison is unavailable use well-hung pheasant meat but cut the initial cooking time to 30 minutes.

450g/1lb venison (from the haunch or saddle if possible)
1–2 onions, peeled and chopped
450ml/¾pt stock
150ml/¼pt red wine
salt and pepper
1 bouquet garni
2tbsp redcurrant or rowan jelly
1 level tsp cornflour
1 recipe quantity shortcrust pastry (see page 16)
1tsp freshly chopped mixed herbs or parsley (optional)
beaten egg or milk to glaze

1 Cut the venison into small dice and place in a saucepan with the onions, stock, wine, seasonings, bouquet garni and jelly. Bring to the boil, cover and simmer until the meat is tender—about 45 minutes.
2 Strain off the liquor, return it to a clean pan and boil hard until reduced to about 200ml/⅓pt; then thicken with the cornflour blended in 1tbsp cold water and bring back to the boil.
3 Roll out the pastry and cut it into four 18cm/7in circles.
4 Place a portion of meat and onions on one side of each pastry round and sprinkle each one with freshly chopped herbs or parsley.
5 Damp the edges of each pasty and fold over the pastry to enclose the filling. Press all the edges firmly together and crimp.
6 Place the pasties on a greased baking sheet and brush with egg or milk.
7 Make a slit in the top of each pasty and bake in a fairly hot oven (200°C/400°F, Gas Mark 6) for about 30 minutes.
8 Reheat the sauce and pour a little into each pasty through the slit using a small funnel. Serve hot or cold.

Makes 4

Salmon Envelopes

When there is just a small piece of salmon available these puffs will help eke it out to feed four people.

150ml/¼pt thick white sauce
1 salmon steak (approx 100–175g/4–6oz), cooked, or equivalent amount of cooked salmon, flaked
2 hard-boiled eggs, chopped
1tbsp freshly chopped parsley
finely grated rind of ¼ lemon
1tbsp lemon juice
salt and pepper
⅓ recipe quantity puff, flaky or rough puff pastry (see pages 21, 24)
beaten egg to glaze

1 Combine the white sauce, salmon, eggs, parsley, lemon rind, lemon juice and seasonings and leave to cool.
2 Roll out the pastry and cut into four 15–18cm/6–7in squares.
3 Divide the filling into four and put one portion in the centre of each piece of pastry.
4 Brush the pastry edges with water and bring all four corners together in the centre. Press the edges very well together to seal and form an envelope shape.
5 Place the envelopes on a greased baking sheet and glaze with beaten egg.
6 Bake in a hot oven (220°C/425°F, Gas mark 7) for 20–25 minutes until well puffed up and golden brown. Serve hot or cold.

Makes 4

Rocky Bacon Dumplings

A suet-pastry idea, quick to prepare and bake, just right for the children after school.

100g/4oz self-raising flour
50g/2oz shredded suet
salt and pepper
1 level tsp mixed herbs
175g/6oz lean bacon rashers, derinded and
    chopped
1 egg, beaten
1tbsp water
25g/1oz dripping
40g/1½oz Cheddar cheese, grated

1 Sift the flour into a bowl, mix in the suet, plenty of seasonings and the herbs then mix in the bacon.
2 Add the egg and sufficient water to mix to a stiff dough (rather like for rock buns).
3 Heat a little dripping in 8 patty tins then divide the mixture between the tins, but do not flatten.
4 Sprinkle with cheese and bake in a moderately hot oven (190°C/375°F, Gas Mark 5) for about 25 minutes until lightly browned and crisp.
5 Serve hot or warm with a crisp salad.

Serves 3–4

6
Starters and Cocktail Snacks

6

Many people become worried at the propect of planning the menu for a dinner party or even about what to serve to eat at a drinks party. It is really very simple if you bear a few simple points in mind. One pastry dish out of the three courses for a dinner party is fine, but not more; do not serve more than one very creamy course ie a creamy soup, creamy main course or creamy sweet—not all three, although the addition of whipped or pouring cream to the dessert does not really count; and soup followed by a sloppy main course with a mousse type of sweet does not give a correct balance. So use pastry as part of the starter, main course or sweet and try to balance the rest of the meal to help your guests' digestion, not upset it by cooking too much rich, creamy and heavy food.

When it comes to cocktail snacks it is a good idea to produce a selection of hot and cold bits and pieces most of which can be prepared well in advance, and those which are to be served hot should only require heating in the oven with the minimum of attention so that the hostess doesn't spend the whole of the time tied up in the kitchen. One or two hot snacks and three to four cold ones is probably the ideal and of these, two or three can be pastry-based. A typical balanced selection could be pâté fleurons, cheese shorties, cocktail bouchées; with a cheese dip, bowls of olives and peanuts, with perhaps prune and bacon rolls and, if time permits, cheese aigrettes.

A recipe for sausage rolls, which are always popular, appears in the chapter on Suppers and Picnics; and some of the other recipes from that chapter can be adapted to serve at a drinks party—quiches, for instance, can be cut into small pieces to make ideal cocktail snacks.

The recipes given here are just a few to show how pastry can play an important part in so many aspects of feeding the family from the everyday pies which everyone loves, through the well-known and more unusual cocktail snacks, to starters for an elegant dinner party.

Leek and Bacon Tart or Tartlets

These can be served as a starter or cut into pieces for a cocktail party.

¾ recipe quantity shortcrust pastry (see page 16), or 1 recipe quantity one-stage shortcrust pastry (see page 21)
25g/1oz butter or margarine
1 leek, approx 225g/8oz, thinly sliced and washed
100g/4oz streaky bacon rashers, derinded and chopped
2 eggs, beaten
150ml/¼pt single cream
150ml/¼pt milk
salt and pepper
pinch ground nutmeg
50g/2oz mature Cheddar cheese, finely grated

1 Roll out the pastry and use to line 15–18 patty tins or a 20cm/8in flan ring or dish.
2 Melt the butter or margarine in a pan and fry the leeks and bacon gently for 3–4 minutes until soft. Drain well and divide between the pastry cases or put in the large flan.
3 Beat the eggs with the cream, milk, seasonings and nutmeg and pour over the filling.
4 Sprinkle a little cheese into each tartlet.
5 Bake in a fairly hot oven (200°C/400°F, Gas Mark 6) for 20–25 minutes or until set and golden brown. For the large flan reduce the temperature to moderate (180°C/350°F, Gas Mark 4) after 20 minutes and continue to cook for 20–25 minutes until set. Serve hot or cold.

Serves 4–6 for a starter or makes 15–18 tartlets which can be halved for cocktail snacks.

This recipe will keep in the freezer for up to 2 months.

Smoked Salmon Flans

These individual flans make a good starter, or one large flan can be baked and cut into tiny pieces to serve at a cocktail party.

¾ recipe quantity shortcrust pastry (see page 16), or 1 recipe quantity one-stage shortcrust pastry (see page 21)
100–175g/4–6oz smoked salmon pieces or trimmings, chopped
2 eggs
300ml/½pt single cream
1tbsp freshly chopped parsley
salt and pepper
pinch cayenne
lemon twists to garnish

1 Roll out the pastry and use to line four individual flan dishes or tins or individual Yorkshire pudding tins (approx 11cm/4½in) or an 18–20cm/7–8in square shallow sandwich tin.
2 Divide the smoked salmon between the pastry cases, or place it in the large tin.
3 Beat the eggs with the cream, parsley, plenty of seasonings and cayenne and pour the mixture over the salmon.
4 Stand on a hot baking sheet and cook in a hot oven (220°C/425°F, Gas Mark 7) for 10–15 minutes then reduce the temperature to moderate (180°C/350°F, Gas Mark 4) and continue to cook for a further 20 minutes or so for the small flans or 25–30 minutes for the large one until set and lightly browned.
5 Serve hot or cold garnished with lemon twists.

Serves 4 or makes 25–30 cocktail snacks.

This recipe will keep in the freezer for up to 2 months.

Samosa

An Indian favourite, these crisp fried pastry parcels with lamb and mint filling make a good starter.

Filling
100g/4oz lean cooked lamb, minced
50g/2oz cooked peas
1 small boiled potato, chopped
½ level tsp freshly chopped mint or a good pinch dried mint
salt and pepper
pinch garlic powder

Pastry
100g/4oz self-raising flour
15g/½oz butter
cold water to mix

Curry mayonnaise
5–6tbsp thick mayonnaise
1tbsp mango chutney, chopped
1tsp finely chopped onion
½–1 level tsp curry powder
2–3 tsp lemon juice

oil or fat for deep frying
tomato wedges to garnish

1 For the filling combine the lamb, peas, potato and mint and season well with salt, pepper and garlic powder.
2 For the pastry sift the flour with a pinch of salt into a bowl and rub in the butter finely. Add sufficient cold water to mix to a soft but manageable dough.
3 Roll out the pastry on a well-floured surface to about 3mm/⅛in thick and cut into 7.5cm/3in plain rounds.
4 Put 2tsp filling on each round, damp the pastry edges and fold over the dough to form half-moon shapes. Press the edges well together.
5 Heat the oil or fat to about 180°C/350°F and fry the samosa, a few at a time until golden brown, turning over if necessary. Drain on absorbent paper and keep hot whilst cooking the remainder.
6 Combine all the ingredients for the curry mayonnaise, put into a small bowl and serve with the samosa which should be garnished with wedges of tomato.

Serves 4

Curried Horns

Shortcrust pastry flavoured with curry powder makes a good hot starter. The filling can be fish, meat or eggs as you prefer.

½ recipe quantity curried shortcrust pastry (see page 16–17)
beaten egg to glaze
sesame seeds

Filling
350g/¾lb white fish fillets, skinned
150ml/¼pt milk
1tbsp lemon juice
salt and pepper
25g/1oz butter or margarine
25g/1oz flour
2tbsp cream
½tsp anchovy essence
2 gherkins, finely chopped (optional)
parsley to garnish

1 Make up the pastry and roll out thinly. Cut into strips about 2cm/¾in wide. Brush with beaten egg.
2 Wind strips of pastry around six greased cream horn tins, starting at the tip, and overlapping slightly as you wind, keeping the glazed side outwards.
3 Glaze the horns again, sprinkle with sesame seeds and place on a greased baking sheet.
4 Bake in a fairly hot oven (200°C/400°F, Gas Mark 6) for 15–20 minutes or until lightly browned and crisp. Remove from the tins and cool on a wire rack.
5 To make the filling, first poach the fish in the milk with the lemon juice and seasonings until just tender—about 8–10 minutes. Drain (reserving the cooking liquor) and flake the fish, discarding any bones.
6 Melt the butter or margarine in a pan, stir in the flour and cook for 1 minute. Gradually add the cooking liquor (made up to 150ml/¼pt with milk or water) and bring to the boil for a minute or so.
7 Season the sauce, stir in the cream, anchovy essence, flaked fish and gherkins (if used) and reheat.
8 To serve, reheat the pastry horns in the oven then fill with the hot filling. Garnish with parsley.

Serves 6

Avocado and Prawn Tartlets

½ recipe quantity wholemeal pastry (see page 17), or 1 recipe quantity unsweetened flan pastry (see page 19)

Filling
75g/3oz full fat soft cheese
2–3tbsp thick mayonnaise
salt and pepper
pinch garlic powder
2 ripe avocados
2tbsp French dressing
100g/4oz peeled prawns
6 whole prawns or parsley sprigs to garnish

1 Roll out the pastry extra thin and use to carefully line six individual flan dishes or tins or individual Yorkshire pudding tins.
2 Bake blind (see page 32) in a fairly hot oven (200°C/400°F, Gas Mark 6) for 15 minutes. Remove the paper and beans and return the pastry cases to the oven for about 5 minutes to dry out. Cool on a wire rack.
3 Cream the soft cheese then add the mayonnaise, seasonings and garlic powder. Spread the mixture over the bases.
4 Halve the avocados, peel and dice the flesh. Dip immediately in the dressing.
5 Add the prawns, toss lightly and spoon the mixture over the cheese filling in each tartlet. Garnish each with a whole prawn or a sprig of parsley.

Serves 6

Quails' Eggs Maison

When available, quails' eggs with their rich flavour make an unusual starter; quartered hard-boiled chicken's eggs may also be used.

½ recipe quantity shortcrust pastry (see page 16), or ½ recipe quantity wholemeal pastry (see page 17)
12–16 quails' eggs or 4 chicken's eggs
100g/4oz soft fine liver pâté
25g/1oz butter, softened
pinch garlic powder (optional)
1–2tbsp thick cream
8 midget gherkins
few lettuce leaves

1 Roll out the pastry and use to line four individual Yorkshire pudding tins.
2 Bake blind (see page 32) in a fairly hot oven (200°C/400°F, Gas Mark 6) for 15 minutes. Remove the paper and beans and return to the oven for about 5 minutes to dry out. Cool on a wire rack.
3 Boil the quails' eggs for 5 minutes or the chicken's eggs for 10 minutes then drain and run under cold water. Shell carefully; leave the quails' eggs whole; quarter the chicken's eggs.
4 Beat the pâté and butter together until smooth then season to taste with garlic powder, salt and pepper and add the cream to give a spreading consistency.
5 Pipe or spread the pâté into the tartlet cases making a mound in the centre.
6 Arrange 3 or 4 quails' eggs in the pâté or 4 quarters of chicken's egg keeping them back-to-back and slanted so they join in a point in the centre.
7 Halve the gherkins then cut the ends to represent fans and place one of these between each egg or quarter egg.
8 Serve on lettuce leaves.

Serves 4

Haddock Talmouse

A delicious filling of smoked haddock makes these puffy cocktail snacks something a little different to try.

225g/8oz (approx) smoked haddock fillet
15g/½oz butter or margarine
15g/½oz flour
150ml/¼pt milk
2 level tsp freshly chopped parsley
salt and pepper
¼ recipe quantity puff or flaky pastry (see page 21)
beaten egg to glaze

1 Cook the fish in a little milk or water until tender then drain. If using milk, reserve and use as stock for the sauce. Cool the fish, then remove the skin and any bones and flake.
2 Melt the fat in a pan, stir in the flour and

cook for 1 minute, then gradually add the milk (or cooking liquor) and bring to the boil for a minute or so.

3 Remove from the heat, stir in the fish and parsley and season to taste. Leave to cool.

4 Roll out the pastry thinly and cut out as many 7.5cm/3in plain rounds as possible.

5 Brush the rim of each circle with beaten egg then put a teaspoon of the filling in the centre. Bring the edges together in the centre to make a tricorn and press well together. Glaze with beaten egg.

6 Place on lightly greased baking sheets and bake in a fairly hot oven (200°C/400°F, Gas Mark 6) for 15–20 minutes until golden brown and puffy.

7 Cool on a wire rack and serve warm or cold.

Makes about 25

Note Any cooked filling can be used in this recipe; spinach and cheese or curried egg make good alternatives.

Advance preparation Make the day before and refrigerate, or make in advance and freeze for up to a month. Thaw before reheating.

Prawn Bites

More like cheese straws or biscuits with a special topping.

½ recipe quantity cheese pastry (see page 17), or 1 recipe quantity rich cheese pastry (see page 18)
beaten egg or milk to glaze
50g/2oz butter, softened
100g/4oz full fat soft cheese or cream cheese
dash Tabasco sauce
½ level tsp tomato purée
salt and pepper
100g/4oz peeled prawns, fresh or canned

1 Roll out the pastry to a rectangle approx 30 × 20cm/12 × 8in and cut into strips 2.5cm/1in wide. Cut these strips into 5cm/2in lengths and place on greased baking sheets. Alternatively cut into circles, crescents, stars etc using small cutters.

2 Brush with beaten egg or milk and cook in a fairly hot oven (200°C/400°F, Gas Mark 6) for about 15 minutes or until golden brown. Cool on a wire rack.

3 To make the filling, first cream the butter and cheese together then beat in the Tabasco, tomato purée and seasonings to taste.

4 Sieve, purée or very finely chop the prawns and beat into the filling.

5 Put the filling into a piping bag fitted with a large star nozzle and pipe lines of prawn butter along the length of the pastry or into a whirl in the centre of other shapes.

Makes about 40

Advance preparation Make cheese bases a day or so before required and store in an airtight container.

Pissaladière

This is a classic French flan but the filling resembles an Italian pizza topping. Traditionally it is baked in a scone-like pastry but I like to use wholemeal pastry.

1 recipe quantity wholemeal pastry (see page 17), or 1 recipe quantity unsweetened special short-crust pastry (see page 19)

Filling
450g/1lb onions, peeled and thinly sliced
2 cloves garlic, crushed
3tbsp oil
425g/15oz can tomatoes or 350g/¾lb fresh tomatoes, peeled and sliced
1–2tbsp tomato purée
salt and pepper
pinch sugar
½ level tsp dried mixed herbs (optional)
75–100g/3–4oz mature Cheddar cheese, grated
1 can anchovies, drained
black olives

1 Prepare the pastry and chill whilst making the filling.

2 Fry the onions and garlic gently in the oil in a saucepan until soft, stirring from time to time; this will take about 20 minutes. They should not be allowed to brown.

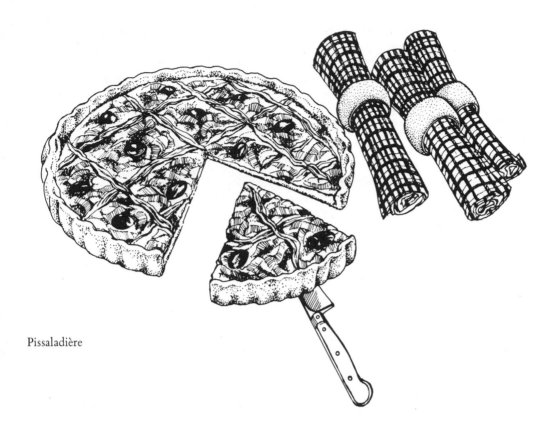

Pissaladière

3 Add the canned tomatoes and their juice or fresh ones plus 2–3tbsp water, the tomato purée, seasonings and sugar.

4 Cook gently until most of the liquid is absorbed, stirring occasionally; stir in the herbs if used and leave the mixture to cool a little.

5 Roll out the pastry and use to line a 23–25cm/9–10in flan ring, tin or dish.

6 Bake blind (see page 32) in a fairly hot oven (200°C/400°F, Gas Mark 6) for 15 minutes.

7 Remove the paper and beans and spoon the tomato filling into the pastry case. Sprinkle with the grated cheese, arrange the anchovies in a lattice pattern over the filling and dot with olives.

8 Return the flan to the oven for 25–30 minutes until the cheese is beginning to brown. Serve hot or cold.

Serves 8

Pâté Fleurons

Crescents of puff pastry topped with a soft pâté piped in shells or stars.

¼ recipe quantity puff or flaky pastry (see
  page 21)
beaten egg to glaze
100g/4oz fine pâté (any type)
75g/3oz butter, softened
1 clove garlic, crushed (optional)
salt and pepper

1 Roll out the pastry thinly and cut out as many 4cm/1½in fluted rounds as possible.

2 Brush the rounds with beaten egg and fold each in half. Place on greased baking sheets and leave to stand for 30 minutes.

3 Glaze with beaten egg and cook in a hot oven (220°C/425°F, Gas Mark 7) for 12–15 minutes until golden brown.

4 Remove to a wire rack to cool and slit each fleuron open a little to allow the steam to escape.

5 To make the filling, cream the pâté and butter together until smooth, then add the garlic (if used) and seasonings to taste.

6 Put the pâté into a piping bag fitted with a star nozzle and pipe a series of shells or stars across the top of each fleuron.

Makes about 50

VARIATIONS

Use tuna fish, salmon, sardines etc. in place of pâté.

Advance preparation Make pastry fleurons a day or so before and store in an airtight container.

Savoury Choux Puffs

Choux pastry makes delicious cocktail bites but if possible bake the puffs on the day required otherwise make the day before and refresh in the oven before filling.

1 recipe quantity choux pastry (see page 29)
175g/6oz full fat soft cheese or cream cheese
75g/3oz butter, softened
1 clove garlic, crushed
1tsp lemon juice
salt and pepper
50g/2oz blue cheese, crumbled
1 can sardines in oil, drained and mashed
1tsp tomato ketchup

1 Put the choux pastry into a piping bag fitted with a 1cm/½in plain vegetable nozzle and pipe 25–30 small buns onto greased baking sheets.

2 Bake in a hot oven (220°C/425°F, Gas Mark 7) for about 20 minutes until well puffed up and golden brown. Pierce each bun to allow steam to escape and cool on a wire rack.

3 To make the fillings, first cream the soft cream cheese and the softened butter together until smooth then beat in the garlic, lemon juice and seasonings. Put one-third of the mixture into another bowl.

4 Add the blue cheese to the larger quantity of cheese mixture and mix well. Put into a piping bag fitted with a small plain vegetable nozzle. Make a hole in the bases of 12–15 of the choux buns and pipe in the filling. Alternatively cut each bun in half, spread in the filling and reassemble.

5 Mash the sardines and beat into the remaining cheese filling together with the ketchup. Use to fill the rest of the choux buns in the same way.

Makes 25–30

Cheese Aigrettes

These are quite delicious and always disappear rapidly at a cocktail party. The traditional flavouring is cheese but I have added my favourite variations too. They can be served plain, sprinkled with grated or Parmesan cheese or with a dip. The mixture can be prepared in advance but do not fry more than 30 minutes before required.

1 recipe quantity choux pastry (see page 29)
1 level tbsp grated Parmesan cheese
50g/2oz mature Cheddar cheese, finely grated
oil or fat for deep frying

1 Make the choux pastry as usual and then beat in the Parmesan and Cheddar cheese, leave to cool.

2 Put the choux mixture into a piping bag fitted with a 1cm/½in plain nozzle or large star vegetable nozzle.

3 Heat the deep oil or fat until a cube of bread browns in about 20 seconds (about 180°C/350°F).

4 Pipe small balls of the mixture—about 1cm/½in in diameter—or drop small teaspoons of it into the hot fat, a few at a time and cook for a few minutes until well puffed up and golden brown all over; turning over during frying if necessary.

5 Drain on absorbent paper and keep warm whilst frying the remainder. Serve warm.

Makes 30–40

VARIATIONS (these are best served with a flavoured mayonnaise dip—see page 143).

Cheese and Prawn Add 100g/4oz finely chopped prawns to the above mixture.

Smoked Mackerel or Kipper Use basic choux pastry recipe—no cheese—and add about 100g/4oz finely flaked smoked mackerel fillet or cooked kipper fillets.

Bacon Fry or grill 175g/6oz streaky bacon rashers until very crispy then crumble. When cold add to the above cheesey choux mixture.

DIPS

Add *one* of the following flavourings to 150ml/¼pt thick mayonnaise mixed with 1tbsp lemon juice and plenty of seasonings: 2 level tsp creamed horseradish; 1½–2 level tsp tarragon mustard; 1 level tbsp tomato purée; 1–2 level tsp curry powder.

Cheesey Boats

Use boat-shaped moulds which come in several sizes (or patty tins if unavailable) to make the pastry cases, and fill as you like. Sails can be made with a slice of tomato or processed cheese and a cocktail stick.

½ recipe quantity shortcrust or cheese pastry (see pages 16, 17)
1 can sardines in oil, drained
75g/3oz full fat soft cheese, softened
1tbsp lemon juice
pinch garlic powder
salt and pepper
paprika
mini parsley sprigs

1 Roll out the pastry and use to line boat-shaped moulds. (The rolling out may have to be done several times depending on the number of moulds available.)
2 Prick the bases and bake in a fairly hot oven (200°C/400°F, Gas Mark 6) for 10–15 minutes until golden brown. Remove and cool on a wire rack.
3 Mash the sardines thoroughly then beat in the cream cheese until smooth. Add the lemon juice, the garlic powder, and the seasonings to taste.
4 Fill the boats and level the surface.

5 Garnish with lines of paprika, and/or mini parsley sprigs.

Makes approx 20 boats

VARIATION

Egg and prawn filling: Mash 3 hard-boiled eggs with 2tbsp thick mayonnaise, ½ level tsp curry powder and plenty of seasonings. Spread into the boats and top each with 1 or 2 peeled prawns.

Cocktail Bouchées

Also called vol-au-vents, they are delicious when served hot with drinks as a single mouthful. They can also be made larger for serving as a starter and larger still for a main course. The range of fillings is unlimited.

½ recipe quantity puff pastry (see page 21)
beaten egg to glaze

1 Roll out the pastry to about 5mm/¼in thick and cut out as described on page 36. Use 4cm/1½in rounds for cocktail bouchées and 8–10cm/3½–4in if to serve as a starter.
2 Place on lightly greased or dampened baking sheets and leave to stand for 5 minutes.
3 Brush with beaten egg and bake in a hot to very hot oven (220–230°C/425–450°F, Gas Mark 7–8) for about 15 minutes or until well puffed up and golden brown.
4 Remove the centres and cool on a wire rack or if to use at once, keep warm.
5 Add the hot filling and serve. If to be served cold, allow *both* bouchées and filling to cool before combining.

Makes approx 24 cocktail-size bouchées.

FILLINGS

Chicken or Turkey Add 100g/4oz finely chopped or minced cooked chicken meat to 150ml/¼pt well-seasoned thick white sauce with a dash Tabasco sauce and 1tbsp chopped capers.

Salmon or Tuna Add one 90g/3½oz can salmon or tuna fish, drained and flaked, to

Assorted cocktail snacks

150ml/¼pt well-seasoned white sauce, with a dash anchovy essence and 1tbsp freshly chopped parsley.

Crab Add one 90g/3½oz can crab meat, drained and flaked, or about 100g/4oz fresh or frozen crab meat to 150ml/¼pt well-seasoned thick white sauce with a little grated lemon rind and 1tbsp lemon juice added.

SAVOURY HORNS

Use shortcrust, cheese pastry or one of the flaked pastries to make the horns and serve hot or cold for a starter. 'Mini' horns for cocktails are made by winding the pastry only halfway along the tins.

½ recipe quantity shortcrust or cheese pastry (see pages 16, 17), or ¼ recipe quantity puff, flaky or rough puff pastry (see pages 21, 24)
beaten egg or milk to glaze

1 Roll out the pastry thinly and cut into long strips about 2cm/¾in wide.
2 Brush the strips lightly with beaten egg or milk and wind them, glazed side outwards, around the greased cream-horns tins, beginning at the tip and overlapping the pastry a little as you wind. If the strip is not long enough, join on a second piece.

3 Place the horns on greased baking sheets with the end tucked underneath and glaze again.
4 Bake the flaked pastries in a hot oven (220°C/425°F, Gas Mark 7) for 10–15 minutes or until well puffed up and golden brown; bake the other pastries in a fairly hot oven (200°C/400°F, Gas Mark 6) allowing about the same length of time.
5 Carefully slip the pastry horns off the metal horn tins and cool them on a wire rack. Fill with your chosen filling and serve hot or cold.

Makes 8 for a starter or about 16 'mini' horns

Ham Horns

150ml/¼pt thick white sauce
2tbsp thick mayonnaise
1 level tsp tarragon mustard or horseradish sauce
100–175g/4–6oz cooked ham, minced or finely chopped
6–8 stuffed Spanish olives, chopped
salt and pepper

Combine all the ingredients and spoon or pipe the mixture into the pastry horns; if to serve hot, first heat in a saucepan and use to fill the warmed horns.

Curry Horns

150ml/¼pt thick white sauce
1 onion, peeled, finely chopped and fried until
  crispy
4 hard-boiled eggs, finely chopped
1½–2 level tsp curry powder
salt and pepper

Combine all the ingredients and use the
mixture to fill the horns as for the ham
filling.

Mushroom Horns

150ml/¼pt thick white sauce
1tbsp snipped chives or freshly chopped parsley
175g/6oz button mushrooms, finely chopped and
  fried in 1tbsp oil
½tsp Worcestershire sauce
salt and pepper

Combine all the ingredients and use the
mixture to fill the horns as for the ham
filling.

Anchovy Twists

These can be made from trimmings of any
flaked pastry or from shortcrust if you prefer.

100g/4oz any flaked pastry or shortcrust pastry
  (100/4oz flour etc)
1–2 cans anchovy fillets
1 egg, beaten

1 Roll out the pastry and cut into strips
measuring approx 10cm × 5mm/4 × ¼in.
2 Drain the anchovies on absorbent paper
and cut each in half lengthwise.
3 Brush the pastry strips with beaten egg and
place a piece of anchovy on each one.
4 Twist the anchovy and pastry together and
place the twists on greased baking sheets.
Brush with beaten egg.
5 Bake in a fairly hot oven (200°C/400°F,
Gas Mark 6) for about 10 minutes or until
golden brown. Cool on a wire rack.
6 Serve hot, warm or cold.

Makes up to 50 twists

Pinwheel Puffs

A good way to use up the puff pastry
trimmings from making bouchées.

100g/4oz (approx) puff pastry trimmings
Gentlemen's relish, Marmite or yeast extract
  spread
little beaten egg to glaze

1 Roll out the pastry to a rectangle keeping
to about 15cm/6in on two of the sides. Trim
to a neat shape.
2 Spread all over the pastry lightly with
Gentlemen's relish, Marmite or yeast extract
spread.
3 Carefully roll up into a neat roll beginning
with the long edge, but not too tightly.
4 Cut the roll into neat slices about

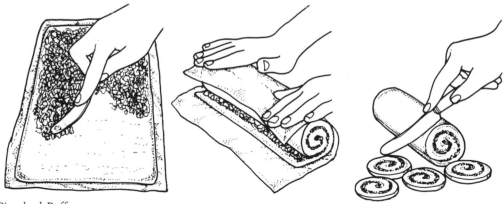

Pinwheel Puffs

145

1cm/⅓in thick and place, cut side downwards, on greased baking sheets.

5 Flatten each one slightly with a palette knife, brush with beaten egg and bake in a hot oven (220°C/425°F, Gas Mark 7) for about 10 minutes or until well puffed up and golden brown.

6 Cool on a wire rack and serve warm or cold.

Makes about 30

Cheese Straws

These are very more-ish and children love them at their tea parties as a change from sweet cakes. Any type of cheese can be used but a strong one obviously adds more flavour.

1 recipe quantity rich cheese pastry (see page 18)
beaten egg or milk to glaze
sesame seeds or Parmesan cheese

1 Roll out the pastry fairly thinly (3–5mm/⅛in thick) and cut into narrow strips. Size is a matter of preference, the width is usually from 1–2.5cm/⅓–1in and the length generally 5–7.5cm/2–3in.

2 Place the straws carefully on greased baking sheets, either flat or with one or two twists.

3 Either leave plain or glaze, or glaze and sprinkle with sesame seeds or grated Parmesan cheese.

4 Bake in a fairly hot oven (200°C/400°F, Gas Mark 6) for 10–15 minutes or until golden brown and crisp. Cool on a wire rack.

Makes about 3 dozen

Cheese Shorties

These are good served just as they are or to use as 'dunkers' with a creamy dip.

150g/6oz plain flour
salt and pepper
½ level tsp dry mustard
150g/6oz mature Cheddar cheese, finely grated
150g/6oz butter, softened
2tbsp (approx) top of the milk to mix

1 Sift flour, salt, pepper and mustard into a bowl and mix in the cheese.

2 Add the butter and work into the dry ingredients with the milk using the fingertips to squeeze and mix. Alternatively place in an electric mixer or food processor.

3 When smooth roll out on a floured surface (or between two sheets of polythene if difficult to handle) to 5mm/¼in thick. Cut into small circles or other shapes measuring approx 2.5–4cm/1–1½in and place on lightly greased baking sheets.

4 Cook in a moderately hot oven (190°C/375°F, Gas Mark 5) for about 15 minutes or until golden brown. Cool on a wire rack then store in an airtight container. After 2 or 3 days the shorties are best refreshed in a warm oven before use.

5 Serve as they are; topped with a cheese and onion mixture; or with a cheesey dip.

Makes about 45

Cheese and Onion Topping Grate a small onion into a bowl, beat in 75g/3oz softened butter, 150–175g/5–6oz finely grated Cheddar cheese and 1tbsp mayonnaise or salad cream. Season well and spread over the shorties.

Cheesey Dip Mash together 225g/8oz cottage cheese and 75g/3oz crumbled blue cheese; add 2tbsp mayonnaise, seasonings, pinch garlic powder, dash Worcestershire sauce, little cream, 1tsp grated onion and 1 stick very finely chopped celery. Turn into a bowl and serve.

Cocktail Canapés

These are attractive bite-sized cocktail snacks with the bases made from either pastry, pieces of toast, bread, pumpernickel or cocktail biscuits topped with a variety of savoury items such as cucumber, tomato, slices of egg, prawns, pieces of crab, smoked salmon, anchovies, gherkins, asparagus spears, olives, small slices of savoury sausages, pâté, ham etc. Piped cream cheese and mayonnaise are used for decoration and sometimes they are glazed in aspic. The canapés are usually made in a selection of designs with a variety of toppings made from whatever ingredients are available at the time.

Pastry bases can be made from most types of pastry—puff, flaky, rough puff, short-crust, wholemeal, yeast, quick, one-stage, cheese etc. Use either pastry made specially or just the trimmings from something else—only a small amount is required; roll out thinly and cut to various shapes with cocktail or small biscuit cutters—try circles, triangles, stars, diamonds, hearts, crescents etc, the size being about 2.5–5cm/1–2in. Place on greased baking sheets, brush with beaten egg or milk and bake in a hot oven (220°C/425°F, Gas Mark 7) for flaked pastries or a fairly hot oven (200°C/400°F, Gas Mark 6) for other pastries, allowing about 10 minutes cooking time or until golden brown and crisp. Cool on a wire rack.

These bases will store in an airtight container for several days but should be refreshed in a warm oven before use if stored for longer then 24 hours. They will also keep in the freezer for up to 2 months.

7
Traditional Recipes

Many of our dishes are very old ones, slightly adapted to suit modern tastes. As far back as Elizabethan times, we hear of the famous raised pies gracing all banquet tables; the fillings were probably very different from those we favour today but they were in a type of pastry that we still use—hot-water crust. The Elizabethans also liked artichokes and made two differing types of pies with them, both with cream added at the end of the baking process, obviously to prevent curdling. The first was rather bland and would be liked by most people, but the second contained dates, grapes and eggs as well as artichokes, and although it may sound a strange combination it is in fact delicious.

In the South of England we find the suet puddings of Kent and Sussex, similar in a way but quite different in flavour; the Flead Cakes which used to be a feature of tea tables early this century, particularly in the Kent area, have largely disappeared, the problem being to find an old-fashioned type of butcher who can supply the flead; if you can find it, then give them a try—the sweet and crispy squares of this special type of puffy pastry are delicious. Dorset produces an interesting bacon-and-egg flan with the eggs baked unbroken in it, quite different from our usual quiches and bacon-and-egg tarts. Oldbury in Gloucestershire was famous for its little gooseberry pies baked in hot-water-crust pastry (most unusually used for a sweet recipe), while further west we find the Cornish Stargazey Pie; this may not immediately appeal, for the heads of pilchards or herrings peering out of a pastry crust are not everyone's idea of an inviting meal—but if you try this dish you will be surprised how good it really is.

The Welsh used the leek—their national emblem—frequently in pies, tarts and pasties, sometimes alone but often with chicken or bacon. Moving up to Scotland, Forfar produced, and still makes, its famous bridies, a version of the pasty, and little mutton pies which probably rival our pork pies, though they are traditionally served warm or hot even though they are baked in hot-water-crust pastry. Scotland also has a very famous pastry-encased cake called Black Bun, which should be baked several months before Hogmanay when the cake is well matured and is served in slices to the 'first footers' who call to offer their good wishes, and probably hope to knock back a 'wee dram' or two along with the cake!

These are but a few of the recipes featured from around the country, some really old and others more modern, but all traditional and all based on pastry. This shows too how regional recipes have appeared with certain types of food. One good example of this is that Somerset recipes often include apples—obviously because of the number of apples grown for cider making. There are other traditional and regional recipes throughout the book which have been put into other chapters because, although they could equally well be featured here, this chapter would swell to an unmanageable size. They include all the raised pies, Eccles cakes, sausage rolls, scones, Bakewell tarts, mince pies etc.

Stargazey Pie

This rather strange pie, consisting of whole pilchards or herrings complete with heads and tails baked in a double-crust pie, belongs to Cornwall where pilchards were readily available from the local fishermen. It is said that, with the heads left on, the oil from the fish runs back into the flesh during cooking instead of being lost when the heads are removed. These days, a round dish is used with either the heads arranged around the edge and tails all joining together in the centre, or all the heads in the centre standing up in a bunch, but whichever way you choose they are all gazing upwards. Cornish markets long ago sold Stargazey pies baked in long strips so the fish could be easily cut off singly or in groups to sell.

1½ recipe quantities shortcrust pastry (see
    page 16)
4–6 pilchards or small herrings
1 onion, peeled and finely chopped (optional)
1 level tsp mixed herbs (optional)
salt and pepper
beaten egg or milk to glaze

1 Roll out two-thirds of the pastry and use to line a fairly large round pie dish or cake tin approx 4cm/1½in deep.

2 Remove guts, fins and scales from the fish but leave the heads and tails on.
3 If using, combine the onion, herbs and seasonings and spoon a little of the mixture inside each fish.
4 Lay the fish in the pastry-lined dish with the heads protruding over the edge and the tails overlapping in the centre. Season well.
5 Roll out the remaining pastry to form a lid and position it carefully over the fish. Trim around each fish head, sealing the pastry edges between the fish with water.
6 Crimp the edge around the heads, glaze and bake in a moderate oven (180°C/350°F, Gas Mark 4) for 40–50 minutes or until the pastry is golden brown and the fish cooked through. Serve hot or cold.

Serves 4–6 (one fish per portion)

Elizabethan Artichoke Pie

Both globe and Jerusalem artichokes can be used for this pie, but of course giving differing flavours and textures to the filling. With globes it is better to use the canned variety in order to save a lot of effort and time. The true Elizabethan filling added hard-boiled eggs, grapes and dates to the artichokes which makes this an excellent

Stargazey Pie

main course. The simpler artichoke pie is creamy and flavoured with herbs and nutmeg and good to serve as an accompaniment to roast meats or game. I prefer the flavour of Jerusalem artichokes in the baked pies.

350g/¾lb Jerusalem artichokes
salt and pepper
1 small onion, peeled and chopped
25g/1oz butter or margarine
100g/4oz white grapes, halved and depipped
50g/2oz dates, stoned and roughly chopped
1 recipe quantity shortcrust pastry (see page 16)
2 hard-boiled eggs, sliced
1 level tsp mixed herbs (optional)
beaten egg or milk to glaze
4–6tbsp single cream

1 Peel the artichokes, then plunge them immediately into salted water to prevent discoloration, and cook them gently until tender-crisp—about 12 minutes. Drain well.
2 Fry the onion gently in the fat until soft but not coloured, stir in the grapes and dates.
3 Roll out two-thirds of the pastry and use to line a 20cm/8in shallow pie dish or flan tin.
4 Spoon the artichokes into the pastry case, cover with slices of egg and then top with onion mixture, seasonings and herbs.
5 Roll out the remaining pastry to form a lid, damp the edges and position the lid; press the edges firmly together, then crimp.
6 Make a fairly large hole in the top, decorate with pastry trimmings then glaze.
7 Bake in a fairly hot oven (200°C/400°F, Gas Mark 6) for 35–40 minutes or until golden brown.
8 Heat the cream gently and pour into the pie through the hole in the top using a small funnel. Serve hot or cold.

Serve 4–6

Artichoke Pie For a plainer pie to serve as an accompaniment to meats or on its own, omit the eggs, grapes and dates and increase the quality of artichokes to 675g/1½lb.

Scottish Mutton Pies

These are the Scottish equivalent of our own pork or veal-and-ham pies, the main difference being that they are more often served hot than cold. All Scotsmen know and love these pies and enjoy them equally as a snack with a pint or as a meal with vegetables. They should be made with hot-water-crust pastry but the English versions which were very popular up until the First World War and said to be a great favourite of George V were more often made with shortcrust or puff pastry.

350g/¾lb lean raw lamb
1 small onion, peeled
1tbsp dripping or oil
150ml/¼pt (approx) stock
salt and pepper
2 level tsp freshly chopped parsley
1tsp Worcestershire sauce
25g/1oz fresh breadcrumbs (optional)
50g/2oz mushrooms, chopped (optional)
¾ recipe quantity hot-water-crust pastry (see page 26)
beaten egg or milk to glaze

1 Mince the lamb and onion then fry gently in the melted fat for 3–4 minutes. Add sufficient stock to moisten, season well and simmer for 4–5 minutes.
2 Stir in the parsley, Worcestershire sauce, breadcrumbs and mushrooms (if used) and leave to cool.
3 Make up the pastry, divide into six portions and keep in the bowl covered with a cloth to keep warm.
4 Take two-thirds of each piece of pastry and either roll out to fit a 7.5cm/3in patty tin or ring mould or mould round the base of a tumbler.
5 Fill each pie mould with one-sixth of the meat mixture and cover each with a lid made from the remaining pastry, damping the edges and pressing well together.
6 Trim the edges, crimp simply and make a hole in the top for steam to escape.
7 Glaze with egg or milk and bake in a fairly hot oven (200°C/400°F, Gas Mark 6) for about 20 minutes.

8 Glaze again and return to a moderate oven (180°C/350°F, Gas Mark 4) for about 30 minutes or until cooked through and well browned.

9 Remove from the tins (if baked in tins) and add 1tbsp of hot stock to each pie through the central hole, using a funnel, if liked. Serve hot or warm, if possible.

Makes 6

Note If hand-moulded pies become mis-shapen,tie a piece of greased double foil or greaseproof paper around each one for most of the cooking time.

Huntingdon Fidget Pie

The farmers' wives of Huntingdonshire are said to have invented this combination of streaky bacon, apples and onions which turns into a thick sauce whilst baking under a flaky-pastry crust, providing a cheap but satisfying meal with an unusual flavour. They used also to add pieces of chopped rabbit or other meat if available along with oddments of vegetables needing to be used up. It is also known as a Fitchett pie by some people and may be related to the Squab pie.

675g/1½lb cooking apples, peeled, cored and sliced
2–3 onions, peeled and sliced
450g/1lb streaky bacon (or bacon pieces), derinded and diced
salt and pepper
2–3tbsp water
½ recipe quantity flaky or puff pastry (see page 21)
beaten egg or milk to glaze

1 Layer the apples, onions, bacon and seasonings (only a little salt) in a pie dish with a funnel in the centre. Press the filling down evenly and add the water.
2 Roll out the pastry to about 7.5cm/3in larger than the top of the dish, cut off a strip about 2.5cm/1in wide all round and lay this on the dampened pie-dish rim.
3 Brush the pastry rim with water and position the lid, pressing the edges well

together. Trim off the surplus pastry, knock up the edges and scallop. Make a hole in the centre of the lid over the funnel and decorate the top with the pastry trimmings.
4 Glaze and bake in a hot oven (220°C/425°F, Gas Mark 7) for 15 minutes then reduce the temperature to moderate (180°C/350°F, Gas Mark 4) and continue to cook for 1½ hours, covering the pastry with foil or greaseproof paper when sufficiently browned.

Serves 5–6

Note If the apples are very tart add 1–2tbsp sugar to the pie.

Chicken Pudding

Early this century a whole chicken or goose would be encased in a suet-crust pastry, wrapped in a pudding cloth and boiled for about 2 hours. It may sound strange to us nowadays but with the small tender chickens available and with a few herbs added to the pastry it makes an interesting way to serve a chicken. I don't think I would try it with a goose; they are best roasted.

1.25–1.5kg/2½–3lb oven-ready chicken
2 onions
few cloves
2 recipe quantities suet-crust pastry with 2–3 level tsp dried herbs added to the flour (see page 25)

Cider sauce
40g/1½oz butter or margarine
50–75g/2–3oz mushrooms, chopped
40g/1½oz flour
425ml/¾pt cider or half cider and half stock
salt and pepper
2–3tbsp cream (optional)

1 Wipe the chicken inside and out, making sure it is completely thawed if using a frozen bird. Stud the onions with 4–5 cloves each and place them in the cavity of the chicken.
2 Make up the suet pastry with the added herbs, roll out and use to completely encase the chicken, sealing the edges with water.
3 Either place on a well-greased sheet of foil

or a well-floured pudding cloth, wrap up and secure the ends tightly.

4 Boil for about 2 hours with water coming halfway up the bird and replenishing with more boiling water as necessary.

5 To prepare the sauce, first melt the butter or margarine and fry the mushrooms for a minute or so. Stir in the flour, cook for 1 minute, then gradually add the liquid and bring to the boil for 2 minutes. Season well, stir in the cream and keep warm.

6 Unwrap the pastry-encased chicken carefully and carve as usual, serving some of the crust with the flesh, accompanied by the cider sauce.

Serves 4–6

Squab Pie

This is a West Country dish found mostly in Devon and Cornwall. A squab is a young pigeon and although squabs were sometimes used in the pie it was more often made with neck of mutton or lamb chops about the same size as a squab. The pie also contains apples and onions and spices, probably reminiscent of the old days when meat was often mixed with spices to help with preservation. Up to the nineteenth century it was common to cook mutton with apple or oranges to help draw off the fat and this may be another reason for this combination of ingredients. The Cornish squab pie often has raisins added whilst in another locality the pie is made with pork in place of lamb and is called Dartmouth pie.

900g/2lb neck of lamb or mutton chops
900g/2lb cooking apples, peeled, cored and sliced
3 onions, peeled and sliced
salt and pepper
good pinch dried thyme
good pinch ground allspice
good pinch ground cinnamon
1 level tbsp sugar (optional)
150ml/¼pt water, stock, cider or white wine
1 recipe quantity shortcrust pastry (see page 16)
beaten egg or milk to glaze

1 Cut the lamb into small pieces and layer up in a pie dish with the apples and onions, seasoning each layer and sprinkling with herbs, spices and sugar (if used).

2 Add the liquid, then cover with shortcrust pastry (see page 32).

3 Glaze and bake in a hot oven (220°C/425°F, Gas Mark 7) for 20 minutes, then reduce the temperature to moderate (180°C/350°F, Gas Mark 4) and continue to cook for about 1¾ hours, covering the pastry with foil or greaseproof paper when sufficiently browned.

Serves 6

Note If squabs are used, allow 6–8; they should be browned in a little fat before layering up with the onion, apples etc.

Leek Turnovers

6 leeks, trimmed and washed
1tsp lemon juice
2tbsp cream
100g/4oz lean bacon rashers, derinded and chopped (optional)
salt and pepper
1 recipe quantity shortcrust pastry (see page 16)
beaten egg or milk to glaze

1 Trim the leeks to approx 15cm/6in in length and chop the remaining green part.

2 Cook the whole leeks for 5 minutes in boiling salted water with the lemon juice added; add the chopped leeks for last 2 minutes. Drain carefully and thoroughly and cool.

3 Mix the chopped leek, cream, bacon (if used), and seasonings together.

4 Roll out the pastry and cut into six rectangles each measuring approx 15 × 10cm/6 × 4in.

5 Spread the leek mixture along the length of the pastry and place a whole leek on top.

6 Damp the edges of the pastry and bring together at the top, press well together and crimp.

7 Place the turnovers on greased baking sheets and glaze with egg or milk.

8 Bake in a fairly hot oven (200°C/400°F, Gas Mark 6) for 20–25 minutes until golden brown. Serve hot or cold.

Makes 6

Leek Tart

The Welsh have a way with leeks for it is their national emblem and it often appears in recipes in combination with bacon and cream. In the northern part of France and Brittany leeks have also been used widely over the years, perhaps showing that the former link between these countries still exists in some ways. In addition to Leek tart, turnovers were also popular in Wales; in Devon and Cornwall the Likky pie was similar although was more usually leeks and bacon baked in cream under a pastry crust rather than in a tart, flan or turnover.

4 leeks, trimmed, sliced and well washed
25g/1oz butter or margarine
¾ recipe quantity shortcrust pastry (see page 16)
50–75g/2–3oz cooked bacon or ham, chopped
2 eggs
salt and pepper
300ml/½pt single cream

1 Fry the leeks gently in melted fat for about 5 minutes without colouring, stirring them occasionally.
2 Roll out the pastry and use to line a 20cm/8in flan ring, tin or dish.
3 Lay the leeks in the pastry case and sprinkle with the bacon or ham.
4 Beat the eggs, seasonings and cream together and pour the mixture into the tart.
5 Bake in a hot oven (220°C/425°F, Gas Mark 7) for 15 minutes, reduce the oven temperature to moderate (180°C/350°F, Gas Mark 4) and continue to cook for 25–30 minutes until golden brown and set. Serve hot or cold.

Serves 4–5

Note A little grated cheese may be sprinkled over the tart before baking, either in addition to or in place of the bacon.

Dorset Flan

Whether this flan really originates in Dorset or not I can't be sure but it is an unusual way of making a bacon (or ham) and egg flan.

¾ recipe quantity shortcrust pastry (see page 16)
4–5 eggs
100g/4oz cooked ham or bacon, chopped
150ml/¼pt milk
2 level tsp semolina
salt and pepper

1 Roll out the pastry and use to line a 20cm/8in flan ring, tin or dish.
2 Beat one of the eggs and brush the mixture liberally over the base of the flan then sprinkle with the ham.
3 Break 3 or 4 eggs into the flan over the ham (without breaking the yolks).
4 Whisk the milk, semolina and seasonings into the remainder of the beaten egg and pour the mixture into the flan.
5 Bake in a moderately hot oven (190°C/375°F, Gas Mark 5) for 30–35 minutes or until set and browned. Serve hot or cold.

Serves 4–5

Forfar Bridies

These are the Scottish version of the Cornish pasty, mainly baked and sold in the Angus area of Scotland. The filling is much meatier than traditional Cornish pasties, with added suet and none of the vegetables except onion.

300–350g/10–12oz best raw minced beef or rump steak, very finely chopped
25g/1oz shredded suet
1 onion, peeled and finely chopped
1tsp Worcestershire sauce
salt and pepper
pinch ground nutmeg
1 recipe quantity shortcrust pastry (see page 16)
beaten egg or milk to glaze

1 Combine the minced or chopped meat, suet, onion, Worcestershire sauce, plenty of seasonings and the nutmeg and divide into four equal portions.

155

2 Roll out the pastry and cut into four 18cm/7in circles.

3 Place a portion of filling in the centre of each, damp the edges and bring together at the top. Press firmly together and crimp.

4 Stand on a lightly greased baking sheet, glaze with egg or milk and bake in a hot oven (220°C/425°F, Gas Mark 7) for about 30 minutes or until golden brown. Serve hot, warm or cold.

Makes 4

Quorn Bacon Roll

Traditionally this bacon and onion roly-poly was served to the huntsmen and farmers of the Quorn hunt in Leicestershire to satisfy their huge appetites after a busy day. It was cheap and simple to prepare which in those days was essential. A similar form of roly-poly appears in many other parts of the country especially in farming areas.

1 recipe quantity suet-crust pastry (see page 25)
225g/8oz lean bacon rashers, derinded
1 large onion, peeled and chopped
1 level tsp dried sage
salt and pepper

1 Make up the pastry and roll out to a thickness of 5mm/¼in on a well-floured surface.

2 Lay the rashers evenly over the pastry then sprinkle with onion, sage and seasonings.

3 Roll up the pastry carefully and place on a well-floured cloth or a piece of greased foil. Roll up so that the roll keeps it shape but has a little room to expand (make a pleat along the length of the foil) and then secure the ends tightly.

4 Place the roll in a saucepan of boiling water and cook for 2 hours, adding extra boiling water as necessary; do not let the water go off the boil.

5 Unwrap and serve hot with vegetables and gravy or a savoury white sauce.

Serves 4–6

Richmond Maids of Honour

The exact recipe for these tartlets was kept a closely guarded secret and for many years they were baked only by one shop in Richmond, Surrey where I believe they are still available. They became very popular in the reign of Henry VIII with the Queen's maids of honour at Hampton Court—hence their name. The recipe varies now but should include curd cheese, ground almonds and brandy.

¼ recipe quantity puff or flaky pastry (see page 21)
100g/4oz curd cheese
75g/3oz butter, softened
2 egg yolks
1tbsp brandy
75g/3oz caster sugar
40g/1½oz cold mashed potato
40g/1½oz ground almonds
grated rind of ½ lemon
1tbsp lemon juice
good pinch freshly grated nutmeg

1 Roll out the pastry and use to line 16–18 patty tins.

2 Beat the cheese and butter together until smooth, then gradually beat in the egg yolks and brandy.

3 Add the sugar, potato, almonds, lemon rind, juice and nutmeg and beat until smooth.

4 Spoon the mixture into the pastry cases and bake in a moderately hot oven (190°C/375°F, Gas Mark 5) for about 30 minutes or until well risen and golden brown.

5 Cool on a wire rack. They tend to sink a little on cooling but this is correct.

Makes 16–18

Flead Cakes

These have largely disappeared nowadays but they are remembered by some of my friends whose grandmothers baked them for special Sunday teas. Flead cakes are a type of semi-flaked pastry, flavoured with sugar and spice and baked in squares. Flead used to be widely available from the pork butcher for it is the inner membrane of the pig's inside, being a thin skin dotted with little pieces of pure lard. Flead also makes an excellent pastry for savoury dishes if you add a good pinch of salt and omit the sugar and spice. The pastry requires the same proportions of flead (cleaned from the membranes) to flour as fat to flour in shortcrust pastry but has a much shorter texture. Flead cakes are best known in Kent and south-east England.

200g/8oz plain flour
100g/4oz flead (cleaned from the membranes)
50g/2oz caster sugar
1–2 level tsp mixed spice or ground cinnamon
cold water to mix
egg white to glaze
granulated sugar for dredging

1 Sift the flour into a bowl. Add the flead cut into tiny pieces, the sugar and the spice and mix well.
2 Mix to a firm dough with water and turn onto a floured surface.
3 Roll out the pastry, banging it hard to break up the flead, then fold up and reroll as for puff pastry.
4 Repeat the rolling, banging and folding process until the hard pieces of flead are well blended with the flour. This cannot be done quickly.
5 Roll out the pastry to about 1cm/⅓–½in thick and cut into 4–5cm/1½–2in squares. Lightly score the tops, place on greased baking sheets and glaze with egg white.
6 Dredge with granulated sugar and bake in a fairly hot oven (200°C/400°F, Gas Mark 6) for about 20 minutes or until puffed up and golden brown. Cool on a wire rack.

Makes 12–16

Note Some butchers will still be able to find you the necessary flead for the cakes. Pure lard, which has been melted down, is not the same.

Coventry Godcakes

Godparents were thought to give these triangular pastry cakes to their godchildren on New Year's Day as a gift to bring good fortune throughout the coming year. They come somewhere between an Eccles cake and a mince pie, having a mincemeat filling.

½ recipes quantity puff or flaky pastry (see page 21)
450g/1lb (approx) mincemeat
1 egg white, lightly beaten
caster sugar for dredging

1 Roll out the pastry fairly thinly and cut into triangles with a base of approx 20cm/8in.
2 Place a spoonful of mincemeat on one side of the pastry, damp the edges and fold the pastry over to enclose the filling and make a smaller triangle.
3 Press the edges firmly together and flake, then flatten the pastry a little.
4 Brush with egg white, dredge with caster sugar and then place the triangles on lightly greased baking sheets.
5 Cut two or three small slits in the tops and bake in a hot oven (220°C/425°F, Gas Mark 7) for about 20 minutes or until golden brown. Serve warm or cold.

Makes about 12

Oldbury Tarts

These unusual gooseberry tarts are an old Gloucestershire speciality—one of the rare uses of hot-water-crust pastry for a sweet recipe.

450g/1lb gooseberries, topped and tailed
½ recipe quantity hot-water-crust pastry (see page 26)
75g/3oz soft brown sugar
beaten egg to glaze

1 Wash the gooseberries and drain well.
2 Roll out the pastry in batches about 40–50g/1½–2oz at a time (whilst keeping the remainder warm in a covered bowl) and

shape into a small pie case with a lid to fit.

3 Put 3–4 or as many gooseberries as will fit into the pie, add a little sugar and position the lid after damping the edges with water.

4 Press the edges firmly together, crimp and place the tarts on a greased baking sheet.

5 Make as many tarts as possible then glaze them with beaten egg.

6 Bake in a fairly hot oven (200°C/400°F, Gas Mark 6) for 20–30 minutes or until browned and the pastry is crisp. Serve hot or cold with cream.

Makes 10–12

Sussex Pond Pudding

Although from Sussex, I know this pudding better as Grandmother's Lemon Bomb Pudding —which is in fact more explicit, for it is a suet pudding baked in a basin with a filling of a whole thin-skinned lemon and brown sugar. The lemon should explode during cooking giving a splendid sugary lemon sauce when the pudding is cut open. It is most important to use a very thin-skinned lemon and it helps to lightly score the rind lengthways in several places to ensure an explosion!

1 recipe quantity suet-crust pastry (see page 25)
1 very thin-skinned lemon
175g/6oz soft brown sugar

1 Make up the pastry, reserve a quarter for the lid and roll out the remainder to fit a 900ml/1½pt pudding basin. Grease the basin and carefully line with the pastry.

2 Wipe the lemon, cut off the top and tail, and with a sharp knife lightly score the rind from top to tail all round. If preferred, it can be cut into pieces.

3 Add some of the sugar to the pastry-lined basin and bury the lemon in the sugar as you add the remainder.

4 Roll out the remaining pastry to form a lid, damp the edges, position the lid and press the edges firmly together.

5 Cover with greased greaseproof paper and then foil or a pudding cloth.

6 Place in a saucepan of boiling water with the water reaching halfway up the outside of the basin. Cook for 1¾–2 hours, adding more boiling water as necessary.

7 Remove and either turn the pudding out or serve it straight from the basin. The lemon should have exploded (if it was not cut into pieces) and formed a sauce with the sugar.

Serves 4–5

Note For those with a very sweet tooth 40–50g/1½–2oz caster sugar may be added to the suet pastry dry ingredients; 100g/4oz currants may also be added.

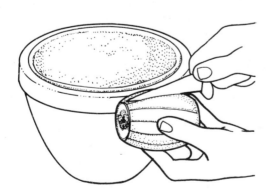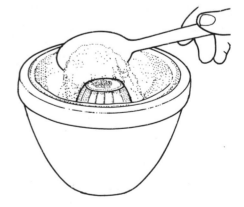

Sussex Pond Pudding – score the lemon lengthways to ensure an explosion!

Kentish Well Puddding

A suet-crust steamed pudding with added currants and a surprise centre of butter which melts during cooking and spills out when served.

450g/1lb self-raising flour
½ level tsp salt
150g/6oz shredded suet
150g/6oz caster or soft brown sugar
150g/6oz currants
water to mix
150g/6oz butter, well chilled

1 Sift the flour and salt into a bowl and mix in the suet, sugar and currants.
2 Add sufficient cold water to mix to a pliable dough.
3 Remove a quarter of the dough, roll out thinly and use to enclose the butter, damping the edges with water to seal.
4 Roll out the remaining dough and use to enclose the encased butter, again sealing with water.
5 Place on a well-greased sheet of foil, with a pleat down one side to allow for expansion, and secure the side and ends tightly; alternatively wrap in a well-floured pudding cloth and tie the top tightly.
6 Boil or steam the pudding for 2–2½ hrs.
7 Remove carefully, unwrap and make a hole in the top of the pudding for the steam to escape, otherwise it will crack.
8 Serve in slices with the butter sauce which will pour out and sink into the pudding. Serve with brown sugar.

Serves 6–8

Note 1–1½ level tsp of ground cinnamon, mixed spice or ground ginger may be added to the dry ingredients.

Black Bun

At Hogmanay in Scotland the 'first footers' who call to wish a family a Happy New Year may well be welcomed with a slice of Black Bun and a glass of whisky, sherry or port. It is a rich fruit cake baked in a pastry case which should be made up to 6 months before required to give it time to mature and mellow before cutting. This recipe uses shortcrust pastry but sometimes a plainer pastry is preferred.

1 recipe quantity shortcrust pastry (see page 16)
450g/1lb currants
450g/1lb raisins
50g/2oz chopped mixed peel
100g/4oz blanched almonds, chopped
100g/4oz soft brown sugar
225g/8oz plain flour
1 level tsp ground ginger
1 level tsp ground cinnamon
1 level tsp ground allspice
1 level tsp cream of tartar
1 level tsp bicarbonate of soda
1 egg, beaten
150ml/¼pt whisky, brandy or sherry
4tbsp (approx) milk
beaten egg to glaze

1 Grease a 20cm/8in round cake tin, and line the base with greased greaseproof paper.
2 Roll out three-quarters of the pastry to a circle approx 35cm/14in in diameter and use to line the tin carefully.
3 To make the filling, first mix together the fruits, peel, almonds and sugar in a bowl. Sift the flour with the spices, cream of tartar and bicarbonate of soda and mix evenly through the fruit.
4 Add the egg, whisky, brandy or sherry and sufficient milk to just moisten and then carefully pack the whole into the pastry case.
5 Roll out the remaining pastry to form a lid, brush the edges with beaten egg, position over the fruit, pressing it down evenly and sealing the edges.
6 Trim the edges and crimp then brush the surface with beaten egg. Using a skewer, make 6–8 holes right through the cake to the base and prick the lid all over with a fork.
7 Glaze again and bake in a moderate oven (180°C/350°F, Gas Mark 4) for 2½–3 hours, covering the top with foil or double greaseproof paper when sufficiently browned.
8 Cool in the tin for at least 30 minutes before turning onto a wire rack. Store in an airtight container or wrap in foil and keep in a cool place for at least a month before use.

8 What Could Go Wrong?

Sometimes when baking pastry—or indeed anything else—the result isn't quite what you were hoping for. What went wrong? You probably followed the recipe correctly, but you could have made some small slip or perhaps wandered between the metric and imperial measures—an easy fault when reading down a list or ingredients giving both versions. Do remember never to mix them—always follow one set or the other; they have been tested separately to ensure success. If you still can't understand where you have gone wrong, then here are some of the causes of common faults in pastry making.

Shortcrust Pastry

1 HARD AND TOUGH Not enough fat or insufficient rubbing in—the mixture must resemble fine breadcrumbs, not be lumpy and uneven. Too much water added, over-kneading or over-handling; baking in too cool an oven, or over-cooking.

2 SOFT AND CRUMBLY Probably caused by not enough liquid or too much fat. The pastry might also be overmixed and kneaded.

3 SOGGY Too much water in the pastry or the filling. Oven too cool or the pastry not sufficiently cooked. When making quiches there are various thoughts on how to prevent a soggy base. Some people brush the pastry with egg-white or milk before adding the filling, others partly bake blind; but I prefer to stand the filled quiche on a hot baking sheet which has been preheated in the oven for at least 10 minutes.

4 SHRUNK The pastry has been over-stretched during the rolling or shaping process.

Suet-Crust Pastry

1 LUMPY PIECES OF SUET IN PASTRY Suet too coarse—grate it very finely or use a commercially shredded suet and make sure it is well mixed before adding the liquid.

2 TOUGH Overhandled or cooked too quickly. When baking, cover with grease-proof paper when sufficiently browned, and use a cooked filling.

3 SOGGY Water not kept boiling during the cooking process. Pastry not covered tightly enough to prevent water getting in. If water boils dry, do not pour extra boiling water into the pan over the pudding, only to the side of it.

Hot-Water-Crust Pastry

1 DIFFICULT TO MOULD OR HANDLE Too little fat or water. Water not boiling—this is most important. Too much water or flour. Pastry cooled too much before moulding. Use rubber gloves (after cleaning thoroughly) if the pastry is too hot to handle. Remember to cover the pastry in the bowl with a cloth to keep in the warmth.

2 CRACKED SURFACE Too little water or water too cool. Insufficient kneading—the dough must be smooth before rolling out or moulding.

3 HARD AND TOUGH Too little water or too much handling.

Choux Pastry

1 CRACKED SURFACE Oven too hot.

2 SOFT OR SOGGY Insufficient beating of the mixture or cooling before adding the eggs. Oven too cool or insufficient baking time.

3 UNCOOKED Usually incorrect proportions of ingredients or too little or too much egg added; mixtures do vary in consistency and the size of eggs also varies.

Flaky, Puff and Rough Puff Pastry

1 HARD AND TOUGH Same possible causes as with shortcrust, or too much flour used during rolling out. The pastry not kept cool during rolling, with insufficient chilling.

2 HARD OUTSIDE, SOFT INSIDE Oven too hot or position in the oven too high. But probably just insufficient cooking.

3 UNEVEN RISE Fat unevenly distributed, the rolling and folding not kept even and the sides and corners not kept straight and square during rolling. Edges must be cut with a sharp knife before use.

4 INSUFFICIENTLY FLAKY The fat was too warm and greasy or the pastry was rolled out too heavily, thus pushing out all the air. Insufficient chilling between rolling; it is safer to allow longer than to cut down the chilling time, particularly in warm weather.

5 SOGGY Too short a baking time or the oven too cool.

6 SHRUNK Rolled out too harshly, causing over-stretching. Insufficient chilling. If the pastry is soft after shaping, chill it again.

Index

Page numbers in italic indicate illustrations

Anchovy:
  anchovy scones, 120
  anchovy twists, 145, *103*
  egg and anchovy pasties, 126
Apple:
  apple and apricot pudding, 73
  apple and marmalade jalousie, 82, *83*
  apple crunch, 111
  apple strudel, 78, *78–9*
  blackcurrant and apple pudding, 73
  double-crust apple pie, 81
  French apple flan, 81, *67, 82*
  Huntingdon fidget pie, 153, *104*
  single-crust apple pie, 80
Apricot:
  apple and apricot pudding, 73
  apricot and date pies, 101, *85*
  apricot sauce, 84
  apricot tart, 87
  beignets with apricot sauce, 83
'Armoured' foods, 126, *86*
Artichokes:
  Elizabethan artichoke pie, 151, *104*
  plain artichoke pie, 152
  turkey and artichoke pie, 52
Asparagus:
  ham and asparagus flan, 124
  pheasant and asparagus parcels, 53
Avocado and prawn tartlets, 139, *103*

Bacon:
  bacon aigrettes, 143
  bacon and mushroom pizza, 128
  bacon and onion pudding, 42
  bacon and tomato pasties, 126
  cheese and bacon slice, 129, *86*
  Dorset flan, 155
  Huntingdon fidget pie, 153, *104*
  leek and bacon pasties, 125
  leek and bacon tart or tartlets, 137
  Quorn bacon roll, 156
  rocky bacon dumplings, 134
Baked lemon cheesecake, 93
Bakewell tart, 76
Bakewell tarts, mini, 102
Baking blind, 32, *32*
Beef, *see also* Steak:
  beef and horseradish pielets, 131
  beef and tomato pie, 43, *50*
  beef Wellington, 45, *46*
  cidered beef with dumplings, 44
  Cornish pasties, 124, *68, 125*
  Forfar bridies, 155
  pheasant and beef pie, 54
  spiced beef pie, 44
Beignets with apricot sauce, 83
Black bun, 159, *104*
Blackcurrant and apple pudding, 73
Bouchées, 36, 143, *103, 144*
Breasts of wild duck en croûte, 55
Broccoli hollandaise vol-au-vent, 66

Canapés, 146, *103*
Carrot and bean pie, 61
Cheese:
  baked lemon cheesecake, 93
  cheese aigrettes, 142, *103*
  cheese and bacon slice, 129, *86*
  cheese and olive rolls, 131
  cheese and onion pasties, 125
  cheese and onion quiche, 123
  cheese and prawn aigrettes, 143
  cheese and tomato pizza, 127
  cheese scones, 120
  cheese shorties, 146
  cheese straws, 146, *103, 144*
  curd tarts, 105
  honey cheese slices, 117
  savoury choux puffs, 142
  Stilton quiche, 123
Cheese pastry, 17, 18, *18*
Cheesey boats, 143, *144*
Cheesey dip, 146
Cherry almond flan, 75
Cherry nut pinwheels, 118
Chestnut:
  chestnut tartlets, 105
  steak and chestnut pie, 43
Chicken:
  chicken and ham pie, 48
  chicken and ham pudding, 43, *50*
  chicken and mushroom pasties, 125
  chicken and pineapple vol-au-vent, 69
  chicken and sweetcorn flan, 124
  chicken bouchées, 143
  chicken pudding, 153
  curried chicken and egg pies, 132
  drumsticks 'armoured', 126
  ham and chicken gougère, 52
  tarragon chicken pie, 53
Chocolate:
  chocolate caramel squares, 110, *85*

chocolate éclairs, 99, *101*
chocolate sauce, 91
Choux pastry, to make and freeze, 29, 41, 160, *29, 49*
Choux pastry:
  cheese aigrettes, 142, *103*
  choux rings, 100
  gâteau St Honoré, 90, *90*
  profiteroles, 91, *67*
  Raymond's gâteau, 91, *67, 92*
  savoury choux puffs, 142
Cider sauce, 153
Cidered beef with dumplings, 44
Circular edging, 37, *37*
Cocktail bouchées, 36, 143, *103, 144*
Cocktail canapés, 146, *103*
Coconut tartlets, 100
Coffee:
  coffee éclairs, 99, *101*
  coffee walnut boats, 106
Colonial goose in a crust, 51, *50*
Confectioner's custard, 89
Cornish pasties, 124, *68, 125*
Coventry godcakes, 157, *104*
Covering a pie dish, 32, *33*
Crab:
  crab bouchées, 144
  crab and egg flan, 124
Cream horns, 107, *49, 85*
Cream puffs, 99, *85*
Cream slices, 107
Creamy pheasant pie, 54
Curd tarts, 105
Curried chicken and egg pies, 132
Curried horns, 138
Curried turkey and grape flan, 124
Curry horns, 145
Curry mayonnaise, 138
Curry shortcrust pastry, 17

Danish pastries, 112, *68, 113–16*
Date:
  apricot and date pies, 101, *85*
  lemon and date scones, 120
Decorating pastry, 33, 36–7, *36–7*
Delaware roly-poly, 74
Dips, 142, 146
Dorset flan, 155
Double-crust pie, to make and freeze, 35, 41, *34*
Double-crust apple pie, 81
Drumsticks 'armoured', 126, *86*
Duck, wild, en croûte, 55

Eccles cakes, 109, *119*
Eclairs, 99, *101*
Edgings for pastry, 33, 36–7, *36–7*
Eggs:
  crab and egg flan, 124
  curried chicken and egg pies, 132
  Dorset flan, 155

egg and anchovy pasties, 126
egg and prawn boats, 143
  farmhouse game pie with eggs, 64
  jellied vegetable and egg flan, 124
Elizabethan artichoke pie, 151, *104*
Errors in pastry making, 160

Farmhouse game pie, 55
Farmhouse game pie with eggs, 65
Fat to use, 14
Fidget (Fitchett) pie, 153, *104*
Flaked grouse pie, 56
Flaky pastry, 21, 161, *23, 49*
Flaky raspberry gâteau, 89, *67, 89*
Flan dish, to line, 31, *30*
Flan pastry, 19
Flan sizes, 19
Flead cakes, 156
Fleurons with pâté, 141, *103*
Florentine boats, 106
Flour to use, 14
Floury scones, rich, 119
Forfar bridies, 155
Frangipan fruit flan, 95
Freezing, 41, 120
French apple flan, 81, *67, 82*
Fruit boats, 106, *101*
Fruit cobbler, 77, *77*
Fruit flan, frangipan, 95
Fruit flans, glazed, 94, *67*
Fruit scones, 120

Gable edging, 37, *37*
Game:
  farmhouse game pie, 55
  farmhouse game pie with eggs, 64
  raised game pie, 64
Garlic sausage rolls, 131
Gâteau Pithiviers, 95
Gâteau, Raymond's, 91, *67, 92*
Gâteau St Honoré, 90, *90*
Ginger scones, 120
Glazing pastry, 40
Glazed fruit flans, 94, *67*
Godcakes, 157, *104*
Goose in a crust, colonial, 51, *50*
Gooseberry:
  gooseberry amber flan, 75
  Oldbury tarts, 157
Gougères, to freeze, 41
Gougères:
  ham and chicken gouère, 52
  salmon gougère, 62
Grandmother's lemon bomb pudding, 158, *104, 158*
Grape:
  curried turkey and grape flan, 124
  grape pastries, 93
Grouse pie, flaked, 56

Haddock talmouse, 139
Ham:
  chicken and ham pie, 48
  chicken and ham pudding, 43, *50*
  Dorset flan, 155
  ham and asparagus flan, 124
  ham and chicken gougére, 52
  ham horns, 144
  raised veal and ham pie, 65
Hazelnut:
  hazelnut bars, 118, *85*
  hazelnut galette, 96
Herb shortcrust pastry, 17
Herb suet-crust pastry, 26
Herby scones, 120
Hollandaise sauce, 66
Honey:
  honey and walnut scones, 120
  honey cheese slices, 117
Hot-water-crust pastry, 26, 160, *27*
Huntingdon fidget pie, 153, *104*

Jellied vegetable and egg flan, 124

Kentish well pudding, 159
Kidney:
  quick sausage and kidney pie, 60
  steak and kidney pie, *4*, 43
  steak and kidney pudding, 42, *42*
  steak, kidney and aubergine pie, 43
  steak, kidney and mushroom pie, 43
  steak, kidney and oyster pie, 43
  steak, kidney, tomato and caper pie, 43
Kipper aigrettes, 143

Lamb, *see also* Mutton
  colonial goose in a crust, 51, *50*
  lamb and orange cobbler, 48, *68*
  lamb cutlets 'armoured', 126, *86*
  lamb fillet en croûte, 47
  minted lamb pie, 47
  squab pie, 154
Leaf edging, 37, *37*
Leek:
  leek and bacon pasties, 125
  leek and bacon tart or tartlets, 137
  leek tart, 155
  leek turnovers, 154
Lemon:
  baked lemon cheesecake, 93
  lemon and date scones, 120
  lemon meringue pie, 76
  mayonnaise, 63
  Sussex pond pudding, 158, *104, 158*
Lime meringue pie, 77
Lining a tin, ring or dish, 31, *30, 31*
Little picnic pies, 66

Macaroon crisps, 118, *85*

Maids of honour, 156
Meringue tartlets, 102, *85*
Military pork puffs, 132, *86*
Military rolls, 131
Mincemeat:
  mincemeat sponge tarts, 101
  mincemeat squares, 112
  mince pies, 87, *119*
Mini Bakewell tarts, 102
Minted lamb pie, 47
Minted tomato and sausage flan, 124
Modern spotted Dick, 74
Mushroom:
  bacon and mushroom pizza, 128
  chicken and mushroom pasties, 125
  mushroom and herb quiche, 123
  mushroom and pepper pizza, 128
  mushroom horns, 145
  steak, kidney and mushroom pie, 43
  veal and mushroom cobbler, 59
Mutton pies, Scottish, 152

Oldbury tarts, 157
One-stage shortcrust pastry, 21
Onion:
  bacon and onion pudding, 42
  cheese and onion pasties, 125
  cheese and onion quiche, 123
  Huntingdon fidget pie, 153, *104*
  onion suet-crust pastry, 26
  stuffed onion dumplings, 60
Orange:
  orange chiffon pie, 84, *67*
  orange meringue pie, 77
Oven temperature guide, 8

Palmiers, 108, *108*
Pâté fleurons, 141
Pâte sucrée, 19, *20*
Pecan pie, 88, *88*
Pheasant:
  creamy pheasant pie, 54
  pheasant and asparagus parcels, 53
  pheasant and beef pie, 54
  poacher's pheasant en croûte, 57
Picnic pies, little, 66
Pigeon:
  squab pie, 154
  steak and pigeon pie, 45
Pinched crimp edging, 37, *36*
Pineapple:
  chicken and pineapple vol-au-vents, 69
  pineapple streusel tarts, 105
Pinwheel puffs, 145, *103, 145*
Pissaldière, 140, *103, 141*
Pizza, to make:
  Italian pizza dough, 126
  scone pastry for, 127
  yeast pastry for, 127

Pizzas:
    bacon and mushroom, 128
    cheese and tomato, 127
    mushroom and pepper, 128
    sardine and tomato, 128
    tuna and tomato, 128
Plain scones, 120
Poacher's pheasant en croûte, 57
Poacher's roll, 129
Pork:
    military pork puffs, 132, *86*
    pork fillet in a crust, 59
    raised pork pie, 65
Prawn:
    avocado and prawn tartlets, 139, *103*
    cheese and prawn aigrettes, 143
    egg and prawn boats, 143
    prawn bites, 140
Profiteroles, 91, *67, 92*
Puff pastry, 21, 161, *22, 49*

Quails' egg maison, 139
Quiches:
    basic quiche Lorraine, 123, *86*
    cheese and onion, 123
    mushroom and herb, 123
    sausage and tomato, 123
    spinach, 123
    Stilton, 123
    tunafish, 123
Quick-mix pastry, 25, *25*
Quick puffy pastry, 25
Quick sausage and kidney pie, 60
Quorn bacon roll, 156

Rabbit:
    rabbit pasties, 125
    rabbit pie with prunes, 58
Raised pies, to shape, 27, *28*
Raised game pie, 65
Raised pork pie, 65
Raised turkey pie, 69
Raised veal and ham pie, 65
Raspberry gâteau, flaky, 89, *67, 89*
Raymond's gâteau, 91, *67, 92*
Rich cheese pastry, 18, *18*
Rich floury scones, 119, *119*
Richmond maids of honour, 156
Rocky bacon dumplings, 134
Rolling pastry, 14, 31
Roly-poly, Delaware, 74
Rough puff pastry, 24, 161, *24*

Sacristans, 109
Sacristans, savoury, 109
Salami and sausage rolls, 131, *86*
Salmon:
    salmon bouchées, 143
    salmon cocktail bouchées, 120

salmon envelopes, 133
salmon fleurons, 142
salmon gougère, 62
Samosa, 137
Sardine:
    sardine and tomato pizza, 128
    sardine fleurons, 142
Sausage:
    'armoured' sausages, 126
    minted tomato and sausage flan, 124
    quick sausage and kidney pie, 60
    poacher's roll, 129
    salami and sausage rolls, 131, *86*
    sausage and tomato quiche, 123
    sausage and tomato tart, 131
    sausage rolls, 130, *86, 125*
Savoury choux puffs, 142
Savoury horns, 144, *144*
Savoury sacristans, 109
Scallop edging, 36, *36*
Scone pizza, 127
Scones, *119*:
    anchovy, 120
    cheese, rich, 120; plain, 120
    fruit, 120
    ginger, 120
    herby, rich, 120; plain, 120
    honey and walnut, 120
    lemon and date, 120
    plain, 120
    rich floury, 119
    spicy, 120
    wholemeal, 119
Scottish mutton pies, 152
Seafood puff, 61, *50*
Shaping pastry, 30, *28*
Shoofly tart, 117
Shortbread, 110
Shortbread sponge fancies, 111
Shortcake, strawberry, 94
Shortcrust pastry, 16, 19, 21, 160, *16, 49*
Single-crust apple pie, 80
Smoked mackerel:
    smoked mackerel aigrettes, 143
    smoked mackerel plate pie, 130
Smoked salmon flans, 137
Somerset fish pie, 64
Special shortcrust pastry, 19
Spiced beef pie, 44
Spicy scones, 120
Spicy shortcrust pastry, 17
Spinach quiche, 123
Spotted Dick, modern, 74
Squab pie, 154
Stargazey pie, 151, *151*
Steak:
    Forfar bridies, 155
    steak and chestnut pie, 43
    steak and kidney pie, 43, *68*

steak and kidney pudding, 42, *42*
steak and pigeon pie, 45
steak, kidney and aubergine pie, 43
steak, kidney and mushroom pie, 43
steak, kidney and oyster pie, 43
steak, kidney, tomato and caper pie, 43
steak parcels, 46
Steamed blackcurrant and apple pudding, 73
Stilton quiche, 123
Strawberry shortcake, 94
Streusel tarts, pineapple, 105
Stuffed onion dumplings, 60
Suet-crust pastry, 25, 160, *73*
Sultana bars, 116
Sussex pond pudding, 158, *104, 158*
Syllabub tartlets, 92
Syrup tart, 80

Tarragon chicken pie, 53
Tomato:
    bacon and tomato pasties, 126
    beef and tomato pie, 43, *50*
    cheese and tomato pizza, 127
    minted tomato and sausage flan, 124
    sardine and tomato pizza, 128
    sausage and tomato quiche, 123
    sausage and tomato tart, 131
    tuna and tomato pizza, 128
    steak, kidney, tomato and caper pie, 43
Treacle tart, 80
Triangular gable edging, 37, *37*
Trout en croûte, 62

Tunafish:
    tuna and tomato pizza, 128
    tuna bouchées, 143
    tunafish fleurons, 142
    tunafish quiche, 123
Turkey:
    curried turkey and grape flan, 124
    raised turkey pie, 69
    turkey and artichoke pie, 52
    turkey bouchées, 143
    turkey drumsticks en croûte, 126

Veal:
    raised veal and ham pie, 65
    veal and lemon pudding, 43
    veal and mushroom cobbler, 59
Venison:
    venison en croûte, 56
    venison pasties, 133, *125*
    venison pie, 57
Vol-au-vent:
    broccoli hollandaise vol-au-vent, 66
    chicken and pineapple vol-au-vent, 69
    cocktail vol-au-vents, 36, 143, *103*
Vol-au-vents, to shape, 36, *34, 35*

Weights and measures, 8
Wholemeal pastry, 17
Wholemeal scones, 119
Wild duck en croûte, 55

Yeast pastry, 26
Yeast pastry for pizzas, 127